The Retirement Handbook

The
Retirement Handbook

A COMPLETE PLANNING GUIDE
TO YOUR FUTURE

By Joseph C. Buckley

HARPER & BROTHERS PUBLISHERS NEW YORK

Library of Congress catalog card number: 53-10669

To my wife Bertha S. Buckley

Contents

Preface

More than two years of research on the varied aspects of retirement preceded the writing of this book.

My deep interest in the subject stems from a casual talk with a friend during one of our daily-commuter train rides to New York City. He is an executive vice-president of one of the nation's leading corporations. After telling me about the many problems encountered in establishing a company retirement plan for his employees, he brought up the question of what each of us would do when it came time to retire. It turned out that neither of us had any definite plan for those important years that lie ahead.

The problem of advanced planning for retirement stuck with me. I took upon myself the challenging assignment of asking a hundred people past middle age what plans they had for their retirement. To my surprise, only six of the hundred had what might be called organized programs. The great majority had no conception of how to go about making a practical plan for their retirement years.

And so began the gathering and organizing of the latest data on the many factors involved in getting ready for and living in the years following compulsory or voluntary retirement. With no ax to grind, I gathered material from manifold sources. I was amazed at how few "how-to-go-about-it" books had been published on the vital subject of retirement. Through correspondence, personal talks and study of professional and general literature, I went directly to those who know the answers in their special fields.

From this survey I learned a great many practical facts about what to do and what to avoid. A number of people with whom I discussed the retirement problem suggested that the ideas collected be set down in a practical book on the subject. The data accumulated has been boiled down into the basic material of this book.

I also found that the public feeling towards retirement is changing to one of increased awareness and interest. This interest will increase as more and more men and women come to realize that the sixty-five-years-and-over age group is increasing on a percentage and numerical basis at a greater rate than other age groups. It will increase as more people come to understand and grasp the values of a fuller and more secure life in retirement. Each year will see a greatly increased number of men and women reaching retirement age, the majority of them destined to live more years as retired individuals.

My purpose in writing this book is to fill a growing need for background information at the practical level to serve as a guide in planning and preparing ahead for better living in the retirement years. Successful planning and preparation for retirement requires a sound knowledge of the basic needs of retirees—financial security, living arrangements, retirement activities, usefulness, health, recreation, use of leisure time, companionship, religious experience and the best places to live in retirement.

Individuals need to evaluate these basic needs in the light of personal desires, ambition and capacities. There is no single solution, no one prescription that meets the needs of all retirees. Planning and effort by the individual himself are so fundamental to getting the most out of retirement that everyone should formulate his own goals and the means for their attainment.

Retirement, approached from its constructive side, is based on the concept that people retire *to* a new way of living rather than retire *from* the present way of life. Retirement is a journey not a destination.

It is hoped the present volume will be found stimulating and profitable by:

1. Men and women in the thirty-five to sixty-five year age group who are interested in long-range planning for financial and psychological security, for better living and happiness in retirement. Now is the time for them to make such plans. The closer they approach the day of retirement, whether it be on a compulsory or a voluntary basis, the more vital retirement planning becomes.

2. Those who have retired already or are about to retire. This book may point out to them some shortcomings in their present plans or may confirm the validity of a well-chosen program. Those who have no definite plan will find this book useful for creating a workable program for contentment in later years.

3. Those who have members of the family, relatives and friends retired or about to retire. This book will be helpful as a guide for aiding the retiree to make adjustments with greater facility and happiness.

The bibliographical listings at the end of the chapters will serve as useful references for those who want additional information on specific topics. Grateful acknowledgment is made to many individuals and sources for supplying material and advice that made this book possible. In addition to those mentioned in the text, thanks are due to several bureaus of the United States Department of Agriculture, Department of Commerce and Federal Security Agency and to the Committee on Aging and Geriatrics. They are due also to the Second International Gerontological Congress, the Marshall

College Conference on Old Age, the state research and development boards, the state agricultural colleges, the chambers of commerce, the realtors and the many others who contributed valuable information and assistance.

Thanks also to John H. Morse, of New York City and Saluda, N.C., for constructive suggestions on farming, and to Lionel Day, of New York City, for comments in the preparation of the manuscript.

Joseph C. Buckley

January, 1953

The Retirement Handbook

CHAPTER I

Getting Ready for Your Harvest Years

Success or Failure in Retirement

Today's concept of retirement is entirely different from that of a generation ago. The old notion that retirement is a state of suspended animation in which doddering invalids or semi-invalids whittle time away in their rocking chairs waiting for the undertaker is obsolete. No active, able-bodied person could stand an existence like that today.

The modern idea calls for retirement *to* a new life rather than retirement *from* life. When a person retires now he simply changes to a new occupation or a new career in which he can continue to grow in personal value and usefulness.

Today we know it's possible to derive great enjoyment from these years of life, years that can be the richest, fullest and happiest of our lives. Robert Browning referred to them this way: "The best is yet to be; the last of life, for which the first was made." They are the years for enjoying the harvest of a life's work.

Your success and happiness in retirement, as in any period of life, depend on the effort, knowledge and common sense you bring into play. Preparation for retirement is fully as important as preparation for a career in a trade, profession or business. You must learn how to live in retirement just as you learned to live in other stages of your life.

However, there is no single formula for happiness in retirement. Retirees, like all people, have individual needs, wishes and desires. They represent infinite variety in their

1

personalities and in the ways they seek and obtain satisfaction.

Deciding what's best for you in retirement requires objective thinking about yourself, your ambitions, your requirements and abilities. Adjustments to a new way of life and provision for financial security must be made. The problems involved call for a mature attitude toward life in general and toward retirement life in particular.

The basic decisions to be made are purely personal and must be made by you. But a great deal of study and research has been devoted to helping you reach wise decisions. Doctors, psychologists, climatologists and other experts have combined to bring you a rich store of background information which you can use in planning your future life. Much of this material you will find in succeeding pages of this book.

Our Responsibilities as Individuals

One fact we must keep in mind is that profound changes are taking place in the structure of the population of the United States. One significant change is the increase in the number of persons sixty-five years of age and over, due largely to the control of infectious diseases, the discovery of new drugs and advances in public health services.

Because of this lengthening of life expectancy, more people are reaching that period of life when they must accept either compulsory or voluntary retirement. More persons will live to reach retirement and will live longer as retired individuals.

At the same time, more and more people in the lower-income brackets are moving up the scale into a big new middle class where they are getting a larger share of the total income than ever before. This middle class has introduced a new and growing group into the economy with more money and savings than average families had twenty-five years ago.

Individuals of this group have the responsibility, during their productive years, of providing financial protection for their retirement. As we shall see in a later chapter, Social Security benefits and pensions need to be supplemented by private income for a secure, worry-free life in retirement.

But, living in the later years is more than a money problem. Retirement living is concerned also with the psychological aspects of adjustment, of finding our place in the community, of understanding ourselves and shaping our retirement goals. We should be ready to assume our full share of responsibilities for ourselves, our dependents and society to avoid finding ourselves in critical circumstances that may hinder our pursuit of happiness in retirement.

Plan Your Retirement Ahead

Since neither Social Security nor pension income can solve all the problems presented by the man or woman who is still active at sixty-five or seventy, we must look to additional means to assure happy and productive lives in the years which are so rich in leisure time. Just sitting around in a rocking chair without anything to do means being thrown on the scrap pile. Most Americans want to stay useful after they retire. Only a small percentage want complete leisure.

Some prior study and education is necessary to master the basic concepts, problems and techniques of retirement living. Too many jobs are so specialized and narrow today that they do not provide any significant carry-over in the phase of living called retirement.

You should begin the planning in a practical and positive way while you are still "in harness." You should cultivate a wholesome attitude toward retirement for the day when you find yourself laying down the tools of your trade, business or profession.

There is a law of the harvest that says "Like produces

like." If it is not possible to set out tomato plants and dig potatoes from under them, by what sort of magic can we expect to gather personal happiness and security out of a pre-retirement attitude which ignores the necessary preparation for retirement?

Nine Steps in Successful Retirement Planning

1. *Define Your Concept of Retirement.* You will be more contented and prouder of your accomplishments if you first clearly understand the meaning, purpose and opportunities of retirement. There are two main classes of needs which motivate men: (1) Those which have to do with survival—food, clothing and shelter; (2) Those which have to do with approval of one's fellow men and acceptance in an in-group, whether it be at work or in the community. When you retire from work, you still have these basic needs to satisfy. Your big problem in retirement is making the adjustment required to fill these needs under changed living conditions.

2. *Make Decisions on the Basis of Fact.* Find out as much as you can about retirement. Search out friends, acquaintances, friends of friends who have retired—ask them for advice. Try to translate what they did into fundamental principles. Analyze their techniques. Read books and articles devoted to retirement. Sift all the information you can gather. Separate the important from the unimportant. Make decisions on the basis of fact rather than on hunches or guesses. Decisions based on factual data are more likely to develop into a workable and individualized plan for you.

3. *Be Open-minded in Collecting Retirement Ideas.* Encourage family, relatives and friends to contribute ideas. The more ideas you have to consider, the easier it will be to select a practical pattern that best fits your personal goal and purpose. You can profit greatly from the experience and practical advice of those who have retired. You can work out

a plan in complete detail guided by worth-while successes and weak spots from the observations you make.

4. *Do Your Own Advance Planning.* A study of company retirement programs indicates that most companies do not give detailed individual counseling to employees on retirement problems. Most company activities are limited to keeping their employees informed on pension rights and a routine interview prior to leaving the company. Don't depend upon your employer to counsel and guide you on what you should do with your retirement time. Plan your own program. Retirement rewards men in proportion to their attitudes toward it. Retirement offers a rosy future for those who plan and work for it. As you progress in planning your retirement career, you become more realistic about the opportunities that lie ahead and less and less responsive to the emotional fears of difficult adjustments and boredom.

5. *Consult Your Wife.* Work out your program with your wife. While men may retire from a routine schedule of work or business, women usually find their schedule of cooking, house cleaning, shopping, etc., remains pretty much the same. It may be more difficult operating on a reduced income, in smaller quarters, in a community where the wife is a stranger. During the years when the husband works, the wife sees him for only a few hours during the day, except on week ends and during vacations. After retirement the husband may be around the house a good deal of the time. This may be a new experience for both of them and may require a period of adjustment. Such changes in the mode of living for both husband and wife should be considered and planned for ahead of retirement.

6. *Make a Long-range Plan.* The earlier you make a general plan of what you would like to do, the better off you will be when retirement becomes an actuality. Start by writing down activities you would like most to do if circum-

stances permit. Work out a detailed program even though it is only tentative. You probably will make many such lists. But each time you revise your original plan you will come nearer to developing a program that will be practical for you.

7. *Don't Set Your Financial Goals Too High.* The wise person values good living, comfort, rest, freedom from hard work, freedom from struggle above monetary gain in retirement. Plan for financial independence, or at least financial security to meet the basic living standards and social values suited to your own desires. In retirement it is foolhardy to set up standards and values on the basis of "keeping up with the Joneses," or living beyond your ability to provide the financial means. Set down the amount needed monthly to satisfy your minimum standard of living in retirement for food, housing, taxes, heat and utilities, house furnishings, household operation, clothing, medical care, hobbies and entertainment, transportation and travel, auto expenses, gifts and contributions, tobacco and liquor, personal care, such as haircuts for husband and beauty shop for wife, and other goods and services. See if your projected income is sufficient to cover your minimum requirements. If it is not enough, you will need to adjust your overall plan to provide additional money. Try to estimate what the value of the dollar will be when you retire. Think in terms of what spending money will buy. Those who make financial security plans today will find themselves in better financial circumstances than those who do little or no planning.

8. *Choose a Location to Live in.* Your decision on where to live when you retire can have a great deal to do with your future happiness. Where would you like to live after retirement? Should you move to a new location, offering a more favorable climate for your health or for better living? Would you prefer a restful location in a region where out-of-doors living can be enjoyed the year round? Do you want to live

formally or informally? Do you count on living with a son or daughter? Do you want to own your retirement home, rent an apartment or live in a hotel or boarding house? What is your preference for residing at or near the seashore, in an interior valley or at the foothills of a mountain? What about moving to a place where you can save money on your living expenses? Perhaps you would like to retire to a small farm or operate a small business enterprise. If so, what locations offer the best prospects? How about roaming the United States in a trailer? If your principal hobby is fishing or hunting, where are the best locations for you to follow these pastimes the year round? Would you feel depressed clinging too closely to your present neighborhood? Would a fresh start in a new place be best for you? Do you plan on a home garden supplying you with a large part of food for your table? If you do, you should plan to locate in a region with a growing season of ten or more months. Would you like to live in a college town, in a community with an active program of sports or of cultural activities or in a community where numerous social get-togethers offer opportunities to meet new people? What contributions would you like to make to community progress? What are your plans for continued development and growth in personal happiness? What is your goal in life? These are but a few of the important questions that must be answered before you can finally decide on a choice of where to live or what to do in retirement. Nobody can answer these questions for you. Your answers and your decision should be formed considerably in advance of your retirement.

9. *Follow Through on Your Plan.* Having visualized and worked out a plan of action, follow it through to its conclusion. Set down tentative dates for the completion of the various parts of the entire program. Don't alter the course or stop the program entirely because of discouragement or seeming failure. But, on the other hand, never hesitate to

revise your plan when to go ahead with the original version is obviously foolhardy. Correct retirement planning enables you to work out your full destiny in living a valuable, happy and successful life. An analysis of the statements and advice of a great number of retired persons brought out the fact that the majority of those who were contented and better adjusted to life in retirement had planned their retirement living in advance. Individuals who were most frustrated, generally speaking, were those who squandered away their retirement futures. They were without a definite plan to guide themselves.

Bibliography

How to Retire and Enjoy It by Ray Giles (McGraw-Hill, N.Y.)

Retire and Be Happy by Irving Solomon (Greenberg, N.Y.)

How to Retire and Like It by Raymond P. Kaighn (Association Press, N.Y.)

Man and His Years, Account of First National Conference on Aging (Health Publications Institute, Raleigh, N.C.)

Living Through the Older Years by Clark Tibbitts (University of Michigan Press, Ann Arbor)

Planning the Older Years by Wilma T. Donahue and Clark Tibbitts (University of Michigan Press, Ann Arbor)

Growing in the Older Years by Wilma T. Donahue and Clark Tibbitts (University of Michigan Press, Ann Arbor)

MAGAZINES

Lifetime Living, Lifetime Living, Inc., 27 E. 39th St., New York 16, N.Y.

Changing Times, The Kiplinger Magazine, 1729 H Street, Washington 6, D.C.

Journal of Living, 1819 Broadway, New York 23, N.Y.

CHAPTER II

Health and Long Life

One of the most heartening statements on the subject of aging is by Senator Thomas C. Desmond, Chairman, New York State Joint Legislative Committee on Problems of the Aging. In the legislative document, *Age Is No Barrier*, Senator Desmond writes:

From the surgeon's operating table comes new appreciation of the hardiness of aging tissues. And out of the new enlightenment of many of the aged themselves is coming a demonstration of the agelessness of human spirit.

Old age is preventable. Not the outward signs, the weathering of skin or the dimming of the eyes' focus, or the tiring of the legs. But the inner self that largely determines one's own TRUE age.

The thermostat of true aging is set by one's mind. By serenity of spirit. By continued "growth." By purposeful activity. And underlying these, financial security.

These are for the most part, responsibilities of the self. One cannot legislate peace of mind, nor can youthfulness be allocated like roads and bridges and post-offices by legislative fiat.

If your health is reasonably good, the chances are that you can expect, if a man, to live to be about sixty-eight years old; if a woman, to the age of seventy-one. On the basis of recent strides in biological and medical research on old age, the predictions of life expectancy for 1975 have now been stretched to about seventy-eight years.

In the early days of human history, for most people life was over by the age of thirty or forty. But now, largely because of spectacular advances in curative and preventive medicine, as well as public health services, a steadily increasing number of people are living to old age. On the average, people are living today about twenty years longer than they did in 1900. The next twenty years may see life expectancy stretched an additional ten to twelve years.

Scientists today are inclined to disagree with the psalmist reference: "The days of our years are three score years and ten." This popular estimate of the natural span of life seems to be contradicted by the third verse of the sixth chapter of Genesis: "And the Lord said, My spirit shall not always strive with man, for he also is flesh: yet his days shall be an hundred and twenty years."

It is easy to confuse the terms *life expectancy* and *life span*. The span of life for man is the longest possible number of years of life from birth to death. Just how long an individual lives may be determined by circumstances such as accident, violence, disease or an hypertensive approach to living. Life expectancy is the average length of life being lived by the entire population at any given time. Life expectancy has not yet caught up with life span.

"Death for any person under 45 may soon become a rarity in the western world, except from accident or violence," United States Government officials told the Second International Gerontological Congress, September 1951. Experiments conducted in St. Louis, particularly with diets for the aged, have led specialists of gerontology to believe that the day is coming when individuals one hundred years old will be in good health, "and as physically capable of maintaining themselves, both socially and economically, as an individual of 50 at present."

Someday it may be possible for a doctor to go to the deathbed of a man of sixty-five and tell him, "There has been a mistake. You have another 50 years to live." This miracle, of course, can only come to pass after chronic disease—the nation's number one health problem—has been put to rout.

The human body is built to last a great many years. Leading medical scientists are of the opinion that man still has not nearly approached the optimum of the possible life span, since he averages only 68 years. Man should have a life expectancy of 150 years, six or seven times his age at maturity, just as any animal has.

Numerous cases could be cited to prove that individuals do live to a ripe chronological age and still maintain their intellectual functions. There is an "amazingly alert" man in St. Louis, Missouri, 106 years old who was active as a chef until he was 90. Though a widower with three of his six children still living, including a lad of 78, this oldster "prefers not to live with his children as he feels it deprives him of his independence." Then there is the 118-year-old gentleman from Texas who journeyed into town to see if he was old enough for an old-age pension. In Tulsa, Oklahoma, it is reported there is a widow of 100 who turned down a proposal of marriage from an old friend aged 82. "He's much too young," she said. And there is the 102-year-old senior citizen of Long Beach, California, who jumped on his motor scooter and drove to the local police station to file a complaint when somebody smashed a window in his home.

Average Life Expectancy Today

The most recent data of the United States Public Health Service, National Office of Vital Statistics, reveals that in 1948 the remaining average life expectancy for selected age groups was as follows:

At Age of	Years Remaining for Men	Years Remaining for Women
35	35.4	39.9
40	30.9	35.3
45	26.5	30.5
50	22.4	26.2
55	18.8	22.0
60	15.4	18.1
65	12.4	14.4
70	9.8	11.2
75	7.5	8.3
80	5.4	5.8
85	3.6	3.7

A man fifty years old today has a 74 per cent chance to survive to the normal retirement age of sixty-five. And having lived until he reaches sixty-five, he has better than an even chance to survive to the age of seventy-five. Recent advances in geriatrics offer good prospects for further retarding illness and mortality of senior citizens.

The excellent chance that a middle-aged man has of surviving to retirement age, and the number of years he can then expect to live, point up how important it is to plan and prepare for the basic wants and needs of retirement living.

It should be noted, too, that women tend to live longer than men. Each year about half a million wives in the United States become widowed. This fact should be taken into account by married couples contemplating retirement. A personal program should take into consideration the needs and problems that may confront the widow upon the death of her husband. At the husband's death, major income sources are reduced or vanish. Unless some provision has been made for the widow, she may have to face a future filled with fear, want and anxiety.

Among the privileges of being born and living in the United States is the opportunity for longevity. The average life span in Bolivia is estimated to be thirty-three years. In

Russia in 1940, only 9 per cent of the population was estimated to be over fifty-five; in the United States for 1950, the figure was 25.5 per cent. India's estimated current life expectancy, twenty-seven years, is not believed to be much higher than life expectancy for Rome two thousand years ago.

Factors in Longevity

Gerontologists point out that the number of years we live is largely tied up with heredity, environmental factors, the use we make of our creative capacities, how we use our strength and energy and the degree of our optimism.

At present, we can do little about heredity as it applies to the longevity characteristics inherited from our ancestors. Geriatrics and other branches of medical science, however, are working on ways to compensate for lack of hereditary factors in longevity.

We can do a great deal about environmental conditions. We can move to a climatic location that is more beneficial to our physical and emotional well-being. We can make psychological adjustments to changes in economic and social status. We can guard against contracting diseases and take precautions against accidents. We can take advantage of new achievements of medical science to prolong life after sixty-five. It is natural to assume that those who receive and follow the best in medical care should live longer than the ones who do not. We can regulate our lives to minimize the strains of emotional pressures. We can be ever watchful of our diet, securing the right kinds and quantities of foods, the best nutrition.

We can develop to the maximum our intellectual, creative and constructive capacities and abilities, learn new skills and interests. We can apply our energy to keeping active at an easy pace within the limits of our physical strength and mental capacity in a new career better fitted to our age. We can guide our thinking along channels that are positive, beneficial and optimistic.

Long life in itself is not enough. Without health, vitality, creative activity and recreation, the opportunity of being useful, and financial security, longevity can be a personal tragedy.

Old Age Is Not a Disease

Old age is not in itself a disease. Few people actually die of old age. Aging is merely a phase of the life cycle. Senior citizens are not suddenly afflicted with chronic illness upon retirement and should not be treated as if they were.

Of course, any person of any age who is physically or emotionally ill should receive medical treatment. But old age should not be considered as a period of permanent infirmity or an age of the "handicapped."

A decline in physical capacities occurs in all adult age groups and varies greatly with the individual irrespective of his age group. Even during middle age, practically everyone has to make many adjustments to gradually declining physical powers. These might be wearing glasses, using a hearing aid, giving up vigorous sports or cutting down on specific items in food and drinks. These adjustments to aging are natural and the necessity for them should not be looked upon with grave concern and fear. Older persons may not be as competent in certain activities as they were in their youth. This should not imply that they are totally incompetent. Senility begins when we close the mind to new knowledge and the heart to new emotional experiences. It is most important to keep on growing, to keep moving forward, in intellectual and emotional vigor.

One of the worst diseases of senior citizens is the fear of old age itself. We must realize that we cannot stop aging. But we can enjoy much health and happiness in our senior years if we learn to grow old intelligently and gracefully. Physicians maintain that fear of disease is often a greater menace to a healthful and happy life than the disease that is feared.

Other mental attitudes that shatter the peace of mind of our aging population are the fear of being poor, worry about losing the attractiveness and physical vigor of youth, fear of losing social prestige, hate and resentment against individuals or circumstances, worry about what the future may bring and resistance to taking a back seat in running things.

The University of Wisconsin recently made an extensive study of worry and fear. Here are the results of this scientific study. First, about 40 per cent of our normal worries turn out to be over things that never happen. Second, 30 per cent of our worries and frustrations are over things that happened in the past. They are things about which nothing can be done now. These are the things we hatch up in our discouraged moods. Third, 22 per cent are the little, petty and needless fears. These three lists together account for 92 per cent of our worries and fears. Fourth, this leaves only 8 per cent for the things which might be considered legitimate worries to which individuals must give care and attention.

Health and disease, happiness and despair, have their roots in thought. Fear, hate, jealousy and anger will express themselves through a sickly body. Fear has been known to kill a man as speedily as a bullet. One of the New York City hospitals reportedly conducted a special examination of sixteen hundred patients and found that 79 per cent of the patients evidenced a strong element of hate and resentment. This is good evidence of the truth that the body mirrors the condition of the mind.

Aspects of Aging

Dr. Albert L. Lansing, of Washington University in St. Louis, an authority on the problems of aging, reports in

Scientific American, April 1953, that some theorists attribute aging to a breakdown of the blood vessels or connective tissue; others maintain that organisms age because their cells wear out, as automobiles or shoes do. Lansing points out that the body will continue to rebuild its cells as long as it lives. It is his contention that "in all probability the main reason that organisms age is not a wearing out of cells, but a decline in the body's cell-building efficiency."

The gerontologist, Dr. V. Korenchevsky, of Oxford, England, concludes that the causes of aging are divided into two main groups called basic primary causes and secondary ones. The basic primary causes are those that produce the processes of pure physiological aging. According to Dr. Korenchevsky, these primary causes are unknown at the present time. They can be investigated only when scientists have learned to prevent and exclude the secondary causes of aging from all the aspects of aging. The secondary causes are fairly well known. In this group belong the degenerative diseases that produce heart disease, certain conditions of the liver, kidney and other organs, disorders and deficiencies of glands, effects of nutrition, mental deterioration, etc.

The organs of the human body do not operate and function independently of each other. Many of them control the activities of other organs and tissues. An abnormal change in a controlling organ can start abnormal changes in an organ associated with it. In this way circles of retrogression are formed which complicate and aggravate the process of aging.

In spite of the complex factors involved, medical researchers are making important discoveries and great advances in man's war on the diseases responsible for initiating or accelerating some of the longevity problems of the elderly.

A new branch of medical specialization, named geriatrics, is concerned with the physiologic and disease problems of our older people. Geriatric physicians deal with the health of the aged much as pediatric physicians care for the health of infants and children. It is true that medicine has not as yet been able to prevent and cure the diseases incident to old age to the extent that it can control the diseases of childhood. But definite gains are being made.

With greater frequency we learn of new discoveries—a new treatment for the stubborn arthritis, new chemicals being tested as inhibitors of cancer, new nutritional aids which take the stiffness out of age, experiments with insulin, cortisone and testosterone to improve the stability of the body. Out of these medical advances will come the benefits of new techniques and treatments. Senior citizens of tomorrow will be healthier, stronger, less susceptible to premature senility and premature death.

However, it is doubtful that a miracle drug will be discovered that will automatically extend the life span. Education for better living will probably contribute as much as medication in any great new advance in aging.

Chronic Diseases and the Older Age Groups

There are no diseases that afflict senior citizens that are not found also in other age groups. Illness is no respecter of age, but older persons are subject to more illness than others. Data from the National Health Survey suggest that the incidence of chronic illness among persons sixty-five years and over is likely to be about three times as high as in the general population.

While chronic illness increases with age, not every older person is afflicted. Also, if a chronic disorder is discovered early, medical treatment can often arrest the development of the disease. Hardening of the arteries is a good case for illustration. During World War I, medical examiners found that the arteries were beginning to thicken in 30 per cent of the soldiers in the thirty- to thirty-five-year age group serving in the United States military forces. Corrective treatment for hardening of the arteries in these apparently healthy soldiers arrested the development of the disease in its early stages. Hardening of the arteries was prevented from developing into a chronic ailment when these men reached their sixties or seventies.

Many chronic diseases are the result of neglect and lack of early, effective treatment. Medical science in the future may discover new drugs and treatments for arresting chronic diseases. But, even now much can be done to increase life expectancy and avert human suffering by suitable treatment when the infirmities are in their early stages.

Heart Disease. More than half of all the people who die each year in the United States die from diseases of the heart and circulation. People on the whole are living longer and escaping the diseases that formerly claimed many lives. Many fall prey to heart disease. One bad part of the heart disease picture is that the mortality in middle age from this disease is on the increase. The frequency with which "heart failure" is cited as the cause of death among executives almost gives it status as an occupational disease.

The types of heart disease afflicting adults over forty are arteriosclerotic, resulting from hardening or narrowing of the coronary arteries that supply blood to the heart muscle, or hypertensive, resulting from long-continued high blood pressure. It has not been determined how many deaths are due to coronary artery disease and how many to high blood pressure.

Most of the sudden deaths from heart attacks are said to be caused by the narrowing and blocking of the coronary arteries. Just what causes the arteries to harden, putting too great a burden on the heart, is not yet known. Until the cause is discovered, the disease can't be prevented. Dr. H. M. Marion, past president of the American Heart Association, points out in his book, *You and Your Heart,* that a heart attack is not necessarily fatal, nor does it mean a life of inactivity. About 85 per cent of those having a coronary condition survive an initial coronary attack. Most of them recover to carry on normal business and social activities.

Hypertensive heart disease, resulting from high blood pressure, is not the result of too much blood. Medical research, however, has not yet found the complete explanation for high blood pressure. Emotional strain has something to do with it; so does heredity. High blood pressure may be caused by a number of factors which over a long time irritate or overstimulate the arterioles or little arteries which serve several purposes in the body, among them the control of the distribution of the blood. Considerable progress has been made in finding suitable agents to lower blood pressure.

One of the most important things to know about heart disease is that it can be controlled and its progress arrested. Recovery from some kinds of heart disease has to be natural. Other kinds can be treated medically. Others require surgery. The best way to keep from getting heart disease is to stop worrying about getting it; take good care of your general health; keep your weight down and watch your diet; get plenty of relaxation and the sleep you need; get a good physical checkup once a year. An estimated three out of four persons who think they have heart disease don't. If you have definite symptoms that might mean heart disease, go to your doctor for a thorough examination.

Cancer and Malignant Tumors are not part of the aging process. But since they are chronic diseases, the second leading killer, accounting for 17 per cent of deaths, they should be mentioned. Dr. Clarence W. Lieb* tells us that cancer is almost a universal worry of older people. It may well be that

* *Outwitting Your Years* by Clarence W. Lieb, M.D., copyright 1949 by Prentice-Hall, Inc.

more people have died from the fear of cancer than from the disease itself.

Cancer is a cluster of body cells that somehow have gone wrong and live off surrounding tissues like parasitic gangsters. Not all the various factors which contribute to causing cancer are known. Thousands of people are alive today because their cancers were discovered and checked in time. The odds that your death will be caused by cancer are one to seven. Again the important thing about this disease is to see your doctor, if you think you have cancer. Early discovery is of the greatest importance with this chronic disease.

Other Diseases. Nephritis, diabetes, arthritis and mental diseases also account for chronic invalidism with advancing years. The slow and silent development of these diseases emphasizes the importance of thorough medical checkups, especially during the fifties and sixties. Early discovery is best assured by a regular physical examination, which is one of the most important safeguards in middle and old age.

A study of statistics on accidental deaths according to age and type shows that one-third of the deaths by accident are made up of people over sixty-five years of age. Falls and motor vehicles cause most of the deaths. The odds that you will be killed by accident are one in twenty. Older people should give special attention to the prevention of accidents. Watch out for loose rugs, waxed floors, rickety and narrow stairways and walks. Avoid poorly lighted areas. Keep a night light burning in the bathroom.

Get a Checkup on Your Health Assets and Liabilities

Sickness and accidents are the enemies of long life and happiness. Don't wait until pain warns you that some ailment has progressed to the danger point. That is like waiting for your car to break down before you take the trouble to check the gas, oil, battery and spark plugs.

Periodic checkups are important at all ages. They are of

the utmost importance in the later years. Don't run the risk of shortening your life by being your own doctor. The older we become, the more sensitive our bodies are to drugs. With approximately five thousand different cures for man's various ailments available in a modern drugstore, it is impossible for an individual to know what is safest and best for him to take. Self-medication is dangerous. Different people react differently to the same dosage of the same drug. See your doctor and follow through on his advice. Resorting to leftover medicines, health fads and old-fashioned remedies without a doctor's advice is unsafe.

A Geriatric Examination. Geriatrics deals with the study of medical treatment for diseases of old age. A geriatric examination, if taken in middle age, provides you with an antiaging program. The geriatric examination is far more detailed and comprehensive than the ordinary disease examination which it includes. It usually covers two or three visits with a physician specializing in geriatrics.

At the age of fifty, ask your family physician to recommend a specialist in geriatrics. Or get in touch with your county medical society for names of geriatric-minded physicians.

Other Checkups. "See your dentist every six months" is good advice. Healthy teeth are one of your most valuable possessions. A timely visit to a good dentist may head off such serious ailments as heart trouble and rheumatism. The kind of food you can eat may depend on how well you can chew. Keep your own teeth as long as you can.

Your eyes, too, need checking. A good plan is to have them examined every two years when you get past middle age.

If hearing is more difficult than it was in your younger years, you may need a hearing aid. Modern electronic hearing aids are easy to wear and have proved a great blessing to persons with hearing difficulties.

More health education, directed to the middle-aged and

the older groups, is urgently needed. There is an abundance of knowledge now available in the fields of disease prevention, medical and vocational rehabilitation and mental hygiene which, if widely disseminated, could build a healthier and happier older population. Our senior citizens are entitled to a fair share of the community's educational and medical resources. The older generation has the right of access to available knowledge on how to make the harvest years of life the best years of all.

Medical care and facilities, geriatric clinics and visiting-nurse services for older people are inadequate in practically all sections of the country. The greatest opportunities for controlling chronic diseases in our aged, at the present time, are those that can be made at the local community level.

What an opportunity this problem of developing community health services for the elderly presents to retired educators and executives who wish to devote some time to public service! In this field the retiree will merely change jobs, putting in a great many working hours in a civic career. In some communities, groups of experienced citizens have formed committees to make the initial efforts to familiarize the community with the needs of older people.

Watch Your Diet for Longer, Happier Living

Many men and women in their sixties and seventies are not so healthy and happy as they might be because they don't make an ally of the food they eat. Some overeat because they think an abundance of food will enable them to keep their strength. Others undereat because they are afraid that food upsets their digestions. There are those whose diet is inadequate because they follow some food fad.

A chronically tired feeling, a gloomy outlook on life, anxiety over small things, loss of sleep, result in many instances from being undernourished. The right food helps keep the body at its best. In the event of illness, a well-nourished body responds better to treatment than one in a run-down condition.

The number of older people in the population who suffer from malnutrition is appalling. This results not so much from not eating enough as it does from not eating a balanced diet supplemented, if necessary, by vitamins.

It has been estimated that twenty-five million Americans are overweight, probably far more than are underweight. Overweight is America's number one health problem, according to the findings of public health officials. The solution of the overweight problem, it is declared, might increase the average life expectancy by as much as four years and greatly reduce deaths from heart disease, cancer and other major chronic diseases of the second half of life. Overeating is a common cause of hardening of the arteries and chronic inflammation of the heart muscles. Diabetes is more frequent in the overweight group.

Foods deficient in protein, vitamins and minerals cause chronic fatigue. Overindulgence in fats and carbohydrates invites premature old age. Since food plays such an important part in your life, you can never "retire" from the responsibility of eating the right kinds and amounts of food you need. The best advice to follow is to have your diet prescribed for you by your physician or a trained dietician.

Acquire the Habit of Rest and Relaxation

Long periods of strenuous activity in work or play should not be engaged in after fifty. The older you are, the easier it is to overtax your heart. Laborious physical activities should be avoided when temperatures are above eighty-five degrees and relative humidity is over 70 per cent. Employ labor-saving devices and short-cut methods wherever possible, especially for the heavy or tedious jobs. Let the younger folks do the heavy work. You do the planning and the supervising wherever possible.

Both bodily and mental fatigue can be reduced by scheduled periods of rest and relaxation. Break up physical and mental work with short rest periods or breathing spells. Don't continue when you feel tired. If you are driving a car on a business or pleasure trip, take at least a fifteen-minute rest after every two hours of driving. If you are doing fairly hard work, physical or mental, stop and rest for ten minutes every hour. When you quit for a rest, stop all over. Short periods of total rest and relaxation are one of nature's best tonics.

Relaxation is just as important as rest. To relax properly eliminate all thoughts of worry and excitement. Release all your mental and physical tension. Tense nerves and muscles are the enemies of complete relaxation. Through observation and experiment you will find out the best conditions under which you can enjoy complete relaxation.

Keep Active as You Grow Old

The secret of longevity in retirement is to keep active both mentally and physically. If the mind and the body are allowed to remain inactive for any considerable period of time, the result is a rapid deterioration of their functions. The aging of the brain consists largely of fat formation in the brain cells. The way to avoid or delay that process is to remain active throughout life.

The capabilities of the older age group to learn have been vastly underestimated. There is no truth in the adage, "You can't teach an old dog new tricks." Millions of persons past sixty-five who have the incentive to learn have acquired new skills and new techniques, are learning to live happily on reduced incomes, are learning to effectively use and enjoy increased leisure time. People can and do continue to learn at all ages. The lack of interest in learning rather than biological degeneration is responsible for the myth that older people are slow, or unable, to learn.

Leading psychologists have demonstrated by numerous tests that the ability to learn falls very slowly with the passage of years after reaching its peak. The early twenties are said to be the peak years for learning, but the drop in the ability to learn is so gradual that at eighty we still have the learning ability we had at the age of twelve. One of the greatest obstructions to learning is self-satisfaction with the knowledge already acquired and the fear of competition in our youth-worshiping society. Given sufficient interest, motives and self-confidence, the old dog can learn new tricks and continue to perform them if he really wants to, irrespective of chronological age.

There is a group of older people who spend much of their time rebelling against the bodily process of aging. They attempt to camouflage to keep up with the pleasures, stimulations and taboos of our youth-conscious culture. This they do in their manner of dress, use of beauty preparations, zealous approach to sports, following of diet fads and search for Fountain-of-Youth miracle drugs so that at sixty-five they can look and act as if they were thirty-five. Persons of this group fall into a state of emotional depression and unhappiness when they are forced to face old age as an inevitable period of life. If there were nothing more to the matter of keeping one's youth than clothes, cosmetics and drugs, one would never grow old.

A wiser group of retired individuals live in the present and plan their personal happiness and security on a more stabilized program of intellectual growth and development. They are the rapidly increasing number of retired persons who are revamping conventional attitudes and thinking, and are evolving practical means for making the later years of life the best years of all.

Dr. Lillien J. Martin, a professor of psychology at Stanford University, retired at sixty-five, then went on to become a famous gerontologist and the founder of the San Francisco Old Age Counseling Clinic. She died at ninety-two, after devoting twenty-seven active years to aiding persons to salvage their old age. From over a quarter of a century of experience in rehabilitating the old, Dr. Martin* concludes:

My picture of a fine, old person, one who by his later life gives proof of having lived well, is of the person who has learned much from his sorrows and built them into experiences useful to others, one who has continued his education all through life so that his mind is alive to changing conditions and is able to take on new views, one who has kept up in the race of progress and refuses to lag too far behind, who has outgrown the narrow needs and self-interest of youth, who has become impersonal but by no means indifferent, who can re-evaluate life after much experience, build up a philosophy and develop the spiritual side of his nature and who is willing to struggle for self-improvement and to live according to the highest ideals he has espoused.

Cicero, the ancient Roman orator and statesman, had a kindly eye on old age when, in his *De Senectute,* he wrote: "Old men retain their mental faculties, provided their interest and application continue; and this is true, not only of men in exalted public stations, but also of those in the quiet of private life. Nature has only a single path and that path is run but once, and to each stage of existence has been allotted its own appropriate quality; so that the weakness of childhood, the impetuosity of youth, the seriousness of middle life, the maturity of old age—each bears some of Nature's fruit, which must be garnered in its season. You must become an old man in good time if you wish to be an old man long. As it is not every wine, so it is not every disposition that grows sour with age."

* *Salvaging Old Age* by Lillien J. Martin and Clare de Gruchy, Macmillan Co.

Here are a few examples that disprove the notion that individuals deteriorate in mental alertness and physical abilities when they reach sixty-five or seventy.

Dr. John Dewey, America's foremost philosopher of his day, retired from teaching at Columbia University when he was seventy. But he went on writing and lecturing, publishing more than three hundred books, essays and articles. When Dewey died at the age of ninety-two, his eyes were still keen, his mind was alert and he still typed his own manuscripts and letters. Winston Churchill, at the age of seventy-eight, once again became prime minister leading his country in a great emergency. How does he do it? Churchill has a good philosophy of life, driving ambition, intense pride, a variety of interests, almost limitless enthusiasm for any task he undertakes. The challenge of adversity only increases his vitality. Arturo Toscanini, at eighty-five, can memorize the complete score of an opera in a few days, and once having committed it to memory never forgets it. Grandma Moses, though over ninety, works every day on her paintings. Grandma Moses, America's foremost self-taught artist, started painting in earnest in her seventies. Mr. Justice Holmes, at the age of ninety, took up the study of Greek. Titian painted the *Battle of Lepanto* at the age of ninety-eight. George Bernard Shaw wrote one of his best plays, *St. Joan,* when he was near seventy. Michelangelo was still painting his masterpieces at eighty-nine. Goethe completed *Faust* when he was eighty-two. Bernard Baruch, eighty-two, and Herbert Hoover, seventy-nine, are two examples of public figures who live active lives. James W. Montee learned to fly an airplane at sixty and at eighty-nine was still flying. Adeline De Watt Reynolds, a grandmother, graduated from the University of California at sixty-eight and then took graduate dramatic courses. At eighty she began her movie career.

The Belgian psychologist, Dr. Jean Palus, told the Second International Gerontological Congress that he disputes the idea that intelligence and learning capacity reach their peak during youth and thereafter decline slowly. "I think any progress in maturation and motivation brings about, obligatorily, a corresponding gain in learning capacity and insight," he declared. Dr. Palus goes on to say:

In youth, man is dominated by biological and physiological urges—the needs for acceptance and recognition, for possession and new adventures, sexual satisfaction and self-assertion. If these needs are not seriously checked in youth, then higher needs make themselves felt in maturity and old age.

The forties and fifties and later years, when correctly entered, open the way to the well-balanced individual to new kinds of experience, meditations and accomplishments which are entirely beyond the possibilities of young persons. Many great men have done their best work in maturity. The "man in the street," in later years, becomes more productive in many fields, such as professional work, family relationships, civic life and any creative accomplishment whatever.

But a great number of persons fail to make their old age a success, Dr. Palus admitted. He pointed out that American society in particular puts great stress on youthful characteristics, such as physical vigor and quick adaptability, and that in many modern industries it is difficult for workers to maintain interest in their work, because of its machinelike nature.

Fixative behavior [Palus said], in which the individual clings to an earlier period of life—either because he missed the satisfactions normal to that period or because he got excessive gratification from them—is a major factor in unsuccessful old age. This explains the cravings for money and dominance in many older people. Here lies the explanation for the kind of pathetic regret immortalized in Goethe's "Faust."

People who keep young in spirit as they grow older are younger looking for their age, more charming, more fun and probably live longer. When Solon, the Athenian statesman and one of the Seven Sages of Greece, was asked the secret of long life, his reply was: "Learn some new thing every day."

Vocational Rehabilitation for Disabled Civilians

Not all persons living in retirement or semiretirement do so because of voluntary or compulsory job retirement. Many are forced into a state of unemployment retirement because of disabilities through accident, illness or other causes to such a degree that their disablements constitute job handicaps. There are over a million men and women in this group in the United States today.

To enable the disabled civilian to be self-supporting, the Federal Government and the states have entered into a partnership for vocational rehabilitation. This Federal-state program of vocational rehabilitation is a public service in the same sense as the school systems, visiting-nurse service, health centers, libraries, water systems and police and fire departments. It is not charity. Vocational rehabilitation services are intended as a legal right. Many persons in early retirement because of disabilities can rehabilitate themselves and enter the employment market to work on a self-supporting basis.

Men and women of working age with substantial job handicaps are eligible. The program is available to persons with unseen handicaps, such as tuberculosis, arthritis, heart disease, deafness and emotional disabilities, as well as for those with disabilities which are visible, such as amputees, paralytics, spastics and the blind.

Briefly, the following services are provided:

1. Medical examination in every case to determine the extent of the disability, to discover possible hidden, or secondary, dis-

abilities, to determine work capacity and to help determine eligibility—at no cost to the individual.

2. Individual counsel and guidance to help the disabled person to select and attain the right job objective—at no cost to the individual.

3. Medical, surgical, psychiatric and hospital care, as needed, to remove the disability. Included are artificial appliances, such as limbs, hearing aids, braces and the like. These are paid for from public funds to the degree that the individual cannot meet the cost.

4. Training for the right job in schools, colleges or universities, on the job, in the plant, by tutor, through correspondence courses, to enable the individual to do the job well—at no cost to the disabled person.

5. Occupational tools, equipment and licenses, as necessary, to give the disabled person a fair start. These may be paid for from public funds to the extent that the person is unable to do so.

6. Placement in the right job. Follow-up after placement to make sure the disabled person and his employer are satisfied with one another—at no cost to the individual.

Three conditions must exist before a person is eligible for these services: (1) He must be at an employable age; (2) He must have a disability which substantially interferes with employment; (3) There must be a reasonable chance of his becoming suitably employed. Those interested in further details should write to the State Vocational Rehabilitation Agency, or to the Department of Health, Education and Welfare, Office of Vocational Rehabilitation, Washington 25, D.C.

Retirement Does Not Hasten Death

Reports about some people dying shortly after retirement have created a suspicion that retired individuals die sooner than those who remain "in harness." The fact is not borne out by statistics. The records of insurance companies show that persons retired and living on annuities actually live longer than those who do not have annuities.

To some people, separation from workday life comes as a shock accompanied by a serious emotional block. These people enter this new period of life as rebellious, confused and bitter adults. If this emotional pressure is not checked and released, it can lead to chaos. Unable or unwilling to adjust themselves to the new mode of living imposed by retirement, they wind up with high-tension emotional systems. Being totally unprepared for retirement, they lose all interest in living.

It is the state of your health, your psychological preparation for retirement, the preparations you have made for old age and your diet—not whether you are retired or employed —that are the governing factors in whether or not you live to a ripe old age.

What Is the Best Age to Retire?

The best circumstances for retirement depend upon what your family responsibilities are, the state of your health, your age, your financial resources and probable retirement income, your general attitude toward retirement and a carefully prepared plan. Individual and family needs differ. Goals, ambitions, desires, standard of living—all are personal matters.

There is no natural law that says a person should retire solely on the turn of a calendar page. Retirement on the basis of age alone is socially wasteful.

But if you are employed by a company or organization that has a compulsory retirement program, the question of your retirement is arbitrarily determined for you in advance. The company sets the age when employees must retire. This is usually between the ages of sixty and seventy, most often at sixty-five.

Some organizations, on the other hand, do have retirement programs which allow employees to choose, within certain limits, the date on which they are to retire. If you are covered by this type of pension policy, you have some serious planning to do in the timing of your retirement.

In a survey among approximately five hundred retired persons in Cleveland, Ohio, reported in *Factory Management,* May 1952, the question was asked: "At what age do you think people should retire?" In answering this question, 44 per cent set no definite age for retirement; 24 per cent said at the age of sixty-five; after sixty-five was voted by 9 per cent; before sixty-five was suggested as the best age to retire by 19 per cent.

Tapering-off Retirement Process

Another approach to retirement is that of gradually cutting down in the hours spent working on the job and stretching out off-the-job time and vacation periods.

This sneaking-up, as it were, on retirement is becoming popular in the retirement programs of certain executives, professional men and women and individuals who have major control of small companies.

The tapering-off program of one large organization requires all employees who work beyond the customary retirement age of sixty-five to take an extra month's vacation without pay for each year worked after reaching the time for retirement. That means an extra month for the first year, two months for the second year, etc., in addition to the regular vacation.

Transferring older employees to easier work assignments and reduced responsibilities at the same pay or at slightly reduced pay is another fairly common practice of management. This does not, however, solve the retirement problem. It is only a partial solution and merely postpones retirement to a later date on a fixed basis of age or retains employees on the pay roll until they die.

Still another method of handling retirement is to retire an aging employee at his compulsory retirement date, and then rehire him as a consultant or for research, a staff job or other special assignment on a part-time, full-time or fee basis.

What About Early Retirement?

One good reason for early retirement is the opportunity it provides for getting a good start on establishing an income-producing business or a farm enterprise while you are still young enough to handle the details involved. Though many people in their seventies have established successful small businesses, getting started as early as possible has great advantages.

If your job means just making a living, drives you to nervous exhaustion, is a ball and chain that keeps you from doing the things you really want to do, offers little chance of future advancement in position and income, has a pension plan that is inadequate, adversely affects your mental, emotional or physical health—then you might as well look for a job offering better prospects, or retire right now.

Some people ought to retire when they are fifty or fifty-five, if for no better reason than to protect their health. Results of a survey among pensioners show that 25 per cent retired because of poor health.

There is a small group of headstrong resistors who, because of their emotional temperaments, their refusal to give up power and authority, would never be happy in retirement. They might as well hold on to their current jobs as long as possible or until they die in harness.

Unexpected unemployment may force you into semiretirement at a much younger age than you anticipated. Finding re-employment in business and industry is a serious problem for men over fifty and women over forty. An unemployed person in his or her early fifties should seriously consider establishing and operating a retirement business or a small farm enterprise.

You may have in the back of your mind the desire or urge to do something entirely different from what you are doing in your present employment. It might be the breeding of high-grade cattle, writing a book, the completion of some academic study or work. No matter what it is, retirement will give you the chance to fulfill your desire. Retire while you are young enough to enjoy and complete what you really want to do.

There comes a time in our business or professional lives when we reach the pinnacle of success in our fields. This crest of the wave may come to some in the middle years of life or to others in their late sixties. In any event, the years that follow do not bring forth any gain in income or advancement in professional recognition or reputation. Those who hang on too long begin to fall behind and lose ground to younger colleagues with new techniques, new ideas and growing reputations. For their own physical, intellectual and moral well-being, those who have reached the peak of success would be much better off retiring early, and filling the remaining years with constructive satisfying activities.

With $10,000 to $15,000 cash and a home owned outright, the average man should be able to retire at an early age. He can establish a small independent business, run a small farm or supplement his income with part-time employment. Many persons have started successful retirement careers with less capital than $10,000. Of course, the more capital you have the better off you will be. Early retirement usually means smaller pension benefits from your regular employment. You should determine what your pension benefits will be, along with your Social Security retirement benefits, after you reach sixty-five, and analyze the other resources you have.

There is no one answer to the best age at which to start

retirement. It depends entirely on what you need and want out of life. But, whatever your decision, bear in mind that retirement years can be the best years of your life. You owe it to yourself and your family to make them so.

Bibliography

You will probably find copies of these books in your public library. If you want to buy and keep some of them for reference, check your local bookstore, or write direct to the publisher.

The Anatomy of Happiness by Martin Gumpert, M.D. (McGraw-Hill, N.Y.)

Happiness by William Lyon Phelps (Dutton, N.Y.)

Aging Successfully by George Lawton (Columbia Press, N.Y.)

The Second Forty Years by Edward J. Stieglitz, M.D. (Lippincott, N.Y.)

The Years After Fifty by Wingate M. Johnson, M.D. (McGraw-Hill, N.Y.)

Should I Retire by George H. Preston, M.D. (Rinehart, N.Y.)

Old Age, Its Compensations and Rewards by Adolf L. Vischer, M.D. (Macmillan, N.Y.)

Outwitting Your Years by William Lieb, M.D. (Prentice-Hall, N.Y.)

Commentary on Age by Kenneth Walker (Cape, London)

U.S. Government Publications. Order from Superintendent of Documents, U.S. Government Printing Office, Washington 25, D.C.

Food Guide for Older Folks, Home & Garden Bulletin No. 17. 5 cents.

Health Is Everybody's Business, Cat. No. FS2.7/a:2968. 5 cents.

Hot Weather Comfort, Cat. No. FS2.50:3. 5 cents.

What Every Person Should Know About Milk, Cat. No. FS2.8: 150. 5 cents.

Better Teeth, Cat. No. I 16.29:20. 5 cents.

The Human Heart, Cat. No. FS2.2:H35. 15 cents.

Safety for the Household, Cat. No. Cl3.4:463. 75 cents.

Looking Forward to the Later Years, Public Health Pub. No. 116. 5 cents.

CHAPTER III

Income Planning for Financing Retirement Living

About eighteen million persons aged sixty-five years and over are expected to be living in the United States by 1960. This estimated figure almost reaches the present combined populations of Canada and Australia.

There are now roughly ten million persons in the United States who are sixty-five years of age and over. Of these:

2,800,000 are partially supported by family, friends or private charity.

2,700,000 are self-supporting, working for others or self-employed.

2,500,000 are dependent upon public authorities, chiefly state old-age assistance plans.

2,000,000 are retired on incomes that include employment pension plans, investments, annuities, savings accounts and Social Security benefits.

The 1950 census indicates that the median income of families in the sixty-five and over age group was $986 per year. Data on income further reveals that in the sixty-five-plus age group:

30 per cent had incomes less than $1,000 per year
21 " " " " between $1,000 and $2,000 per year
16 " " " " " $2,000 and $3,000 " "
18 " " " " " $3,000 and $5,000 " "
15 " " " " over $5,000 " "

The Social Security Administration estimates that in 1950 around eight hundred thousand persons aged sixty-five and over were getting an average of $480 a year from their own savings, annuities, investments and other property. About 350,000 were drawing retirement benefits or annuities, averaging $660 a year, from private employers or collective retirement plans.

A country-wide survey of 15,500 persons who received Social Security benefits every month of 1951 showed that less than half of them had cash or bank balances of as much as $500.

From the above, it is obvious that retired persons on the whole have to get by on rather slim budgets. This fact emphasizes how vital it is for individuals to plan in advance how to obtain the income needed to finance the standard of living they desire for themselves in retirement.

How Much Will You Need for a Retirement Nest Egg?

You cannot tell exactly how much money you will require during the years you live in retirement. But you can make an estimate of the size of the reserve fund you will need to see you through.

The President's Council of Economic Advisers in 1952 classified family incomes under $1,000 as substandard. Those of $2,000 and over were classified as minimum or better. $2,000 is below the minimum adequate for a typical city family. But it was considered adequate for a farm family and for elderly two-person families and some single individuals.

A study was made recently by the Bureau of Labor Statistics covering the prices of seventy items in an elderly couple's cost of living budget. This study indicated that from $1,602 in New Orleans to $1,908 in Milwaukee, at 1950 price levels, was needed for a "modest but adequate" level of living. The average yearly rent for a two- or three-room dwelling, plus cost of gas, electricity, water and heating fuel, ranged from $436 in New Orleans to $705 in Milwaukee. The combined cost of food, clothing, housefurnishings and all other items included in the budget ranged from $1,126 in Savannah to $1,269 in Seattle.

The Retirement Research Division, Florida State Development Commission, comes up with some interesting facts on incomes from a study of retired people living in St. Petersburg. Retired men and women reported an average income of $158 per month per family. Two-fifths of the families received from $100 to $199 per month. One-fifth had incomes ranging from $200 to $500 per month. Half of the retired persons had monthly incomes of less than $120.

As for California, most advisors say that a retired couple living there should have an income of at least $2,400 to $3,-000 a year to live on.

Another index to the financial needs of retired persons is that advocated by the Townsend Plan National Convention in 1952. There are twelve thousand Townsend Clubs, with a membership of five million aged persons. The Townsendites want monthly payments of $175 for every person over sixty who is not gainfully employed. Having lived a number of years in retirement, the Townsendites feel that $2,100 a year is the minimum needed for retirement living.

Your standard of living will determine your requirements. People are disposed, as a rule, to regulate their standard of living as their incomes and savings increase or decline. Too great a decline in the habitual standard of life may bring about discouragement and unhappiness. While some downward adjustment of the standard of living may be necessary in retirement because of reduced income, the more near normal the standard maintained, the better are the opportunities for enjoying comfort and contentment.

You Will Probably Need Less Income in Retirement

1. Your living expenses will decrease, particularly if you decide on moving to the South or to a rural area, where the cost of housing, clothing and food will be lower.

2. Work expenses will stop. You will eliminate costs of going to and from your place of employment. You will save the cost of work lunches. Expenses will stop in connection with business or association conventions and trips and clubs. Also with cost of books, equipment or tools.

3. You can cut down on "front" expenses. There is no good reason now for residing in an expensive neighborhood, belonging to expensive clubs, owning a costly automobile, wearing expensive clothes, giving parties to impress people. You can cut the cost of living by cutting the cost of living high.

4. Taxes will be lower. Your federal and state income and Social Security taxes will be reduced; you may even be exempt. If you move into a lower tax-assessment community, your real estate taxes and personal taxes will be reduced.

5. Cost of supporting children in all probability will be reduced. In the majority of cases, children will have grown up and have finished school or college. They will probably be married and supporting families of their own.

6. Good pre-retirement planning will result in considerable savings. You will probably own your home outright. This will eliminate mortgage payments. Your life insurance policies will more than likely be paid up or you may convert them to paid-up policies. Your personal and time-payment accounts should be paid up. You will need less money to operate on and still maintain a comfortable standard of living.

At the age of sixty-five a man's life expectancy is twelve years. For a woman, at the age of sixty-five, life expectancy is fourteen years. With the present cost of living for a two-person family at around $2,400 to $3,000 a year, a man and wife would need, under normal circumstances, $28,800 to $36,000 to provide for their retired years.

Very few families accumulate a cash reserve fund of this size. Some other sources of supplementary income are necessary to make up the difference between the family's cash reserve and the amount required for living while retired.

The Best Years to Accumulate a Retirement Nest Egg

The years between the ages of forty and sixty-five, for the majority of individuals, are the fruitful years of income-earning power. These are the productive years when experience and vigor bring forth the biggest pay envelopes, salary checks or professional fees. They are also the years to plan wisely for retirement so that you may have adequate income in the harvest years of life.

If you desire financial security in retirement, you must first of all find out where you stand *now*. You must know where you are starting from, what you are currently worth, in order to plan successfully how to attain your financial goal.

What Is Your Net Worth *Now?*

Your net worth is a financial statement of what you own and the form in which it exists, together with what you owe and the nature of the obligations, and the surplus that exists between the two. Net worth is, therefore, a balance sheet showing how well off you are financially. An analysis of your personal financial balance statement discloses strength or weakness in the character of your financial program. Knowing where you stand now helps you to plan the steps necessary to guarantee your reaching the level of economic security you set for yourself.

Your net worth statement should look something like this:

Your Assets		Your Liabilities	
Cash on hand	$____	Accounts payable $____	
Cash in bank	____	Notes payable	____
Cash surrender value of your		Mortgages owed	
insurance policies	____	on real estate	____
Market value of stocks and bonds	____	Debts and other	
Annuities and pensions	____	money obligations	____
Market value of real estate owned	____	Claims against	
Mortgages owned		your estate	____
Notes receivable	____	Unpaid taxes	____
Accounts receivable	____		
Cash value of business or other			
interests	____		
Cash value of furniture, automo-			
bile and other salable assets	____		
Social Security benefits	____		
Total Assets	$____	Total Liabilities	$____

NET WORTH (excess of assets over liabilities) $____

Regular rechecks of your net worth statement every five years are a good safeguard against income deficiency. It is important that you be in good financial health as well as physical health to protect your interests today, and to assure yourself a comfortable retirement later on.

Basis for Financial Planning

The next step for you to take in making a plan for financial self-security is to decide how much money you can reasonably afford to put into various classes of estate-building investments and savings. The figure decided upon, of course, should be revised from time to time as your surplus income increases and your family circumstances vary.

Another factor to consider is the necessity for the family to enjoy a reasonably comfortable standard of living while building for the future. It is not wise to overdo things by employing a penny-pinching policy or an "austerity" existence now in the prospect of avoiding income deficiency after retirement. This calls for a certain degree of thrift to accumulate savings, making the most of income-producing capabilities, and at the same time putting the savings to work to produce additional net worth, without interfering with the current standard of living.

For maximum retirement-income security, income sources should be diversified. Fixed income from Social Security benefits, employment pension plans, annuities and cash in the bank decrease in purchasing power as the value of the dollar shrinks in times of inflation. During depressions, other sources of income, like stock dividends and rents, produce lower returns. Persons are wise indeed who, during their greatest earning periods, buy future financial security by investing their money in a carefully planned, diversified portfolio.

Trends in Retirement

Most retirement plans are based on the concept of offering the employee some degree of security in his old age, as a reward for satisfactory service over a specified period of years. Retirement and pension plans are also conceived as a method of purchasing the employee's seniority rights so that the older employee will turn over the rights and duties of his job to a younger man.

The theory is that, in order to attract and retain ambitious younger men, opportunities need to be provided for them to move forward in their careers. Also, there is a feeling strong in many companies that one of the consequences of physical aging, after sixty-five, is a slowing down of vigor. This slowdown, employers say, can reduce efficiency at both the management and the production levels.

If the trend toward compulsory retirement of persons aged sixty-five and over continues, more and more people are going to be pushed into retirement. Unless they prepare themselves for it, many will find this forced retirement a severe financial burden.

Emergency "Cushion" Fund

For a feeling of financial security, it is wise to have a "cushion" fund in which cash is available quickly. The minimum cash reserve you should maintain in the fund during your workday years should be equal to about three times your monthly average family living budget, or at least $1,000. For individuals living in retirement, a cushion fund equal to about the cost of living for two years should provide peace of mind financially. In other words, a retired couple whose living expenses are $200 a month should have between $4,-500 to $5,000 in their emergency fund.

The best place to keep this fund is in a separate savings account in a bank whose savings deposits are guaranteed by the United States-controlled Federal Deposit Insurance Company. Here it will draw interest and is available quickly as emergencies arise.

The best way to build up a cushion fund is to make regular weekly or monthly deposits. The deposits should be supplemented by financial windfalls and other income additions such as legacies, bonuses, etc. When the fund becomes larger than is required, the surplus over and above the minimum needed for the cushion can be withdrawn to pay off the mortgage on a home, or to purchase annuities or other investments.

A Few Things You Should Know About Social Security

The Federal Old-Age and Survivors Insurance provides three different kinds of insurance:

1. *Monthly Retirement Insurance* for workers who retire at or after age sixty-five, and for their families.
2. *Monthly Survivors' Insurance* for families of workers who die.

3. *Lump-sum Payments* to an insured worker's widow or widower, or to the person who paid the worker's burial expenses.

Becoming Insured

To have Social Security protection, you must be insured. This means you must have worked at employment covered by Social Security for a minimum length of time. Social Security measures your time in quarters of a calendar year. One quarter is January 1 through March 31, April 1 through June 30, July 1 through September 30, or October 1 through December 31, in which you were paid wages of $50 or more in covered employment. To receive *maximum* benefits you must have at least forty quarters of coverage.

The Social Security law requires a person in covered employment to pay a Social Security tax on his monthly wages or self-employed earnings up to $300 a month. He must pay the tax regardless of age or how many quarters he works.

For each full year in which a self-employed person's earnings are $400 or more, he will receive four quarters of coverage. If self-employment earnings are less than $400 a year, they do not count toward benefit payments or quarters of coverage. Self-employed persons pay their Social Security tax every year along with their individual income tax.

This Is What You Get

The exact amount of your retirement benefits payable at the age of sixty-five can be determined only after you have filed a claim and the Social Security office has figured and approved it. But you can get a fairly accurate idea of what your benefits will be by using the simplified formula and table given here.

A number of important changes were made in the Federal Old-Age and Survivors Insurance by amendments to the Social Security Act in 1952. As a result there are currently two methods for computing Social Security retirement payments. For the sake of simplicity we will refer to the formula of the 1952 amendment.

Your retirement benefits are figured under the new formula after you have earned six quarters of coverage during the years after 1950. If you do not have six quarters of coverage beginning with 1951, see your local Social Security office regarding the old method of figuring retirement benefits. Beneficiaries who are already receiving payments based on covered earnings beginning in 1937 may have their benefits figured under the new formula. If they have had six quarters of covered work after 1950, higher retirement payments are possible.

Remember: To receive the maximum benefits listed you must have forty quarters of coverage in all.

First step in figuring your benefits by the new formula. Add your wages in covered employment or self-employed income after 1950. Do not include any wages or income over $3,600 for any one year.

Second step. To find average monthly wage, divide by the number of months after 1950 up to the quarter in which you reach sixty-five (if less than eighteen, use eighteen). The average monthly wage cannot be more than $300 per month.

Third step. Take 55 per cent of the first $100 of your average monthly earnings.

Fourth step. Take 15 per cent of the remainder up to two hundred dollars.

Fifth step. Add the amounts obtained under steps three and four. The total you get is your basic retirement payment.

The minimum payment to an insured person who has retired and is eligible for payments is $25 per month. The maximum payment to a retired person without dependents is $85 a month. The total amount paid to members of your family (your wife or children under eighteen) is computed on your basic retirement benefit. The total monthly benefit payment to a retired worker and his family cannot be more than 80 per cent of his average earnings or total more than $168.80.

Under the 1952 law, average monthly earnings over $300 a month per year do not count toward Social Security retirement benefits. The current ceiling of $300 on average monthly earnings, as well as the pension formula method, may be raised in the future.

The table below shows retirement payments figured under the new law as amended in 1952. Amounts in the table for selected average monthly earnings are for persons claiming benefits based only on earnings after 1950.

Retirement Benefits

Average Monthly Earnings after 1950	*Retired Worker*	*Retired Worker, and Wife at 65*	*Retired Worker, Wife and One Child under 18*
Under $ 35.00	$25.00	$ 37.50	$45.00
100.00	55.00	80.00*	80.00
150.00	62.50	93.80	120.10*
200.00	70.00	105.00	140.00
250.00	77.50	116.30	155.10
300.00	85.00	127.50	168.80*

* Reduced to total maximum family benefits permitted by law.

When Payments Stop

If you are under seventy-five years of age, retirement benefits will not be payable for any month in which you come out of retirement to work in covered employment for wages of more than $75 a month.

Self-employment earnings up to $900 in a year will not affect your retirement payments; for each additional $75 or part of $75, one month's benefit is not payable.

After you are seventy-five, your earnings from any source will not affect your Social Security retirement payments.

Payments to dependents based on your Social Security account are not payable for any month in which your check is not payable.

The marriage of any person receiving monthly benefit payments as a dependent or as a survivor will stop payments. If the wife or dependent husband of a retired insured worker is divorced, payments are stopped.

When the child entitled to benefits reaches the age of eighteen or marries before reaching the age of eighteen, payments to the child are stopped.

You Need More Than Social Security Benefits

Many people are coasting along expecting their Social Security retirement benefits to provide enough pension income to live on in retirement. They are in for a big disappointment. Of the four and a half million persons who now receive Social Security benefits, almost a half million must depend upon aid from public assistance funds. Only about one out of every eight persons receiving Social Security has as much as $50 a month income in addition to Social Security benefits.

The average Social Security retirement benefit paid to those entitled to them in 1952 was $47.25 a month for a retired worker and $81.50 for a retired worker and aged wife. For an aged widow it was $36. Even under the law as it was changed in 1952 to permit increases in benefits, the maximum retirement benefit a retired worker can receive is $85 a month as an individual, or $127.50 a month if he has a wife over sixty-five.

If the wife of a man receiving Social Security retirement benefits is younger than he is (in two-thirds of marriages wives are younger than husbands), she cannot get Social

Security benefits based on the husband's basic benefits until she too reaches the age of sixty-five. Of the two million men receiving Social Security retirement payments, only about five hundred thousand have wives old enough to qualify for benefits.

The sixty-five-year-old wife of a man receiving Social Security retirement benefits can receive a monthly benefit equal to 50 per cent of the husband's basic benefit. A child under eighteen years of age of an individual entitled to Social Security benefits is entitled to 50 per cent of the father's basic benefit. When the husband dies, the widow, when she becomes sixty-five, can receive a monthly benefit of 75 per cent of the husband's basic benefit.

Social Security retirement benefits are not paid automatically. You must go to your local Social Security office and file a claim for your benefits. Retirement benefit payments are retroactive only as far back as six months.

Social Security is now compulsory for many types of work-for-yourself activities. The owner of a store, lunch counter, filling station, beauty parlor, rooming house; the independent contractor; the artist and the writer who earns $400 or more in any one year, is covered by the law and his self-employment income will count toward Social Security payments. His contribution toward Old-age and Survivors insurance protection is payable at the time he files his income tax return.

Not Included for Social Security

The following professionals are not included in Social Security: doctor, dentist, architect, osteopath, optometrist, naturopath, veterinarian, chiropractor, Christian Science practitioner, certified public accountant or full-time practicing accountant, funeral director or professional engineer. Self-employment as a farm operator is excluded. Clergymen and members of religious orders are not included. Employees of nonprofit charitable, religious, educational, scientific or literary organizations came under the law only if the employing organization accepts Social Security.

Survivors' Insurance Payments

When a currently insured worker dies at any age, monthly Survivors' Insurance benefits are paid to his unmarried children under eighteen and widow or dependent divorced wife (regardless of age) if caring for a child.

A lump-sum payment is made to an insured worker's widow or widower or to the person who paid burial expenses. This payment may be made even though monthly benefits are also paid.

A worker is currently insured and his dependents are qualified for the Survivors' Insurance feature if he has worked any six quarters (equal to one and a half years) within three years before his death. The amount of the insurance benefits paid to survivors depends upon the insured person's average monthly earnings and the number of dependents who survive him.

How to Increase Social Security Benefits

The amount of your Social Security benefit is determined by your average monthly earnings up to $300.

If a retired worker sixty-five or over is not receiving the maximum benefit payment, it is probably because his average monthly earnings before retirement were not high enough.

You can return to work in covered employment and qualify for a higher retirement payment by increasing your average monthly earnings after obtaining the required six quarters of coverage. If you are over sixty-five but under seventy-five, your Social Security benefit will not be paid for the months you earn $75 or over. But you will qualify for a higher benefit when you quit work. If you are over seventy-five, you can still receive Social Security benefits while earning $75 a month.

If you are sixty-five and are receiving a wife's or widow's benefit, you may go to work and qualify for a higher benefit in your own right after six quarters of coverage.

Another way to increase your income is to work at a job not covered by Social Security. You will then continue to receive your retirement benefits while working. However, you will have to confine your employment.

If you cannot increase your benefit by going to work, you can still increase your income by getting a job not covered by Social Security and still receive your retirement benefits while working. However, you will have to confine your employment to jobs such as those that are not covered under the Social Security Act. You can also add to your income by going to work in domestic employment, provided you do not work for one person more than a part of twenty-three days in a quarter. Be sure to check with the local Social Security field office for complete details.

A self-employed person not covered by the Social Security Act, such as a lawyer or doctor, if he was over twenty-one years of age on December 31, 1950, can go to work for another self-employed person or in covered employment on a salary basis. When he has worked for one-half the time after age twenty-one or December 31, 1950, whichever is later and the attainment of age sixty-five, he can receive Social Security benefits when he retires (minimum of six quarters of coverage required). Consult your local Social Security field office for details before engaging in this type of employment.

A husband and wife may both work in covered employment long enough for each to become entitled to benefits at the age of sixty-five.

For Additional Information

Visit your local Social Security field office or write to Department of Health, Education and Welfare, Social Security Administration, Washington, D.C. There are a number of free pamphlets available explaining how Social Security benefits apply to you and your family.

What's Your Company Pension Worth to You?

Find out early in your retirement planning program how your company retirement or pension plan operates. Check on how much you can expect to receive when you retire.

Pension plans usually require a long period of continuous work service—ten to thirty years—with the pension-paying company. The amount of your pension income is usually determined by the number of years you work for your last employer and, in some instances, the amount of your average wages or salary.

In some industrial and business company pension plans, employees make contributions to the pension fund. Many company pension plans, however, are financed entirely by the company and special trust funds are set aside for this purpose. Some plans make provision for benefits in the case of death or of permanent total disability. Some pension plans contain provisions that pensions can be discontinued or decreased.

Here's what typical company pension plans pay.

The size of retirement pension varies according to the formula on which the particular company plan is set up. Here are a few common methods of figuring the size of retirement pensions:

One hundred and twenty-five dollars a month including Social Security benefits, for workers past sixty-five years of age, with thirty years of service. Proportionally smaller benefits for shorter service.

One hundred and twenty-five dollars a month minimum guaranteed, including Social Security benefits, at age of sixty-five for men, sixty for women, after twenty-five years of service, or 1 per cent of average monthly salary for last ten years of service multiplied by number of years of service.

Many plans provide pension income which, added to Social Security benefits, pay about 45 per cent of annual compensation for those in the $3,000 a year bracket, from 40 to 45 per cent for those between $5,000 and $15,000, and from 25 to 40 per cent for those over $15,000.

The pattern of retirement pension plans, based on an analysis of several of the leading company plans, seems to be in the direction of slightly more than $100 a month for an unmarried worker and about $130 a month for a married man, including Social Security benefits. Some unions have their eyes on retirement pension plans. Increased pension payments to union members will be a big issue in negotiated contracts that come up from now on.

There are other types of company pension plans that are based on deferred compensation on an annual profit-sharing arrangement. A certain sum of money set aside each year for each eligible participant is placed in a trust fund. When the participant retires, his or her interest in the trust fund is paid over in cash or in an annuity.

Executive pensions. Only a small group of high-paid, top-level executives enjoy large pensions. The amount of pension compensation and the method of computing executive pensions varies widely with individual companies and types of business. In general, retirement pensions of the highest paid corporation executives who benefit from company pensions plans range from 10 to 30 per cent of their average compensation. The majority of top-management executives do not, however, have the benefit of company retirement pension plans. The company philosophy has been that top executives receive such high salaries that they should set up their own retirement programs out of savings and investments without benefit of company pensions.

There is no guarantee you will receive a pension. If you are discharged before reaching retirement age, you may lose all rights to your pension. You also run the risk of being forced to leave for health or other reasons before completing the length of service and age requirements. Reorganization of the company, a period of low earnings or lack of work might also call for discharging employees and revamping the pension plan. Pensions can be delayed, or stop, pending union negotiations at any time.

In most industrial retirement pension plans, supported in full by the employer, only those employees who have already retired are provided for in the trust fund and are covered by a guaranteed pension. There is usually no guarantee that those employees currently working will also be covered by retirement pensions, although most employers do intend to continue their pension plans.

War Veterans' Pensions

Public laws provide a free indemnity payment to survivors of men and women who die while in the armed forces.

Compensation is also paid to veterans for approved disabilities incurred in connection with services while in the armed forces, plus additional money in such cases for dependents. Payments are made for service-connected loss of certain parts of the body, such as arms, legs, hands and eyes. Pensions are paid to veterans and their dependents for non-service connected disabilities, if they meet income and other requirements for eligibility. The amount of compensation depends upon the disability classification approved by the United States Veterans Administration.

Federal Civil Service Retirement System

Retirement plans for civilian employees of the Federal Government usually provide benefits based on a formula related to length of service and salary. All employees of the executive, judicial and legislative branches of the United States Government and the municipal government of the District of Columbia are covered, except those who come under other special retirement plans.

Employees contribute 6 per cent of their base salary to the Civil Service Retirement and Disability Fund. They can make voluntary payments up to 10 per cent of total salary to purchase additional retirement benefits. Employee contributions go towards the purchase of a retirement annuity. While retirement benefits are proportional to the number of years of creditable service, at least fifteen years of service is required for various age-retirement benefits.

The Federal Civil Service Retirement Benefit consists of the annuity supported by employee contributions plus a pension paid by the Government. The Government pension benefit is 1½ per cent of the highest five-year average salary for each year of service. The benefit must not be more than 80 per cent of average salary.

Railroad Retirement and Survivor Benefit Plan

Monthly retirement annuities are payable to employees of all railroads who are:

1. Sixty-five years of age and have completed ten years of service.
2. Sixty to sixty-four years of age and have completed thirty years of service. Annuity is reduced for men but not for women.

3. Sixty to sixty-four years of age, have completed ten years of service, are permanently disabled for work in their regular railroad occupation and have a current connection with the railroad industry.

4. Less than sixty years of age, have completed twenty years of service, are permanently disabled for work in their regular railroad occupation and have a current connection with the railroad industry.

5. Less than sixty-five years of age, have completed ten years of service and are permanently disabled for all regular gainful employment.

A monthly annuity is also payable to the wife (or dependent husband) of a retired employee who is sixty-five years of age. The wife must also be sixty-five or have in her care an employee's child who is unmarried, under eighteen and dependent upon the employee.

State and Local Government Systems

It is estimated that almost two out of three state and local government employees are covered by retirement systems. Practically all retirement systems for public employees provide disability as well as retirement benefits. The benefits under most plans are related to years of service and average salary. Sixty is the most common minimum retirement age. There is no standardization in the requirement provisions. Retirement benefits of police and firemen, because of their occupational hazards, are generally more liberal than those for other public employees. The effectiveness of some of the state and local systems has been hampered by the voluntary nature of coverage provisions.

Public School Teachers' Retirement Plans

Public school teachers are covered by state retirement systems, with the exception of retirement plans of a number of large cities. Benefits usually are related to average salary and years of service.

College and University Retirement Plans

The Teachers' Insurance and Annuity Association of America, founded at the suggestion of the Carnegie Foundation, offers a noncashable, nonforfeitable, deferred annuity contract with flexible premiums and maturity date to college and university staff members. Premiums for the purchase of the annuity may be paid either by the staff member or by the college or university having membership in the Teachers' Insurance and Annuity Association.

Some institutions have their own privately controlled pension plans. They are usually established on a joint-contributory basis. A common method is to set aside 10 per cent of the employee's salary shared equally by the staff member and the institution. There are many variations of the percentage set aside and the employee-employer matching. As a general rule the retirement pension is one-half the average salary for the last five or ten years preceding retirement. The normal age of retirement is seventy, though in some plans it is sixty-five or sixty-eight years of age. Most college and university plans have a disability benefit as a secondary feature.

General Observations on Pension Income

The majority of retirement pension incomes by themselves are not sufficient to meet the costs of living for a two-person family. Retired workers, therefore, must supplement the family income from some other source. This is particularly true when the retirement pension includes Social Security benefits.

There are wide extremes in pension plan practices of providing for the pensioner's spouse after the death of the pensioner. Many plans make no provision for pension pay beyond the life of the original pensioner. A few plans provide pensions at a reduced rate for the living spouse. These facts should be taken into consideration in planning sufficient monthly income to replace the pension reduction or termination after the death of the pensioner.

Too much dependence on pension income is unrealistic. If your pension should not materialize, you must be prepared to meet the financial needs of living in retirement through other income sources. By failing to look at all sides of the pension picture, you run the risk of being unable to provide for your economic comfort in the harvest years of life. Many employees and employees' wives are happy in the mere knowledge that they have a retirement pension plan. They don't know what is in the plan. Investigate the details of your plan several years before retirement becomes a fact. This advance knowledge of what to expect places the retirement pension in its true perspective in relation to overall retirement income.

What You Can Do with Life Insurance

The basic reason for buying life insurance is to protect the family by assuring them of an income in case death should take away the head of the family. Many a widow today is living in comfortable circumstances as the result of her husband's planned insurance program. But, in addition to affording this protection, life insurance also has a cash-savings value that can be used for retirement income.

By the time you are ready to retire, your children will probably be grown and earning their own incomes or married and establishing families of their own. The protection value of your life insurance policy is not so important as in the earlier period of your life when the family was young and dependent on you. Under these conditions, you can convert your policy into a life-income policy or an annuity. The rate of monthly cash income, of course, depends upon the cash value of the policy.

In the case of married persons with dependents to be provided for after the death of the insured, a retirement income policy or a joint annuity can be purchased for the cash value of the policy. This would continue the annuity payments after the death of the first annuitant.

For those who continue to need life insurance protection, a policy that is paid up at retirement age can be maintained in effect, at its current value, without the payment of additional premiums. This relieves the drain of current insurance premiums on the individual's retirement income.

Insurance that is not fully paid up can be converted into a paid-up policy and continued in effect but providing a smaller insurance benefit. This policy can also be converted into a retirement income policy or into an annuity. The amount of the monthly annuity payment will depend upon the age and sex of the beneficiary and the cash value of the insurance policy.

Two insurance policies that are valuable in planning a retirement program are the limited payment policy and the endowment policy.

A limited-payment policy calls for premiums during a specified number of years after which the policy becomes fully paid up. An endowment policy pays a specified sum of money at the end of a specified number of years—like $10,000 in twenty years. If an endowment policy were taken out at the age of forty, the money under a twenty-year endowment would be available at the age of sixty.

Insurance policies in many instances have a substantial loan value. Insurance companies will lend you money based on the cash surrender value of your policy; the longer you have paid premiums, the larger the amount you can borrow.

Investigate your job or group insurance plan, and check the features of the plan as they refer to your entire insurance program and especially any features that refer to retirement.

Group insurance is usually term insurance and has no loan or cash surrender value. It is temporary and not permanent protection.

One of America's leading industrial companies has a group-insurance plan with interesting retirement features. For most employees the life insurance amounts to approximately one and a half times straight yearly earnings, with $2,000 as a minimum, and the average amount over $4,500. After normal retirement age (sixty-five for men and sixty for women), life insurance continues on a reduced basis with no further contributions from the employee. The company plan also provides up to $500 for hospital and surgical benefits after normal retirement age at no cost.

A veteran of World War I or World War II carrying National Service Life Insurance has the cheapest form of life insurance he can buy. No insurance company can duplicate its low premium rate. This insurance can be converted into an endowment policy.

In your overall insurance planning program, be sure you have hospitalization, and sickness and accident policies in addition to life insurance. If you already have these policies, examine them to find out whether or not they can be canceled at older ages. Because older persons are more frequently ill than young people, the chances are that sickness, accident and hospital insurance will be of increasing importance to you. A residence policy will protect you against fire and theft in your home. If you, while driving your car, should be involved in an accident causing injury or death to others or damage to another's property, your entire life savings could be wiped out, unless you are protected by automobile liability insurance.

Your insurance policies should be coordinated into a definite planned program. Life insurance offers a combination of protection and investment and is a practical way to create an estate. A reputable and conscientious insurance agent will help you work out a plan in detail. You will be much better off dealing with one agent in whom you have confidence than in buying insurance policies at random.

Annuities Provide Protection Against Running Out of Money

An annuity guarantees a specified income for life, after you reach a specified age or date. You can buy an annuity by agreeing to pay a sum of money in monthly or yearly installments or in a lump sum. For this the company, usually an insurance company, will pay you a specified income, to begin on a specified date and to continue as long as you live. It assures you freedom from investment worries while conserving savings. It assures you that, in retirement, your income will not be wiped out. Payment checks come in every month for life.

Annuities differ from insurance in that they are designed to protect your income as long as you live, while insurance, in addition to savings features, protects your dependents when you die. If a man pays the annuity company $20,000 in a lump sum at the age of sixty-five, the company guarantees to pay him a regular monthly income of around $128 as long as he lives. A woman of sixty-five would get around $110 a month for life for an investment of $20,000, because women on the average live longer than men.

The price of an annuity depends upon your age, sex and the kind of annuity you buy. There are several different types. A straight life annuity pays an income for life but all payments stop at death. Joint and survivor annuities provide an income for life for two or more persons as long as one or more live. Buying an annuity is a practical way to save for old age. If you have enough money, it is a good idea to put part of it into annuities and part into other income-producing investments. If you are not concerned about conserving your estate for heirs, annuities are especially valuable in your retirement planning.

What About Stocks as an Investment?

Nearly six and a half million persons, one in every sixteen adults, own stocks in American corporations. They buy stocks because they believe the stocks will increase in value and provide capital growth. They buy stocks because of the income received from dividends. Some people buy stocks to build up an estate. Others buy stocks as a hedge against inflation. Generally speaking, there is not much chance that the average man will get rich overnight in the stock market.

Don't speculate in stocks to build up your estate. To trade in stocks successfully, which means buying well and selling well, you have to be right twice running. Thousands of persons who have tried speculation with pet theories, formulas and hunches have had their fortunes wiped out. Investing in good stocks for long-term capital growth can be profitable. But, even the stock market experts and the professionals have widely divergent views as to the value of selected stocks and turning points in the stock market.

From an income standpoint, some stocks return 15 per cent on your money; some 1.5 per cent; some have never paid a dividend; some have never missed one. There are risks and rewards in investments in stocks, and in bonds too. Before you start buying stocks for income or capital growth, decide how stocks fit into your overall plan. Any money you put into stocks should be over and above your cash reserve fund. For most people, it is wise to invest in life insurance and a few other stable investments, like a home, before buying stocks.

Don't put more than half your surplus savings into buying

stocks. Managing a securities investment program is a serious
business calling for a full measure of experience, judgment
and objectivity. Good common stocks of reliable, leading and
well-managed American companies bought for holding
and not for speculation are a good investment. Stay away
from new, small or local enterprises and the speculative
stocks of large companies. Diversify your stock holdings. If
you invest in stocks or bonds, the safest way to do it is on the
basis of experienced technical advice. Don't play your own
hunches. Be sure to pick a reputable brokerage house to
handle your transactions. If you have over $50,000, employ a
professional investment counselor to handle your investments
on a fee basis.

Look into Income-building Opportunities of Mutual Funds

The charted record of one mutual fund dealing in common
stocks shows the startling growth of $10,000 invested in
shares of this fund in January, 1941. Had all the distribu-
tions from the fund—both net profits and income—been
reinvested when received in more shares of the mutual fund,
the May, 1951, asset value would have totaled $31,019.

Of course this is past history. And there is no guarantee
that the next ten years will bring the same results. Shares of
mutual funds fluctuate in value with the changing market
prices of the various stocks or bonds owned by the fund.
Dividend income varies according to the income earned from
the securities owned by the mutual fund.

A mutual fund is an investment company through which
you and thousands of others pool money to obtain the diversity and safety you could not have buying stocks alone. You
buy shares that represent a proportionate interest in the many
diversified securities held by the mutual fund. Investment
experts operate the fund and select the stocks and bonds to
be bought based on their intimate knowledge of securities.

Your investment is therefore spread over many companies and industries. Your money instead of being all in one basket is diversified.

There are about two hundred mutual funds, or mutual trusts. Some are good investments, some are highly speculative. The problem is to find the ones that are a good investment for you. One way to find a good one is to compare the long-term performance records of one mutual fund against another and to check the reputation of those operating the mutual fund.

If you have surplus cash to spare, say under $2,000, you would probably be better off buying shares in a mutual fund rather than buying stock directly in a company. You can set up a system of investing your surplus savings automatically by making regular monthly purchases of shares out of your current earnings. For maximum protection divide your purchase of shares between investment funds that are old and reliable, with a good record of paying dividends. A mutual fund or trust composed largely of common stocks would be best for compounding income and the possibility of capital growth. Your banker or a reliable broker will tell you which are the best buys.

Real Estate Is a Good Field for Investment

Your first and most important investment in real estate is to buy and own outright your own home. Investment authorities say that the average family is justified in paying up to two times or at the most three times its annual income as the purchase price of a home. Many home buyers come to grief by taking on more than they can afford to carry financially when buying a home. You should be able to make a cash down payment of at least 25 per cent of the total cost of the home. So start your home buying program as early in life as possible. Pay off the mortgage as soon as you can.

When the mortgage is paid off, you can use your surplus cash for other investments.

If you're getting near retirement age and want to buy a home for your take-it-easy years, you had better have an assured cash income, or some large insurance policies for mortgage security. It is considerably harder for a person nearing sixty-five to borrow on a mortgage than it is for a family head in his forties. Prospective home buyers in the aging group will have to make bigger down payments than is required of younger borrowers. Mortgage lenders generally want the payment schedules worked out so that the mortgage will be paid off by the time the borrower reaches the age of seventy.

The best time to buy real estate for investment purposes is when real estate buying activity is low. Income producing properties bought at such times can usually be sold later at substantial profits. The real estate market operates in a cycle of prosperity and recession generally following the lines of the business cycle. Real estate cycles, however, usually have longer intervals between the top and the bottom of cycle swings.

Most profits in real estate are made by those who buy and sell income-producing properties in growing sections of prosperous cities, towns and communities. It takes keen observation to spot localities that are ripe for increased real estate values—to know what and when to buy and sell. The values of real estate depend on the use made of, and the nature of, useful improvements placed on it. One hundred acres of mountain-range land in Colorado is not nearly so valuable as a fully developed fifty-acre orange grove in Florida or California. The same fifty-acre grove would have still greater value subdivided into desirable business or home-site properties.

The greatest values for investment purposes are not in

lots for residential dwellings but in property that develops into income-producing units such as business districts, sites for gasoline stations, etc. However in many cities, alert operators buy large old homes, and remodel and modernize them into small apartment units. These properties are sold at advanced prices, or kept and rented for income.

Another way people make money in real estate is to buy lots and erect modern homes on them, furnish the homes, live in them for a time and then sell them completely furnished. This method is popular in Florida and California. Homes of this character may also be rented furnished or unfurnished for income. Building two-, three- or more family dwelling units on the same lot, living in one unit and collecting rentals from tenants for the other units is a popular way of securing retirement income from real estate. Still another popular type of real estate investment is the building with stores occupying the ground floor with offices or living units above.

Don't attempt to act as your own broker when buying or selling real estate. The expert, practical advice of a reliable and competent realtor should be sought by those not familiar with local real estate development conditions. A good realtor knows the values and potentialities of real estate in the locality which he serves. If you do not know a competent realtor, ask your banker or the local real estate board to recommend the names of accredited realtors with reputations for honest and fair dealings.

Income from Personal Savings

A savings bank is a safe place to keep money. Your account is protected up to $10,000 by the Federal Deposit Insurance Corporation. Money deposited in a savings bank earns from 2 to 2½ per cent interest. An interest account at compound interest is a growing investment. However, it takes a large principal to provide enough income from interest alone to provide for an adequate standard of living. For one hundred dollars a month, you would need a principal of $50,000 earning 2½ per cent.

A good way to accumulate savings is to take at least one-tenth of what you earn each pay day and deposit it in your savings account. Soon you will see your wealth growing like a tree. A safe return, even though a small one, is more desirable than a risky one for retirement purposes.

United States Savings Bonds

This is another safe place for your savings. The United States Government would have to become bankrupt for you to lose your principal. Series E Bonds which mature in about ten years pay 3 per cent interest if held until maturity. If you buy a Series E Bond for $75, you get $100 for it at maturity. No interest checks are paid on E Bonds so long as they are held by their owners. If the bonds are held until maturity, interest is paid in a lump sum. If they are cashed in before maturity, proportionate interest is paid. E Bonds are ideal for laying away money you don't want to spend. United States Savings Bonds can be had in denominations of $25, $50, $100, $200, $500, $1,000 and, for those who think in higher terms, $10,000.

Investigate Before You Invest

Here's some counsel that experienced investors give: Don't speculate with money you need for insurance, home payments or emergencies. Keep that separate. There is a certain amount of risk in managing money. Even if you bury money in your own back yard, you're still taking a risk—the risk that your money won't buy as much if prices rise and inflation sets in. When investing your money stay away from tips of well-meaning friends. Get the technical information you want about protecting your capital and at the same time putting it to work to earn a return on investments from an unbiased specialist—a reliable banker or investment counsel.

Public Old-age Assistance

There will probably always be some persons in the community who do not have sufficient income to meet the needs of subsistence living. Some of them may not be covered by, or entitled to, Social Security benefits. Some, covered by Social Security and receiving the benefits, may require additional income to meet their minimum needs.

Under the Social Security Act persons who attain the age of sixty-five, are citizens of the United States, have resided within the state for a minimum length of time (different in the various states) and are in economic need may apply for public old-age assistance.

Persons must prove themselves needy to merit this public assistance. In 1951 more than 5,800,000 persons in the United States were receiving public assistance. Of these, more than 2,745,000 persons were receiving old-age assistance. The national average monthly payment for old-age assistance, in 1951, was $43.23 per recipient. There is a wide difference among states ($18.41 to $76.41) in the amount of the average payment made to recipients. This is due to the relative capacity of the state or local government units to finance their public assistance programs, as well as differences in the needs of various individuals. If Social Security benefits are being paid to an individual, this is taken into consideration in fixing the amount of public assistance paid to him.

Winding Up Business Interests

Disposing of personally held business interests at a fair value can be a critical factor when it comes time to retire.

That's why persons who own controlling interest or a large capital investment in business organizations should plan in advance how to dispose of their holdings. The owner of a retail establishment, wholesale business or small factory, for example, may face worry and financial loss if he tries to dispose of his business under unfavorable conditions.

Finding a suitable buyer can be a serious problem. Other factors that should be considered are taxes, proper timing, the transfer of franchise deals with suppliers and customers from present owner to new owner, patent ownership and arrangements, real estate and leases and other conditions peculiar to the type and size of the business.

Winding up a business is no easy matter. Many a man's life work has been sold at fifty cents on the dollar because little or no planning had been given to this problem. If you are a sole proprietor you should ask yourself this question: "What plans have I to dispose of my business at a fair value when I reach the time to retire?"

Importance of Making a Will

After having made provision for security by building up the net worth of your estate, the next most important duty in your financial program is provision for the disposition of these assets in the case of your death. Only about 50 per cent of husbands who die before their wives bother to make a will. This is a careless way of protecting an estate. It can be very painful for the wife and dependents.

Many people fail to make a will because they mistakenly believe that, in the absence of a will, the property will automatically go to the wife or to the children as they would wish it to go. This is not necessarily so. If there is no will providing for the disposition of an estate, then upon the owner's death it will be divided among heirs according to the laws of descent of the state. In some states, the wife would get only one-third of the estate, the remaining two-thirds being divided among all the children on an equal basis. If property is located in two or more states and there is no will, realty is usually disposed of according to the laws of descent of the state in which it is located.

Under these circumstances, serious problems sometimes arise and hard feelings develop among the heirs. The home where the wife lives might conceivably have to be sold to settle the estate. Property you originally intended for your wife or some particular member of the family could easily get dissipated in court actions and lawyers' fees while heirs fight a family feud to determine their rights.

Joint ownership of property is not a substitute for a will. Your wife may have to wait months before she can get possession of property or bank accounts. Banks and probate courts generally freeze all accounts and property at death. It may be several months before the estate is settled. Many a widow finds herself without sufficient cash income to live on or unable to pay for her husband's funeral expenses while his estate is being settled.

See a competent lawyer for expert advice before making a will. Do this while you are in good health and have plenty of time to study the will. This reduces the risk of your will being contested and assures disposition of your assets according to your wishes. If you have a large estate you may want to make certain dispositions of the estate while you are living to avoid high estate and inheritance taxes that otherwise would drain off a substantial part of your assets.

Planning Your Personal Estate

In our society man has assumed the role of protector of, and provider for, the family. To the woman society has assigned the functions of wife, mother and homemaker. Consequently, little effort has been made to train women in estate planning and management.

Life-expectancy records, however, show that women live longer than men. Most family fortunes eventually are inherited by women. Wives should therefore be equipped to handle money and property lest they mismanage or dissipate the estates left to them by their husbands.

Husbands can help their wives to learn by taking them into partnership on all financial matters which have a bearing on the future of the family. Many wives have no idea, until after the husband has passed away, of the extent and nature of the family's financial resources. They are totally unprepared to handle many critical situations that arise when the family estate falls into their hands.

One way for wives to secure training in the investment and management of family finances is to take up a selective reading or study course. They can also enroll in adult education courses on estate planning and management. A number of wives and husbands are using part of their retirement leisure to do this very thing.

Still another method is for the husband to make a gift of money or property to the wife while he is alive. The husband guides the wife in her investments and management of the fund or property. This gives her the practical experience she will need in administering the entire estate when the husband is not there as an active protector-provider. The same idea can be followed in training children to take over estate management.

Since World War I, women have proved their ability to handle business and financial matters by their successful records of achievement in many occupations in the office, factory, government and professions previously reserved for men. Women are fully capable of making a success of estate management, if they are properly trained for it.

To make things easy for your spouse to carry on your original estate planning, keep a detailed record or memoranda of the entire contents of your estate among your personal papers. Go over the entire estate program periodically with your spouse, or the executor of your estate. Let them know where all your personal papers can be easily and quickly found. This may save time, trouble and expensive legal proceedings.

You can dispose of your personal estate in these ways:

(1) Through your will you can make outright disposition of your assets.

(2) You can make outright gifts of parcels of your estate during your lifetime.

(3) You can create a "living trust" by transferring your estate or part of it to a trustee. The income from the estate is paid to you during your lifetime or to a specified person or persons for life, other persons to get the principal later. Some retired persons have established a living trust so that they can live a free life and not be bothered by the responsibilities of managing property and investments, yet be assured that they will have income protection against old age.

(4) You can protect your spouse or other dependents by assuring them an income for life by use of a "testamentary trust." This is done through a trust established by your will. The reason for creating a testamentary trust instead of giving the assets outright is to protect the beneficiary against his or her inexperience or folly in the management of the estate you created.

The disposition of an estate if you are wealthy is by no means a simple matter. The Federal Government imposes a stiff estate tax, above an exemption of $60,000. Some states, in addition, have their own estate or inheritance taxes. In many instances a large part of an estate has to be disposed of to pay these taxes.

Retirement is a good time to give special consideration to the disposition you plan to make of your personal estate. Since financial conditions, laws and family all change with the passage of time, the disposition should be carefully planned. You should seek the guidance of a lawyer in your planning. If yours is a large estate, make sure you select an attorney who specializes in this field of the law.

How to Beat Financial Insecurity

Your conclusion after reading this chapter may be that income planning for retirement living is a difficult assignment. This is true. Money accumulation and money management are by no means easy problems to solve. But if your later years are to be free of financial worries, and you want to enjoy a feeling of independence, then you must begin to gather in financial resources while there is time to do so.

If you suffer from income deficiency now and find it difficult to build up your net worth, some other sources must be found to create a nest egg for retirement.

There is a proverb which says: "Time is money." The weekend interval of Saturday and Sunday plus a few hours each night could be the answer to your problem. Perhaps you can combine your free time with your talents and skills and put them to work in a small but worth-while income producing enterprise.

What you can do. Many small businesses and personal service occupations can be started and operated at home. They can be built to the point where they can provide the additional money you need for protection in the future years. Read the chapters in this book on hobbies, establishing your own business and retiring to a farm. Possibly you will find a practical idea you can use now to bring in supplementary income for increasing your net worth. The spare-time activity you start now could develop into your principal source of income when it comes time for you to retire. Make a hobby out of whatever you propose to do. Be sure, however, that it does not interfere in any way with your regular job, which is your assured source of income.

Lay aside the money you earn from your part-time enterprise. Do not use it for any other purpose than to build up your net worth. Don't use it for current living expenses. Use the cash surplus to build up your emergency cushion fund, to expand the business enterprise, to pay off the mortgage on your home or put it to work in some income-producing investment. The first surplus money you acquire is the seed for starting the growth of your financial tree.

Action is the backbone of your program. Make out a program listing your specific goals for the next three to five years. The younger you are, the more leeway you have in working out your financial planning program. No one can prescribe a definite course of action for you. The purpose of this book is to help you do your OWN planning. Remember that your real wealth is represented by your brain, your energy, your ambition and your character, and not just the number of dollars you may own at the moment.

Bibliography

How to Plan Your Financial Security by Lawrence Washington (Whittlesey, N.Y.)

Managing Personal Finances by D. F. Jordan & E. F. Willett (Prentice-Hall, N.Y.)

How to Lay a Nest Egg by Edgar Scott (Wiston, Philadelphia)

Personal Estate Planning in a Changing World by Rene Wormser (Simon and Schuster, N.Y.)

Buying a House Worth the Money by Frazier F. Peters (Little, Brown, Boston)

U.S. Government Publications. Write to Superintendent of Documents, U.S. Government Printing Office, Washington 25, D.C.

Farm and Home Financial Planning, Cat. No. A 1.38:599. 10 cents

Guide to Family Spending, Cat. No. A 1.38:661. 15 cents

CHAPTER IV

Leisure-Time Activities with a Retirement Perspective

Everyone Should Have a Hobby

An active interest in a satisfying leisure-time activity stimulates the urge to do something, provides a pipeline to carry off emotional pressure and is a place to retreat from the tensions of the day.

Few jobs or occupations, outside of possibly art and music, provide sufficient psychological, social and cultural benefits to satisfy the human needs for a more fruitful and richer life. Interest in hobbies is a long step toward satisfying the thirst for contentment.

There comes a time in middle life, around the forties and fifties, when children have outgrown their stage of childhood, when the confining responsibilities of fatherhood and motherhood slack off somewhat. This presents a good opportunity to use the leisure time available to recapture a hobby started during your earlier years, or to begin to develop new hobbies in fields of special interest, which can be carried over into retirement.

If you dig down beneath the suface and get to the root of the problem of those who say they are unhappy in retirement, you will find that the majority have no satisfying leisure-time activities or hobbies. These unhappy people do not need a hobby as an escape mechanism, or to keep them from falling into a state of boredom, so much as they need a hobby to enrich their lives, to stimulate their thinking, to help them accomplish something positive with their skills and abilities.

Develop hobbies early in life and you will probably not have to search for something enjoyable or satisfying to do when you retire. Doctors and psychiatrists agree that a man or woman with stimulating hobbies can find retirement one of the happiest times of life.

If you have several hobbies, you will not fall into the trap of riding one too long so that it narrows your interests. By keeping several hobbies going, you can switch from one to another whenever you find that your interest in one of them seems to be drying up.

Some investigators, when making a field survey among retired workers, found that reference to the word "hobby" did not always bring favorable answers to questions put to retired persons. Hobbies were considered by these retired persons to be "sissy" activities or beneath their dignity. When the words "outside-of-work interests" or "leisure-time activities" were substituted for hobbies, the responses to the questions showed more positive interest. It makes little difference whether you call them spare-time activities or outside-of-work interests. The important thing is to have them. In retirement you can hardly have too many.

Hobbies are enjoyed by both men and women—and children as well. Everyone should be encouraged to develop hobbies that appeal to him. Many wives are obsessed with the notion that, because their husbands have an absorbing hobby, they have lost interest in their wives and families. Nothing could be further from the truth. Such thinking is largely selfish on the part of the wife. Instead of bickering and criticizing, these wives would be better off developing hobbies of their own. This would provide the couple with new opportunities for interesting topics of conversation. The wise and understanding will encourage their mates to develop a hobby. Also many creative hobbies can be carried on by both husband and wife together.

There seems to be no end to the list of possible hobby pursuits. You can have outdoor hobbies and indoor hobbies, summer as well as winter ones. There are hobbies which involve making things, collecting things, learning things and doing things. No one with hobbies need be lonely or discontented for long.

Hobbies should be taken up for their own sake, for the interests that exist in them, for the development of latent skills or talents, for the pleasure and personal satisfaction derived from them and for their intrinsic value. Most people take up hobbies merely as a form of relaxation and creative expression.

A hobby is one of the best conversation stimulators in the world. It encourages cooperation with like-minded folks and has been the basis for many lifelong friendships. The rewards sought and the satisfactions derived from hobby activities have nothing to do with monetary returns. In fact, many hobbies have no financial merit in themselves. They serve mainly as an insurance against boredom, contribute to cultural development, are activities leading to personal happiness or have some therapeutic value.

On the other hand, there are hobbies which if carried over into retirement, can open the door to income potentialities. They can be made a profitable avocation and can be developed to the point where they become a profitable business.

Popular Hobbies

Stamp collecting is America's number one hobby. There are some three million stamp collectors in the United States. Some people have large sums of money tied up in stamps as a long-term investment or as a form of savings. World famous stamp collectors were the late King George VI of Great Britain and President Franklin D. Roosevelt.

Almost four hundred thousand women collect handmade glass. This is the nation's number two hobby. Other popular collectors' items are coins, old prints, buttons, antique furniture, dolls, phonograph records, china, books, jokes, autographs, shells, miniature objects of all kinds—the list of items for collecting is endless. Collecting is a fascinating and stimulating hobby. Some collectors have correspondents all over the United States and in many foreign countries. A collector of cigarette packages in Chicago has four thousand cigarette packages, representing thirty-five hundred brands from sixty-six nations. He exchanges packages with collectors in Great Britain and Denmark.

The popular creative hobbies include numerous do-it-yourself activities, such as gardening, oil painting, ham radio, model railroading, home craftwork, photography and workshop projects.

A retired New York City banker has a cradle hobby. He has built almost a hundred to date. It takes this retired banker a day to make a cradle. He gives them away to small girls in the Connecticut town where he lives and to little girls in hospitals all over the East from Maine to Cuba. He finds himself busier than ever since retirement. The cradles, which in all cases are presented as gifts, cost him approximately $5 apiece which he feels is $5 well spent.

As a contrast to the retired banker with his cradle-making hobby, there is a retired vice-president, reported in *Fortune*, who commutes almost daily to New York City on the same train he took before he retired. He does this just to meet and talk with his old cronies. After killing most of the day going to movie theaters, he joins the crowd on the five-twenty for the ride and talk back to the suburbs. He has been doing this for seven years. Frustration and loneliness during the hours he used to spend on the job have gotten the better of him. He refuses to accept or to make adjustments to his retirement. This retired vice-president would be much more contented, if, like the retired banker, he had an absorbing hobby. He could, of course, like so many retired executives have done, engage in a small money-making enterprise or give his time and talents to one of his town's community or welfare boards.

An ex-newspaper man in Jackson, Miss., who retired and took up flowers as a hobby, planted a garden of one thousand rose bushes.

Home gardening has always been a popular leisure-time hobby in practically all parts of the world. You will find more books on the various branches of gardening in your public library than on any other hobby classification. It is a hobby you can enjoy with a patch of ground around the house or with a formal garden complete with greenhouse. Poets and philosophers have written much about it. Physicians and psychiatrists recommend gardening to many of their patients. There's nothing like getting your hands into Mother Earth to forget the cares and problems of the world.

A vegetable or herb garden, if large enough, can provide you with relaxation and a source of income. A vegetable garden will certainly keep down expenses by providing food for the table. And flowers, in addition to their beauty and decorative value, have provided many a person with supplementary income from the sale of cut flowers or the selling of novelty potted plants or flats of seedlings. One woman who makes a good living from gardening has a three-acre plot. She divides this into three gardens—spring, summer and fall. She sells cut flowers and plenty of white ones for weddings.

"Uncle Charlie" is a seventy-seven-year-old amateur gardener who for forty years has boarded the Staten Island Ferry to New York City every weekday morning at nine-fifteen with an armful of fresh-cut flowers. These he distributes to his fellow passengers as he walks down the aisle. What price does "Uncle Charlie" ask for his flowers? Just a "thank you" or a smile. Gardening as a hobby has a spiritual virtue as well as a practical one.

You can, in retirement, cash in on your practical gardening experience by establishing a custom landscape service, offering your knowledge and time for hire in pruning, care of shrubs and hedges, lawn maintenance and mowing, seeding lawns, rock-garden work, installation of flagstone walks, etc.

Here are some hobbies with profit-making possibilities and a few items you can make to bring in supplementary retirement income:

CERAMICS—Vases, ash trays, mugs, novelty salt-and-pepper shakers, jugs, bowls, figurines, lamps, tiles, pottery, floral containers.

WOOD—*Carving.* Statuettes, animals, birds, figurines, plaques, picture frames.

Cabinetwork. Reproduction of antique furniture, lawn furniture and ornaments, end tables, tea wagons, colonial, period or modern furniture, coffee tables, pin-up lamps, children's furniture, benches, stools, cupboards, kitchen cabinets, picket fences.

Small Articles. Flower stakes, trays, boxes, colonial kitchenware, lamps, knickknacks, hanging shelves, serving plates, book ends, salad bowls, toys, novelties, rustic birdhouses and feeders, forks and spoons.

METAL—*Copper.* Giftware, trays, teapots, decorative plates with fused-enamel finishes.

Gold or Silver. Jewelry, such as bracelets, earrings, pins, brooches.

Pewter. Plates, jugs, candlesticks, ash trays.

Iron. Hand-forged fireplace sets, hand forging, lanterns, colonial hardware, candlesticks.

LEATHER—Pocketbooks, billfolds, belts, wallets, original-design tooled leather goods.

PLASTICS—Novelties and fashion accessories.

TEXTILES—Needlework, crocheting, knitting, tatting, embroidering, sewing, quilting, braided rugs, woven rugs, stuffed toys, hand-woven place mats, bags, gloves, fabric-painted blouses, aprons, scarfs, ties, coverlets, draperies, luncheon sets, baby robes.

CONCRETE—Birdbaths, pedestals, garden urns, inlaid flagstone sidewalks, garden pools and ornamental objects, pottery, flower boxes.

MISCELLANEOUS—Handmade greeting and Christmas cards, hand-painted trays, shellcraft, perfume, food products, repair work of all kinds, restoration of old houses, writing, painting, composing music and songs.

Your local public library will have reference books on arts and crafts. Some states have state-wide extension services, usually under the Department of Education, to promote and develop arts and crafts in their states. A good how-to-do-it book is *Handicraft Hobbies for Profit,* by Robert Scharff (McGraw-Hill, N.Y.). A good list of over two thousand references to hobby and recreational subjects is *How-to-Do-It, A Selected Guide* by Robert E. Kingery (Bowker, N.Y.).

In home workshops, men and women are turning their hobbies into a source of supplementary retirement income. With modern power-driven bench tools and attachments, jigs and fixtures, new materials and finishes, these hobbyists soon become experts in the quantity production of distinctive and original items, novelties and gadgets of every shape and form. In basements, attached garages and sheds many a retired person finds relaxation and a source of income with project ideas that click with the public.

These products are usually sold direct by the craftsman, through city and resort gift and curio shops, by mail order or through novelty and gift jobbers located in the leading merchandise buying centers. In selling through stores it may be necessary to place the items with the store owners on consignment. This means that after the item is sold the shop owner takes a commission for selling it. Commissions usually are from 20 to 40 per cent of the purchase price. When establishing the purchase price, be sure you have figured in the cost of materials, packaging, if any, and the value per hour you place on your time and artistic ability.

Illustrative Cases of What Others Have Done

A man who lives in Maine was ordered by his doctor fifteen years ago to give up his regular job and retire because of his health. After overcoming his health problem, he started a small sign-painting business lettering advertising cards for local merchants. Eventually he drifted into making small wood novelty items commonly sold at resort spots. He conceived the idea of painting original saucy sayings on rustic wood plaques. These sold like hot cakes at $1.00 to $1.50 each. A silk-screen printing process was developed to turn out the sign plaques in large quantity. One of the largest toy distributors in New York City has ordered thousands of his novelties and souvenirs. They are now sold at novelty and souvenir counters all over the country. Over the years the business has been built up to what it is now—a $100,000-a-year enterprise.

Starting in 1944 with a cheap set of power tools, in a workshop in his home garage in a suburb of Los Angeles, Roy Adams (pseudonym) began making end tables and coffee tables out of Lucite. While Roy designed and made these furniture pieces, his wife hustled around selling them. Business was so good that this enterprising couple interested a few people in investing capital in their venture. Production was moved to larger quarters. Novelty jewelry items made from scrap plastic material were added to the line of furniture pieces. Again the business grew and was successful. Still not satisfied with financial security, Roy and his wife sold out their interest in the company. They then teamed up with a friend who had ideas for manufacturing toy furniture. The real big break came when this new company added a line of musical toys and developed their own music-making mechanism. Today, eight years after starting out in a home garage workshop, they have skyrocketed the current business into a four-million-dollar enterprise.

A New Hampshire hobbyist developed her own formula and method of making realistic-looking flowers. For an orchid corsage of her own creation, her prices range from $3.50 for a single large orchid. She handles her own sales and exhibits at New England fairs and exhibitions. In the three years since she started, this hobbyist has sold over a thousand orchids. In addition, she makes ten other types of flowers from lilies to pansies.

An advertising agency man had a hobby of mixing salads. He developed a combination that was sought after by his friends. For a while he made a hobby of supplying his friends with his original salad mix. Still producing from his apartment kitchen, he tried selling by mail. In less than a year he had over one thousand mail-order customers. With the mail-order business rolling under its own steam, he decided to try direct mail to grocers from names submitted by his steady customers. Five hundred grocers stocked his product. By this time production was too big for the kitchen and it was farmed out. At this point the bulk of the business is now handled by food brokers. What started five years ago as a hobby has now grown into a business valued at $150,000, with four new items added to the line.

A couple in California spent their last dollar to buy a ranch home. They used improvised nail kegs and boxes as furniture for a while. Finally they decided that if they were going to have furniture, it would have to be home built. The husband and wife laid out a pattern for a chair, drawing it on wrapping paper and set to work to make it. It turned out fine. Eventually, they built a lot of furniture for the ranch home, each piece drawn to full size on wrapping paper. Neighbors saw their handiwork, liked it and asked for copies of the homemade drawings. Word spread and the demand for the pattern drawings became so great that eventually the drawings had to be printed. Today, these printed furniture patterns, covering more than sixty articles, are sold by mail order all over the world.

In Florida, a seventy-one-year-old retired white-collar worker who had no special skill in craft work, looking for something to occupy his time, began making novelties out of bamboo. After a little experience, he got courage enough to put some of his items in a gift shop run by a relative. A popular item sold in the gift shop was tiny Guatemalan dolls made up as earrings. This retired man got an idea that bamboo poles cut into narrow slices at an extreme angle would make a good tiny frame for the dolls. As a result he turned out attractive earring frames into which he fits the one-inch dolls. The frames are sanded smooth, lacquered and fitted with ear screws. He now turns out several dozen pairs of bamboo earrings daily which he sells to gift shops at $10.50 for a dozen pairs. Gift shops retail them for $1.50 to $2.00 per pair. Selling the earrings at retail prices, he makes a net profit of $50 on three dozen pairs. By selling to gift shops he makes enough money to pay himself several dollars an hour for his work. This man's hobby provides him with supplemental income which, added to his inadequate pension and Social Security benefits, enables him and his wife to enjoy a decent living standard.

Handicraft is a big business in some communities. Within one hundred miles of Asheville, North Carolina, some six thousand families are engaged in making hooked rugs. Families earn from a few dollars to more than $3,000 a year. The work is almost exclusively spare time, sandwiched between farm and household duties.

Many a hobbyist has found a happy adventure in rejuvenating and selling antique furniture, after mastering the techniques of the trade.

One man's hobby recently saved the United States Army twenty-eight million dollars in practice ammunition. The man, a civilian who lives in Columbus, Georgia, has a hobby of inventing. His invention is a subcaliber device for the Army's recoilless rifles which enabled the rifles to fire a smaller shell than is regularly used.

An Ohioan of seventy-five enrolled in a correspondence law course. After graduating he took his bar examination, passed it and practiced for several years. A beauty-culture school tells of successfully training several retired persons who, after graduating, opened their own businesses. Similar reports come from a professional weaving school about teaching persons up to age seventy who then went into business for themselves.

In Los Angeles, a woman turned her hobby of making medallions into profit by selling her work to fashionable select shops in Beverly Hills and Pasadena. In three months she made $1,300.

A fifty-cent investment in United States Government publications on the Federal income tax started a Virginia woman on a career as a tax consultant. She renders a personal tax service which yields her $1,000 for seventy-five day's work.

Over a twenty-one year period a Lancaster, Pennsylvania, Amish housewife has sold more than twenty-five thousand eggs, dressed up to resemble human and animal faces and figures. The eggs are sold at stalls in Lancaster's farmers' markets.

A garment cutter retired at the age of sixty-eight, after

fifty years in New York City's garment center, and turned his leisure into developing his talent for painting. Within ten years he was giving one-man showings at important art galleries.

Forced to give up his regular line of work because of a heart attack, a Vermont resident, while ill, began making old-fashioned wooden toys for his grandchildren who visited him. They and their friends liked the toys so well that he soon found himself designing toys for mass production. After two years, having recovered his health, he has established "Grandad's Toy Shop" across the road from his home. He doesn't make many toys himself. Instead, his projects keep a woodworking mill busy making and assembling parts. Grandad paints them.

When the Hampton's of Gering, Nebraska, toured the United States in 1939, they decided to get only one kind of souvenir—pitchers. They got a pitcher at nearly every stop they made. And so developed a hobby for pitcher-collecting that now numbers over fifteen hundred. From collecting, Mrs. Hampton developed an interest in ceramics and now sells much of her own work.

An old sailor in Vancouver, British Columbia, spends his days feeding birds. At night he works in a steel foundry to make more money to feed more birds. Aviaries now cover almost the whole acre of his property. The bird count is in the hundreds. It's impossible, he says, to keep an exact count.

You would never think offhand of New York City as good territory for an archaeology hobby. But there's a dentist living in the Bronx who has dug out more than forty-five thousand Indian artifacts in New York's five boroughs. His cottage and dentist's office is an Indian museum. Reading newspaper real estate pages and news columns, he gets tips on where the bulldozers are about to begin foundation excavation. These yield collection items. From New York City's soil he retrieves all manner of minerals—garnets, tourmalines, jaspar, flint and several kinds of quartz—which he fashions into lovely polished ornaments.

After learning the technique of fabric painting, a Brooklyn, New York, woman began painting designs on handkerchiefs and blouses for herself and her friends. Today she buys blouses, scarfs and aprons from wholesalers in dozen or more lots and handpaints the garments with fabric paint in floral effects and designs of her own. These she sells at good profit to a number of New York retail outlets.

Retired from the Navy, a cabinetmaking hobbyist acquired an old schoolhouse near his Virginia residence and converted it into a workshop. Here the hobbyist faithfully duplicates, with modern tools, the construction details and quality standards of craftsmanship of eighteenth-century antique furniture. The mahogany tea caddies and trays, cherry mirrors and other articles he reproduces, are duplicates of antiques two hundred years old. So great is the demand for his antique reproductions, he is swamped with orders. The Reproduction Program of Colonial Williamsburg is his best customer.

If you don't have a hobby now, you will do well to consider developing one. Select a hobby you would really like, not a hobby someone else likes, or one somebody forces you into, or one that happens to have profit possibilities. Most people follow their hobbies for the pure enjoyment they get out of them. Your hobby has to be something that's fun for you, otherwise it won't provide the stimulation, recreation and satisfaction you're looking for. Start to develop your hobby slowly, as a part-time project, to see whether or not you are on the right track. Keep up-to-date on new techniques, new materials, since improved processes can sometimes save you time and money.

There's joy in turning one's mind and hand to the development of one's own style and quality in design and workmanship. The development of intellectual and creative talent and skill, in the hobby field of your choice, will lead you to the reading of many books and magazines, attending instructive exhibitions, comparing your work with that of the masters, and friendly visits with professionals and amateurs who will help you develop into a finer artist or craftsman.

Should you be undecided as to which hobbies to cultivate and develop, attend local hobby and handicraft shows, exhibits and lectures. Local art supply stores, YMCA, YWCA, community workshops, adult education centers or the public library can direct you to local hobby groups, craft guilds or other hobbyists who are glad to assist you in getting started.

Bibliography

You can get a lot of fresh ideas about your hobby and add to your knowledge and experience from tips and illustrated articles that appear in magazines edited to appeal to hobby enthusiasts. Here is a list of magazines devoted to various hobby activities:

All-Pets Magazine, 18 Forest Ave., Fond du Lac, Wis.
American Artist, 24 W. 40th St., New York 18, N.Y.
American Cage-Bird Magazine, 3449 N. Western Ave., Chicago 18, Ill.
Antiques, 40 E. 49th St., New York 17, N.Y.
Art News, 654 Madison Ave., New York 21, N.Y.
Camera, 217 E. 25th St., Baltimore 18, Md.
Craft Horizons, 40 E. 49th St., New York 17, N.Y.
Crafts and Hobbies, 30 E. 29th St., New York 16, N.Y.
Craft, Model and Hobby Industry, 30 E. 29th St., New York 16, N.Y.
Flower Grower, 99 N. Broadway, Albany 1, N.Y.
Handweaver and Craftsman, 246 Fifth Ave., New York 1, N.Y.
Hobby-Model Merchandising News, 1027 N. 7th St., Milwaukee, Wis.
Home Craftsman, 115 Worth Street, New York 13, N.Y.
Lifetime Living, 27 E. 39th St., New York 16, N.Y.

McCall's Needlework & Crafts Annual, 230 Park Ave., New York 17, N.Y.

Mechanix Illustrated, 67 W. 44th St., New York 36, N.Y.

Modern Game Breeding, 28 W. State St., Doylestown, Pa.

Organic Gardening, Emmaus, Pa.

Photography, 366 Madison Ave., New York 17, N.Y.

Popular Ceramics, 417 N. Figueroa St., Los Angeles 12, Calif.

Popular Gardening, 90 State St., Albany, N.Y.

Popular Home Craft, 154 E. Erie St., Chicago 11, Ill.

Popular Mechanics, 200 E. Ontario St., Chicago 11, Ill.

Popular Science Monthly, 353 Fourth Ave., New York 10, N.Y.

Profitable Hobbies, 2401 Burlington St., Kansas City 16, Mo.

The Art Digest, 116 E. 59th St., New York 22, N.Y.

The Home Garden, 575 Madison Ave., New York 22, N.Y.

U.S. Camera, 420 Lexingon Ave., New York 17, N.Y.

Workbasket, 2401 Burlington St., Kansas City 16, Mo.

Easi-Build Jig Saw Pattern Book, Easi-Build Pattern Co., Pleasantville, N.Y.

U.S. Government Publications. Order from Superintendent of Documents, U.S. Government Printing Office, Washington 25, D.C.

You Can Make It, Cat. No. C1.14:L97/9, Vol. I. 20 cents.

You Can Make It for Camp or Cottage, Cat. No. C1.14:L97/9, Vol. II. 20 cents.

You Can Make It for Profit, Cat. No. C1.14:L97/9, Vol. III. 20 cents.

Make It of Leather, Cat. No. C18.27:190. 15 cents.

Home for Birds, Cat. No. I 1.72:14. 10 cents.

Carpentry, Cat. No. W 1.35:5–226. 75 cents.

Modernizing Farmhouses, Cat. No. A1.9:1749. 20 cents.

Growing Annual Flowering Plants, Cat. No. A1.9:1171. 15 cents.

Herbaceous Perennials, Cat. No. A1.9:1381. 20 cents.

Orchids, Culture of, Cat. No. A1.35:206. 5 cents.

Building with Logs, Cat. No. A1.38:579. 20 cents.

Painting, Repairs and Utilities, Cat. No. W1.35:5–618. 30 cents.

Upholsterers, Cat. No. W1.35:10–455. 30 cents.

CHAPTER V

How to Enjoy Leisure

When I asked a number of people, "What are you going to do when you retire?", the majority answered: "Take it easy." No one can dispute their right to relax as they enjoy the fruits of a life well spent. Unfortunately, though, most of them had not given any special thought to what they meant by "take it easy."

Taking it easy should not mean merely eating, sleeping, reading the newspaper, listening to the radio or watching television, chatting with neighbors and sitting on a park bench. These passive activities, if engaged in for prolonged periods, can lead to boredom and frustration. A retired person who consistently follows this pattern of life has no objective, no direction and is drifting into unhappy idleness. Even days of the week will soon lose their significance on such a take-it-easy program.

Writing about leisure, Dr. Edward J. Stieglitz, in *The Second Forty Years,* J. B. Lippincott Co., concluded: "Success or failure in the second forty years, measured in terms of happiness, is determined more by how we use or abuse our leisure than by any other factor." Stieglitz goes on to say that a "superabundance of leisure, or the abuse thereof, has marked and initiated the decadence of cultures throughout history."

It is folly for the retiree to permit himself to be trapped into feeling that the burdens of living disappear when he retires and that peaceful living is a period of continued idleness. Release from the stress and strain of gainful employment is not the answer to happiness and contentment in retirement.

A planned program of leisure-time activities will help you formulate a positive attitude toward retirement. Such a program will insure that you make and keep desirable social contacts; develop and express creative talent, skill and interest; keep from becoming a burden to yourself, your spouse and family, as well as the community; achieve a status of usefulness.

However, in planning leisure time, don't feel that you must have a rigid time schedule for everything you do. It is not desirable that every minute be assigned to a prearranged activity. Don't be a slave to a program. Attempting too much is just as bad as having no program of spare-time activities at all. In arranging your program, be guided by your tastes and natural inclinations. Live one day at a time but live a full, active day. You will find that your schedule will become a habit. That is good if the habit is basically right for you. You should not work too much, play too much, loaf too much— but do a little of each in moderation.

The hours between 9:00 A.M. to 5:00 P.M. are usually the most troublesome ones for the retiree. These are the hours formerly filled with job or housework routines. Unless these hours are planned wisely they are likely to turn into periods of loneliness and boredom, a threat to emotional security. Planned wisely, they can be the richest, happiest hours of your life.

Group Activities

"All who would win joy, must share it; happiness was born a twin," says Byron. Group activities provide a means of doing worthwhile things and an opportunity to enjoy the companionship of congenial people. Group activities provide a focal point where retired persons can receive recognition for personal accomplishments. They are a meeting place for collaboration with others on useful activities. They provide retirees with an opportunity to belong to a socially desirable group in the community.

Many local communities have, or are making provisions for, community facilities for the recreational and cultural needs of older people. These facilities provide for a wide range of activities, such as shuffleboard, horseshoe pitching, card and checker games, hobby workshops, sports, amateur dramatics, concerts, picnics—in fact almost any kind of recreational activity.

Other group activities include social and service clubs and organizations, such as the American Legion, Red Cross, Wednesday Afternoon Music Club, Garden Club, Camera Club, University Club, the Old Guard, Senior Citizens, Golden Age Club, Townsend Club and fraternal lodges, as well as many other cultural, political and church groups.

Those who have been too busy earning a living to devote time to social activities will find wonderful opportunities in these group activities. Here they can enjoy pleasant, stimulating friendships with persons who have interests and backgrounds common to their own.

Find out what social, civic and other groups are active in your locality. Visit several of them until you locate those where you feel at home. Join groups which you think would benefit you. Take the initiative yourself in making known your desire for membership. Sharing companionship with people of similar desires and outlooks is one of the best ways of enjoying a contented retirement.

During most of your workday life, you have probably been associated with a group or team in your business, trade or profession. Much stimulation for planning and accomplishment, as well as peace of mind, has come from these group associations. In retirement, these routine associations will no longer be present. The group or team will be missed. Group activities in retirement can be a valuable substitute.

I know a man who had the reputation of being a successful sales manager. A few years ago he retired to a place he bought in New Hampshire. When I met him in New York City recently, he said: "None of that retirement for me. I just sat around on the porch for months, with a drink always handy, and nothing in particular to do. I like to meet new people. I just couldn't stand being isolated. So I'm back selling again." Had this man planned his retirement to include some kind of group activity, he would have found plenty of opportunities to meet new people and to channel his talents into worthwhile activities.

A certain amount of amusement and pleasure can be bought as one buys food or clothing. Real happiness, however, comes only as the result of personal effort and preparation. Happiness must be lived. Those who cultivate the right kind of leisure-time activities avoid the dullness, loneliness and chronic pessimism that accompany useless idleness.

Clubs for the Retired

Dr. Allen G. Brailey, a Boston physician, stated in an address that there exists a large group of retired people who, while they make no complaint and seem satisfied with life, "taste only a fraction of the zest of life which might be theirs." Dr. Brailey said he advises his patients who have held positions of responsibility: "Do *not* retire from work; retire to more congenial work—for the Community Fund, for the Red Cross, for the church or the schools, for the Scouts."

Too many of his patients, contends Dr. Brailey, are satisfied with edging the lawn, shopping with the wife and visiting with the grandchildren. While these people keep busy enough to escape boredom, "they are too willing to dally away their days, to let their special talents and abilities, perfected by long years of experience, gradually rust away from sheer disuse."

It was Dr. Brailey's suggestion that our senior citizens organize into clubs, along the lines of the National Grange. Some of the functions of such clubs might be to find employment in the business world for deserving jobseekers, to equip hobby shops for woodworking, weaving, jewelry making, painting, etc. Another proposal was that the clubs should provide facilities for dinners, get-togethers and fun, with opportunities for cooking hobbyists to practice their art. The handicrafts which such clubs could turn out might prove self-supporting, but this is not important. Clubs of this kind would enable retired men and women to do congenial work without the requirements of punching a time clock or meeting a deadline.

The San Francisco Senior Recreation Center was planned exclusively for older people. The Center is maintained by a private agency. It is open five afternoons and two evenings a week. Some of the Center's activities include classes in folk dancing, dramatics, crafts and painting, personality and charm demonstrations, millinery and group singing. A poetry group meets each week. Weekly luncheon forums are held with able speakers on subjects of interest to senior citizens. There are service projects such as making quilts for veteran's hospitals. Members enjoy regular programs of music and dancing. Picnics, outings and trips to historic landmarks are scheduled during the year. More than fifteen hundred members have joined since the Center opened in 1948. The ratio is approximately one man to three women, with members coming from all walks of life.

In St. Petersburg, the Chamber of Commerce has initiated programs and promoted facilities for the use of retired groups. Here you will find clubs for every age and a great variety of recreational activities. Cities like New York, Chicago, Boston, Philadelphia and Cleveland, as well as many smaller communities, are offering recreational facilities to new social groups as they are formed.

If there is no Golden Age or Gay Sixties or Senior Citizens or other appropriate club in your locality, you can be instrumental in founding one. Many such social groups have been formed by enterprising people who wrote "letters to the editor" or inserted advertisements in the newspapers. All you need say is: "Persons over sixty, of good character, interested in forming a club to scotch loneliness and cultivate fun come to (street address)." An advertisement such as this was the seed from which sprang an active and flourishing club in a Pacific Coast community.

After forming the club, turn to the local community center for help in finding a regular place to meet and for assistance in handling organization details and setting up a program of activities. Should you be interested in starting such a club, write the National Recreation Association, 315 Fourth Ave., New York 10, New York. Ask for a copy of the booklet, *11% Plus, Recreation for Older People*. (25 cents).

The Old Guard

The Old Guard is a nonsectarian and nonpolitical organization which started over twenty years ago with the founding of the first group in Summit, New Jersey. It is a social club for retired men of fifty and older.

The purpose of the Old Guard is to cultivate good fellowship, to renew old friendships and to form new ones; to preserve mental alertness; to foster deeper interests in the community; and to devise ways and means to be more helpful. The members are retired bankers, chemists, editors, engineers, lawyers, manufacturers, merchants, clergymen, physicians, teachers, railroad officials, salesmen and men in other business and professional occupations. The wealth of diverse experiences represented by these retired men assures stimulating friendships and provides the opportunity for useful community service.

The motto of the Summit chapter is a quotation from Dr. Samuel Johnson: "*If a man does not make new acquaintances as he advances through life, he will soon find himself alone. A man, sir, must keep his friendship in constant repair.*"

Meetings of the Old Guard are conducted in such a manner as to provide the maximum of informal good fellowship. Dues are only one dollar a year. Meetings are held in YMCA buildings once a week in the forenoon. The members do not feel out of place in the YMCA, for many of them have contributed substantially to the erection of the building and some contribute annually to its support.

There is no professional promotion or propaganda of any sort for the Old Guard. The movement has spread of its own momentum to twenty chapters across the country. Chapters are found in such states as New Jersey, Ohio, Pennsylvania, New York, Texas and Florida. There is no intention to make the Old Guard national in scope. Each group remains an independent unit, formulating its own regulations. The Summit chapter has 202 members from all stations in life. The Old Guard Chapter at Princeton, New Jersey, includes many famous retired members of the Princeton faculty among its seventy members.

Beyond a doubt, the Old Guard fills a real need in the retirement life of its members. If no chapter exists in your community perhaps you can help start one. Those desiring more information should communicate with the parent chapter—The Old Guard, % YMCA, Summit, New Jersey.

Additional Ways to Occupy your Leisure Time

National and State Forests and Parks. There are thousands of lakes and ponds, miles of flowing streams in national and state forests and parks for fresh-water fishing and hunting. Thousands of miles of leafy roads and trails await the hiker, horseback rider and picnicker. Mushrooms, berries and edible roots can be gathered in these public playgrounds. You can enjoy camping out in a trailer or tent. You can stay in cabins or other accommodations from de luxe hotels to motor courts located in or near many of these national and state recreational areas.

Adult Educational Courses. Don't overlook the opportunity to add to your education by taking advantage of courses offered by colleges, high schools, trade and vocational schools, both public and private. You are never too old to learn. Many retired people are getting a lot of fun out of retirement living by going back to school or college. Some take up a second career. Others continue their education in order to keep up with cultural and scientific developments of the day.

A school at which all the students are at least sixty years old is operating at Cold Springs, New York. This school offers a course to help men and women make more fruitful use of the years that follow retirement. The curriculum includes lectures and discussions on human growth and development, election issues, international affairs and the United Nations, art, music and the sciences. It also includes gardens, a workshop and other facilities to help students learn new hobbies or expand old ones. This type of project, while at present an experiment in education, is destined to spread throughout the nation. Persons resident in university and college towns might approach educational authorities to inaugurate a similar project in their region.

The Institute for Human Adjustment, University of Michigan, for the past few years has presented a lecture and discussion course, Living in the Later Years. The topics covered provide specific information to help solve current individual problems, to give a philosophy of aging and an understanding of the needs of older people.

A new course, Learning for Longer Living, under the direction of Dr. Wilma Donahue, combines educational experience with social and recreational activities to provide practice in the art of mature living. The course is devoted to a discussion of such topics as health, nutrition, psychological change, mental hygiene, financing the later years, employment opportunities and retirement. Following the discussion, the group has an evening meal together, after which an hour is devoted to practice in social living. The social-recreational activities include games, group singing, square dancing, instrumental music, dramatics, hobby shows and a party. The lectures in the course, Learning for Longer Living, have been recorded on tape. This makes it possible for groups everywhere in Michigan to hear these lectures. The University of Michigan, in conjunction with station WWJ-TV in Detroit, has also offered a series of courses on television. The results of these various educational experiments prove that older people can and do want to learn.

Consult the department of adult education of the public school system in your locality for a listing of courses available. You will be surprised at the range of subjects covered, in classes that meet one or two nights a week, in demonstration laboratories, workshops, forums and informal discussion groups. Lecture courses and forums on the preparation for aging and retirement living, designed for middle-aged people, are offered in many communities. Your interest in the subject is usually all that is required for registration. Going back to school can be one of your most satisfying retirement activities.

The Public Library is said to be the poor man's university. It is the answer to many a retired person's prayer. Here you can find books, magazines and bulletins covering many fields. The range of subject matter is wide, from how-to-do-it books to classics, earning a living, personal finance, biographies, mysteries, arts and crafts, personal growth counsel, fiction, technical subjects, travel, adventure and reference information on practically any subject you can think of. No matter what your tastes may be, your public library can provide provocative reading material. One of the pleasant aspects of retirement is the time and opportunity it affords to catch up on one's reading. It is a good time to increase your knowledge of subjects that fascinated you when you did not have time to pursue them.

Community and Civic Organization Jobs offer opportunities for channeling spare-time energy and abilities. A large number of these agencies operate at a community, state or national level. They welcome volunteer workers even on a part-time basis. Here you will find a chance to be useful. Your help will be appreciated. You will enjoy the rewarding satisfaction of helping in a noble and worthy cause. The chamber of commerce or community social service agency should be able to help you line up worthwhile civic jobs.

Museums and Art Centers are another source of pleasure and education worth looking into, they provide opportunities to further cultural and educational development. Find out whether or not the museum and art centers offer special lectures, classes and discussion groups. One of the richest experiences of living is the development of an appreciation of nature's beauties. Have your name placed on the mailing list announcing new activities.

Local Politics offer opportunities to use training and experience, to engage in activities that are interesting and exciting. Many retired men are doing useful and constructive civic work in city and town elective offices, as well as in state legislatures.

Music is a good medium for recreation and a tonic for the heavy heart. "Music is the fourth great material want of our nature—first, food, raiment, shelter, then music." *Bovee.*

You can enjoy music as a listener at concerts and recitals, on the radio and on television or by playing recordings. You can enjoy music as a participant by joining community singing groups and choruses or glee clubs, or by playing an instrument alone or in instrumental groups.

Local Pageants and Festivals. Don't overlook the recreation and pleasure afforded by the many colorful and historic dramas, pageants, exhibitions, musical festivals, summer and winter theater groups presented in season in many communities. Also, watch for symphony and band concerts, lectures, forums and conventions that may be offered locally.

A university or college town is usually a good location for retirement because of the variety of recreational and cultural activities that are available to local residents.

Travel Trips. In retirement you have plenty of time to travel and see for yourself those far-off places you have daydreamed about. You can do your traveling by plane, train, ship, pleasure craft, bus, trailer or automobile—whichever appeals to you most.

It is possible to enjoy travel trips on a slim pocketbook and not miss any of the high spots in the places you visit. The trick is to know as much about the pleasure potential of the places on your trip as possible. You probably know where to find the best local fun, the best scenic spots and the good eating places in your home town. The same sort of knowledge about the places in your travel trips can make a small budget work wonders.

In your local library you will find many travel and historical books about the areas you plan to visit, which will give you a good background on the growth and life of the area. Write to the chamber of commerce at the places you plan to visit for descriptive and illustrative information. Ask specific questions about cities or towns. Make notes of the scenic, historical, cultural, artistic and eating places that appeal to you. Plan to make your travel trips when the tourist crowds have gone. Accommodations then are easier to get and prices are often lower. Your travel budget will take you a long way, if you plan in advance.

Letter Writing. Retirement is a good time to take up letter writing seriously. Writing conversational letters to relatives and friends is a happy way to use up some of your leisure time. You can visit your friends by mail, exchanging letters that express thoughts as naturally as you would talk to them if you were visiting them. You like to receive letters. So do other people. So keep letters flowing back and forth to friends, relatives and pen pals.

Fishing and Hunting enthusiasts will find numerous opportunities to engage in their favorite sport for recreation or as a means of supplementing the food basket. In many of the retirement locations covered later in this book, fishing may be enjoyed at all seasons of the year. For those who enjoy hunting, the open seasons permit plenty of excitement hunting big game, wild fowl, ducks and game birds.

Golf. Innumerable golf courses at country clubs, resorts and public or municipal links invite devotees of the game to play for relaxation and fun. Don't play too hard. Don't try to defeat every other member in the club. Try to get pleasure, exercise and relaxation out of your game whether you shoot eighty or one hundred and twenty.

Additional Outdoor Sports and Activities. Joseph Lee, the father of the playground movement in this country, said, "We do not cease playing because we are old; we grow old because we cease playing." All of us need a certain amount of physical exercise to keep our bodies in good shape. During retirement we should see to it that we get the kind of physical exercise which is beneficial to body structures and to our muscular and nervous systems. As long as they are not against doctor's orders, not carried out too vigorously or to excess, the following activities are highly desirable:

Archery	Hikes
Auto rides	Horseback riding
Baseball	Horseshoes
Boating	Nature study
Bocci	Picnics
Bowling	Quoits
Camping	Roque
Croquet	Shuffleboard
Excursions	Softball
Gardening	Swimming
Geology	Trips

Commercial Entertainment. There are times when a certain amount of relaxation and enjoyment is to be had by watching others perform for your pleasure and amusement. Some of these activities like attending the theater, symphony concerts, selected radio broadcasts and television programs stimulate creative thinking or provide genuine entertainment. Others are just plain time killers and provide little in the way of satisfaction. A great many amusements and entertainments are built around thrills, sensations and stunts for the purpose of increasing the "box-office take" or the "gate." Avoid these.

Your Own Back Yard. Don't overlook the opportunities in your own back yard to provide recreation, not only for yourself but for neighbors and friends. Outdoor play space can be used for lawn games, outdoor fireplaces for preparing lunches and suppers. The back yard provides space for a variety of leisure-time activities and a place to meet and entertain friends. And don't forget the pleasures derived from home gardening and attracting birds.

Religious Activities. For many, a rich full life does not have a meaning without some form of religious belief. Each individual comes to an understanding of God in his own way. Men may not agree as to the precise needs and goals of the human spirit. But one important thing for each individual to realize is that he has spiritual needs which he can define and fulfill through study, discussion and participation in religious activities. It may be through the path of adherence to the creed of a particular church. Or he may develop his own personal and private approach. The important thing is that man is, by his constitution, a religious creature. He needs spiritual reliance in a power greater than his own, an inspiring force around which to build a philosophy of life.

Religious interest usually increases with age. Those who were too preoccupied with earning a living and making a place for themselves in society during their younger years seem to derive increasing satisfaction from religious experience as they grow older. Churches and synagogues are beginning to recognize the special needs of the rapidly increasing number of older folks in their congregations. They are planning to meet these needs with programs of adult activities. Several religious groups maintain assemblies as well as camps and conferences. These activities attract thousands annually. In making up your schedule for your leisure time, include attendance at church or synagogue services, committees, bazaars or other activities, especially those designed for senior members.

Another Aspect of Leisure

This chapter has attempted to show how leisure activities fit into the retirement program. It has explained how time invested in planned leisure activities, not in idleness, can pay big dividends in helping retirees get more out of life. Many who are lonely, bored and neurotic, or suffering from psychosomatic illness, would not be so afflicted, if they learned how to keep active and to develop self-expression and desirable social contacts.

Physicians and psychiatrists tell us, "Illness is often the result of maladjustments rather than organic disease." Writers in gerontology strongly emphasize that the rest cure for retirement ills has been condemned by medical science in favor of stimulating and invigorating recreational or leisure-time activities.

A distinguished specialist in geriatrics, as well as a renowned writer on the subject, Dr. Martin Gumpert recently had this to say: "The chief bar today to happiness in old age is our defective understanding of retirement—with its bleak connotations of enforced leisure and idleness. Leisure should never be more than the passive counterpart of active work."

What we must do is to plan our retirement to include productive activities in the later years.

Bibliography

Give Yourself Background by F. Fraser Bond (Whittlesey House, N.Y.)

Second Honeymoon by M. M. Musselman (Crowell)

MAGAZINES

Holiday, Independence Square, Philadelphia 5, Pa.

National Geographic Magazine, 16th & M Sts., Washington 6, D.C.

National History Magazine, Central Park West & 79th St., New York 24, N.Y.

Nature Magazine, 1214 Sixteenth St., Washington 6, D.C.

General Federation of Clubwomen, 1734 N St., Washington, D.C.
Townsend National Weekly, 6875 Broadway, Cleveland 5, Ohio.
Trailer Life, 3107 W. Sixth St., Los Angeles 5, Calif.
Trailer Topics Magazine, 28 E. Jackson Blvd., Chicago, Ill.
Travel, 45 W. 57th St., New York 19, N.Y.
Travel America, 71 Vanderbilt Ave., New York 17, N.Y.
Field and Stream, 383 Madison Ave., New York 17, N.Y.
The Fisherman, Box 70, Oxford, Ohio.
Outdoor Life, 353 Fourth Ave., New York 10, N.Y.
Outdoor Sportsman, 109 Commerce St., Little Rock, Ark.
Hunting and Fishing, 230 E. Ohio St., Chicago 11, Ill.
Motor Boating, 572 Madison Ave., New York 22, N.Y.
Yachting, 205 E. 42nd St., New York 17, N.Y.
Golfing, 407 S. Dearborn St., Chicago 5, Ill.
Lifetime Living, 27 E. 39th St., New York 16, N.Y.

U.S. Government Publications. Write to Superintendent of Documents, U.S. Government Printing Office, Washington 25, D.C.
Catalog of National Park Service Publications, C35. Free.
Tent and Trailer Campsites, Cat. No. 1 29.2/AC158/1–2. 10 cents.
Camp Furniture and Furnishings, Cat. No. 1 29.2/AC15/2–2. 10 cents.
Recreation Areas of U.S. (map), Cat. No. 1 29.8:R24/948. 25 cents.
National Forest Vacations, Cat. No. A 13.2:V13/4/950. 25 cents.
Geographic Guide to Floras of the World, Cat. No. A1.38:401. 75 cents.
Guidebook of Western United States, Cat. No. 1 19.3:614. 50 cents.
Attracting Birds, Cat. No. 1 1.72:1. 10 cents.
Basic Fish Cookery, Cat. No. 1 49.39:2/2. 20 cents.
Camp Stoves and Fireplaces, Cat. No. Y3.EM3:2C15/1–2. 50 cents.
Fish and Shellfish of South Atlantic and Gulf Coasts, Cat. No. 11.72:37. 15 cents.
Planning Recreation for the Rural Home, Cat. No. A1.75:20. 30 cents.

CHAPTER VI

A Small Business of Your Own

Select the Right Field

So you think you would like to own and operate a small business! Many others have done it. You can too. In fact, if you plan on retiring in your fifties or sixties, you may even develop a small business into something more profitable than anything you've done before.

A business of your own will bring you a sense of independence, an opportunity to use your ideas. It may mean a chance for higher income because you can collect a salary plus a profit or return on your investment. You will experience a pride of ownership. You will achieve great satisfaction and a sense of usefulness to the community. You will not be bored by having nothing to do. Like hundreds of other retired men and women, you can find life fascinating and stimulating in a small business of your own.

What business should you choose? Technical or professional training, previous experience in business, special skills and talents, hobby interests or a deep-seated longing to engage in a definite type of business—these are the motivating factors that should influence you in the choice of a business to own and operate.

Pick a field you know something about. Skill, experience and adaptability are essential for success. The best way to obtain operating knowledge of a business is through actual experience. The necessary experience can be acquired before you retire, by part-time work on week ends or during vacations.

You should have sufficient capital to establish the business, to finance it and to provide for your own living expenses for the six months to a year that it usually takes to get a business to stand on its own feet. In many cases, the necessary equipment, tools or furnishings to operate the business can be acquired well in advance of your retirement. It is best not to start your retirement business by contracting large obligations, thereby running too great a risk with your money, your time and your future.

Before you plunge into business, investigate the potential demand for the products or services you have for sale. If your prospective clients do not want or need your products or services, your chances of success are slim indeed. Your opportunities are favorable if business conditions in the locality where you plan to locate are good, and if there is a definite need for the line of business you are considering.

While the success stories that can be told about small businesses are legion, another side of the picture must be given serious consideration. Studies indicate that approximately one-fourth of new businesses do not survive the first year, and over half operate less than three years. The success or failure of a business venture is determined by many factors. The most important single factor is the ability of the owner-manager to apply sound principles of business management and promotion in the operation of his business. If you do not know how to run a business, you had better work first for someone who is successful and learn his methods. Many persons fail because they pick a business that is not suited to their temperament and past experience. Lack of working capital to adequately equip and operate the business causes many a businessman to go broke. Finding the right town to support the kind of business contemplated, the best street and the best location on the street are extremely important for the success of the venture. Failure to keep records, slipshod service and too liberal credit policies are roads that lead to failure.

The financial returns from a business of your own range from the bottom to the top of earning power. You should remember that, as a self-employed person earning more than nine hundred dollars a year, you will have to forego your Social Security benefits until you reach the age of seventy-five. If yours is a growing and prosperous business, you can afford to let Social Security benefits lapse while you are operating the business.

Keep away from fields calling for physical strength, long hours and a daily grind of close attention to many small details. This is of serious importance to retired folks. Stay away from the usual crowded fields, like gasoline stations, corner groceries and dry-cleaning establishments where competition is likely to be intense. Make or sell specialty items whose volume is not great enough to interest the larger stores or factories. Operate a service type of business in which your skill, talent and specialized equipment are too personalized for competition by large organizations.

Keep the operation small enough so that you can always run the business and so that the business does not run you ragged. Don't try to compete with others organized for large-scale volume. Remember your object in retiring is to get away from aggressive activity and nervous tension so that you may enjoy the rewards of living a comfortable, easy-going way of life. If you feel like going fishing or on a trip for a few days, you should not be so tied down that you cannot do these things.

Don't think, however, the business is going to be profitable if left completely to run itself. You must devote time, attention and managerial control to the business to keep it running smoothly and to pay you a profit for your time and trouble. But there is no need to break your neck trying to make a financial killing. You should launch your small business as much for the fun in it as for the money you make out of it.

Besides the financial returns from operating one's own small business, there is another factor to be considered. That is the desire of many people to some day be in business for themselves. This desire in many cases never gets beyond the daydreaming stage, particularly during the period of one's regular working career. When you embark on retirement, you have a real chance to fulfill this ambition. If you are well qualified to conduct a business of your own, you can anticipate not only making a decent living, but also building up a business that has a resale value and that can be carried on perhaps by your wife or children.

You will find much helpful information in the many good books in your public library on the subject of organizing and operating various types of small business enterprises. The United States Government has a great interest in the welfare of small businesses and publishes a great many bulletins which can be profitably applied to small business procedures.

You Don't Need a Lot of Money to Launch a New Business

If you have a specialty that your friends rave about— whether it is a food specialty, like party or gift cookies, a home-recipe salad that's out of this world or unusual hand-woven rugs or mittens—you might have the makings of a good small business. And you don't need a barrel of money to get it started on the road to producing a good income for you.

There is a woman in Connecticut who has an enviable reputation among her neighbors and church associates for baking excellent and unusual cookies. Friends always called on her to bake cookies for parties and special events. When the friends of friends sampled these fancy cookies, the demand for them snowballed.

Two years ago this woman and a church friend decided they would go into business together, one to bake the cookies, the other to sell them. A local department store with a lunchroom was lined up as a customer. When patrons of the lunchroom asked to buy some of the cookies to take home, the cookie baker knew that she was off to a good start. The country club was the next large customer. This was followed by several wayside inns noted for their fine foods. In each instance, patrons of the establishments inquired about buying cookies to take home. By word-of-mouth this homemaker became famous locally for her tasty cookie specialties. At this stage, the baking of the cookies was a home-kitchen operation. But the mixing, baking, packaging and storage of ingredients soon outgrew the kitchen. To keep up with the demand, they moved the growing cookie business to a small, low-rent neighborhood store, and fitted it out with the necessary equipment for greater production.

With business thriving, sights were set for retail distribution in the quality grocery stores. A local concern bought one hundred one-pound boxes of cookies to be used as Christmas gifts. Some customers wanted cookies sent by mail to friends in distant cities and to relatives in the military services overseas. A couple of food brokers dropped in, asking for the line to sell to retail stores.

This home-kitchen venture, started two years ago, has developed into a profitable small-store neighborhood enterprise with current sales around two hundred to two hundred and fifty one-pound boxes of cookies each week.

How a Musical Recital Started a Strudel-baking Business

Amazing circumstances sometimes lead directly to one's establishing a small business. Take the case of a young con-

cert pianist in New York City who planned a Sunday afternoon musicale at her home. Her mother, as a contribution
to the success of the musicale, decided to bake and serve
Viennese strudel made from a family heirloom recipe.
"What's this?" the guests asked. "It's one of mother's home-
made strudels," the pianist replied. "Do you think she would
make some to sell?" Mother said she would be glad to bake
each guest one of her strudels. The guests protested. They
wanted to buy several to serve as refreshments at their own
parties. The mother and daughter talked it over in the
kitchen—and decided it might be a good idea for pin money.
A few orders were taken right then and there. For over a
year, the mother has baked Viennese strudels to order. She
now has two kinds: the sweet to serve with tea or coffee, the
unsweet to go with cocktails. From morning until night the
kitchen oven is kept busy baking strudels to fill special orders. This is just another example of how a special home-
baking skill was turned into a profit-making opportunity.

There are thousands of these personalized proprietor-
operated small businesses in the United States. The success
of these small enterprises depends on having a good idea
and an outstanding quality product, and sticking to it en-
thusiastically, continuously through a period of years.

There's Money in Personal Service Businesses

You can prepare in your spare time for a retirement career
in a service business of your own. There are a number of
personal service businesses that offer opportunities for financial security, independence and working hours regulated to
your own desires. Many of these service businesses can be
run from a home workshop, garage shed or basement. Age or
minor physical handicap is no barrier. The work is light,
pleasant and profitable.

It doesn't matter whether you have had previous experi-

ence. Very little capital is required to start them. You can
learn the how-to-do-it techniques from practical, down-to-
earth home-study courses offered by reliable and accredited
correspondence schools. In many of the larger cities, private
trade schools and vocational and technical high schools offer
classes in some of these occupations.

Television and Radio Servicing is one field in which there
are more good-paying jobs and opportunities than there are
trained and experienced men to fill them. Industry experts
have estimated that over 130,000 qualified TV technicians
will be needed for the installation, trouble shooting and repair of television receivers in use by 1955. There are far
fewer than fifty thousand fully trained TV servicemen available today. Many men without any previous radio or TV
experience or special talent have learned TV and radio servicing at home or at school. Hundreds of men operate TV and
radio service businesses of their own with capital earned in
spare time.

Electrical Appliance Repairing is another field offering opportunities for you to start your own business and earn
money while you learn the short-cuts and time-saving techniques. There are millions of electrical equipment units in
daily use in homes, office buildings and farms. Skilled technicians are needed to keep this equipment in good running
condition. If you are mechanically inclined, you can learn
by correspondence how to repair vacuum cleaners, washing
machines, motors, refrigerators, etc. I know a man who quit
his job as a bank teller over twelve years ago and has made
a good living ever since, working from his home, as an
electrical repair specialist.

Automatic Saw Filing and *Lawn-mower Sharpening*. With
only a small investment you can start a general repair shop
specializing in saw filing. This is another one of those personal service businesses you can start at home in your spare

time, and build up to a full-time business asuring you an income to cover your living expenses. Overhead and operating expenses are low. Prospective customers include furniture and other factories, newspapers and printers (they use circular saws to trim printing plates), building contractors, carpenters, manual training departments of schools, farmers and home owners. Between April and September, lawn-mower sharpening is a profitable business. You can add other services like key making, knife and tool sharpening. This type of small business offers opportunities to earn from $15 to $30 a week in spare time, or $60 to $85 and more a week for full time. For information on how to promote and develop this type of business write to Foley Manufacturing Company, Inc., 3300 Fifth Street, Minneapolis, Minnesota. Ask for a copy of *Money Making Facts About Automatic Saw Filing*.

Oil-burner and Air-conditioning installation, repairing and servicing also offer good opportunities for retired men. Other types of service businesses are *venetian blind laundry, farm machinery repairing, rug and upholstery washing*. Manufacturers who sell special equipment to do these specialized jobs assert that many men have built profitable businesses with their equipment. You can obtain their names and addresses from advertisements in popular and crafts magazines. It is advisable to investigate these service propositions thoroughly before devoting time to them and investing money in special equipment.

What to Charge for Service Work

How much should you charge for service-repair jobs? The prevailing rates for house calls range from $5 for the first half hour to $5.75 for the first forty-five minutes. The usual charge for more than a half hour is $1.25 to $1.50 for each additional fifteen minutes. For shop repairs, $5 per hour is the average charge. Pick-up and delivery charges range from

$3.30 to $7.50. Many service companies add 10 to 25 per cent to protect themselves against call-backs. The cost of replacement parts are of course additional. Charges for service jobs may vary considerably in different parts of the country.

A Sewing Shop Can Be Profitable

In many cities, towns and villages throughout the nation there is a real shortage of skilled dressmakers, competent seamstresses and experienced milliners. Women handy with the needle, adept with the sewing machine and its attachments, having a knowledge of style and design, can use their time and skill profitably sewing for others.

In the custom-made field there are opportunities for making made-to-order bridal costumes, odd-size and invalid clothes, party and regular dresses and costumes, children's dresses, infants' wear and sportswear. Innumerable opportunities exist for sewing slip covers, draperies, smocks, coveralls, aprons, lingerie, monogramming, embroidery, invisible weaving, medallions, gloves, quilting, hand-painted blouses, toys, handbags and novelties.

Some enterprising, creative dressmakers have pyramided their original custom-made creations into a line that finds ready sale in local specialty dress shops. Unusually good design or style, good materials and high-quality workmanship are the essentials for success in operating a custom-dressmaking or sewing shop. The finished product should look handmade not homemade. Original styling and attractive design gives the product talking points over factory-made products. Concentrate on high-profit items. Stay clear of the low-profit, highly competitive market, especially fashion items on the way out.

There is also a growing market for mending and alterations. Some women are successfully conducting sewing classes. The scarcity of competent seamstresses is so great that a woman skilled with the needle can usually find plenty of work doing alterations for specialty dress shops and department stores.

A sewing shop is a small business you can establish and operate from your home. All you need do to get customers is to advertise in the classified section of local newspapers. List your shop in the yellow pages of the local telephone book. Send postal cards to specialty shops and women's clubs. If you live near a boarding school, college or hospital, send postal cards to students and nurses who are usually too busy to do their own wardrobe repairs.

Display an attractive sign in the front of your home. You should be sure to price your products or time at the prevailing scale for similar work of skilled craftsmen, so that you can make a reasonable profit.

Tutoring Service

Retired college, grade and high school teachers earn from two dollars to five dollars an hour tutoring children, students and adults in special subjects. A clientele can be developed by advertising in the school page or classified section of local newspapers, and also from contacts with local schools and colleges.

Additional Personal Service Activities

Here are a few other activities that can be operated on a part-time or full-time basis from the home: addressing envelopes for mail-order businesses and businessmen, telephone answering and soliciting for local business concerns or professional men, typing manuscripts for authors, practical nursing, taking care of children during the day—children called for and returned, balanced meals, boarding home for children, boarding home for elderly people, curtains washed, stretched and hand-ironed—pick-up and delivery, dresses and blouses hand-ironed, cooking special diet meals, teach auto driving with dual-controlled car, furniture refinishing, floors sanded and refinished, attics, cellars and yards cleaned, sewing machines repaired, construction, alterations and remodeling for homes, writing articles for professional or trade magazines, market research for advertising and research organizations, physical therapy, convalescent care, renting furnished or unfurnished rooms, photographic studio, developing and photo printing.

How About Establishing a Small Retail Business?

Gift Shop. Here is an opportunity for men and women with an appreciation of art and craft values to cash in on their knowledge. To be a successful operator of a gift and art shop, you should specialize in items that are unusual and unique. If you can get the exclusive rights for a number of these items in the city or county where your store is located, so much the better. Your best chance to obtain an exclusive is to act as the sales outlet of experienced craftsmen. They might be individual craftsmen who work alone. They could be members of an organized homecraft or art group. You might be able to arrange to be the exclusive representative in your locality for the many products of a regular state or local homecraft industry or association. Many gift shops are also workshops where original items are produced on the premises.

You probably will not be able to obtain enough products from individual craftsmen alone to profitably operate a gift and art shop, so you will be dependent also upon manufacturers who produce in volume for the national gift shop market. Even in this type of merchandise, many gift shop operators can and do obtain exclusive items. In any case, the proprietor must create an appealing atmosphere for the items on sale that idealizes even the commonplace items as pieces of merchandise.

The majority of gift and art stores are run by owner-managers without the aid of paid help. While there are many gift shops that do a large volume of business, the smaller gift shops do an average business from $10,000 to $20,000 a year, which usually provides a good income for one person. Gift shops do best in college towns, towns with an historical background, recreational and resort centers, and the local shopping center of towns where the standard of living is high. Many gift shops are associated with roadside tearooms and fine restaurants. Others operate as drive-in gift shops and are located on highways where tourist traffic is heavy. The important ingredients for success are location, capitalization, adequate and unique stock-in-trade, credit facilities, merchandising ability, modern methods of management, display of merchandise and accounting and the personalities of the owner and assistants.

Capitalization will vary with the location and the size of the business establishment. For a business that can reasonably expect to do $10,000 in sales volume, the investment for the first year should not be less than $3,000, of which $2,000 should be available to pay for merchandise and expense bills when due. The average salary taken by the proprietor of a gift-shop business of this size is 15.4 per cent of net sales. In other words, on a volume of $10,000, the salary of the owner-manager would be $1,540. Net profit for the average gift shop doing this volume in sales is about 6.3 per cent. This would give the owner an additional $630 which he can use to supplement his salary or to increase working capital.

Some profitable gift shops, however, yield higher incomes than the average figures stated above. With net profits of

10.1 per cent and a salary of 14.7 per cent, the proprietor of the profitable gift shop doing a $10,000 sales volume would have a monthly income of about $207.

Bookstore. Bookselling is a business which will not make unusual physical demands upon you. You may have to spend a good many hours on your feet, but if your health is average you won't find this too taxing. Those who patronize a bookstore are usually intelligent people who are interested in the world of ideas. If you have similar interests you will find the work fascinating and stimulating.

The majority of small bookstores that feature new books for sale also have a rental library and sidelines of allied merchandise, such as gifts and greeting cards. Generally, in a large city it would be unwise to start a neighborhood bookstore with less than $5,000. In a smaller city the amount might be less, around $4,000. The overall profit figures for bookstores are not high. They indicate that $10,000 net sales will probably be necessary to provide you with an $1,800 annual salary.

A small bookstore can make out fairly well in a neighborhood shopping center. The best location here is next to a "necessity" store, such as a grocery, drugstore or laundry. While there are a few successful bookstores in towns of less than ten thousand population, your chances of success are better in towns of not less than twenty-five thousand population.

Retired persons living in a college or a university town can build up a small but profitable business selling used textbooks. The books can be bought from students at the end of the school year. Many students will have no further use for their books. Offer to buy the books at one-quarter of the current list price. At the beginning of the following term, sell the books at one-half to three-quarters the new-book price, depending upon their condition. Advertise in the college paper. You will not get rich on this scheme, but you can build up a profitable little business and have fun making friends with college students.

Confectionery-Tobacco Store. Here's a business you can own, if your capital is limited and your training is nontechnical and unspecialized. For the individual who lacks capital to finance a store in a busy location, opportunities exist in growing residential areas. A store of this kind can be operated by a physically handicapped person. It offers the possibility of reduced living costs for a family which is satisfied to live adjoining the store, and an opportunity for family participation in a common enterprise. The disadvantages are long hours and limited income. Also, many people turn to retail candy and tobacco stores when business conditions are poor, with the result that there may be too many stores of this type. The net profits in a candy-tobacco store in a large city may run from 15 per cent to 30 per cent of gross sales, closer to 15 per cent if the store has no soda fountain, and nearer 30 per cent if the store sells soft drinks, ice cream and light lunches.

The investment required to finance the establishment of a candy-tobacco store ranges from $1,000 for a neighborhood store modestly fitted with secondhand fixtures to fifty times that amount for a de luxe shop on a busy downtown street. If the store includes a soda fountain, then the investment will be greater. The business can be expanded to include food items such as coffee, tea and cocoa, canned soups and sandwiches. The sale of periodicals and newspapers brings in a small but steady amount of cash.

Woodworking shop. An almost unlimited number of articles can be made and sold or repaired in a well-equipped woodworking shop operated by a skilled craftsman. Here are some of the things that can be done: furniture and cabi-

netmaking and repair, repairing and restoring antiques, upholstery and repair, novelty toy and bric-a-brac manufacture,
hobby products. To succeed, you should be a skilled mechanic or craftsman. A small woodworking shop can be
successfully operated in any community where there is a
demand for your products or services.

It is impossible to say with any degree of accuracy how
much capital is required to open a shop of this kind, because
there are too many variables. With good business judgment,
shrewd management and rigid economy, you might be able
to begin business with as little as $1,000 or $2,000. However,
experience shows that more than half of the ventures set up
within too narrow capital margins fail within the first year.
If you attempt to set up shop on $1,000, your equipment will
have to be bought on the installment plan. This is a bad way
to start business for a retired person. It is safer to start with
sufficient capital to cover all initial expenses. This should include cost of equipment and materials and rent if you lease
a shop or building, and a capital checking account of at least
$500 with another $500 as a reserve for emergencies.

The success of a business of this kind, to a large extent,
will depend upon your ability to accurately estimate and
quote prices to customers. Some of the rule-of-thumb methods are: (1) double the estimate for labor and material; (2)
double the labor estimate and add materials estimate; (3)
multiply the labor estimate by a given factor and add estimate of materials. It must be remembered that the final
quoted price must include an amount to cover both the pro-
rated overhead and the profit anticipated.

Some of the articles that can be made in a small woodworking shop are garden and lawn furniture, doghouses,
birdfeeders and birdhouses, driveway arches, gates, lattice
fences and trellises, covered sandboxes, ironing boards, fold-

ing seats, poultry nests, clothes-drying racks, workbenches, bookcases, breakfast tables and benches, wall bookracks and many similar items. These articles may be sold completely assembled or knocked down. Knock-down kits containing all the material cut to size will appeal to customers who prefer to assemble and paint the articles. Wooden articles can be sold to roadside-stand proprietors, mail-order houses, hardware and paint stores and other retail stores that can be induced to take on a line of articles made from wood.

Metal-working Shop. A skilled machinist or craftsman in metal can handle a great variety of jobs operating his own shop. With a little ingenuity in adapting attachments and special tricks with tools, he needs comparatively little equipment. He can do general repair work and service work on machinery, household equipment and farm implements.

Those who have an artistic sense can add ornamental iron fabrication equipment for making handmade products such as lighting fixtures, wrought-iron lamps, hinges, latches and hardware, stair rails, gates and the like. Architects and builders, antique dealers, garden shops and lighting fixture stores are prospects for ornamental metalwork.

In rural communities the proprietor can operate a traveling (truck-mounted) shop with a power take-off from the engine of the truck.

For estimating and quoting, generally speaking, the same rule-of-thumb methods can be used as for the woodworking shop mentioned above. A small business of this kind will need a community population of at least twenty thousand to support it.

A Letter Shop. Retired advertising men, reporters, printers, office managers, stenographers and salesmen might consider establishing and operating their own letter shop. A small shop with one or two persons in addition to the proprietor, which offers typewriting, duplicating, addressing and mail service, could provide income for a fair living for the owner.

In order to start a small but well-equipped letter shop offering these services, you would need about $5,000 capital. This would provide for new equipment, supplies, shop furnishings, working capital, personal reserve and miscellaneous expenses. A great deal of this equipment can be bought in the working years before you retire. Successful letter shops can be established in both large and small communities.

Paint and Decorating Store. In many communities, especially small towns, there are not enough paint stores. Most of the retail paint sales in these communities are handled by hardware stores, lumberyards, farm implement dealers and building-supply dealers. As a rule such stores do not have specialized paint salesmen and often lack the interest and facilities to exploit the full potentialities of this business.

Enterprising retired painters and builders who learn the principles of selling and merchandising will find opportunities to start their own paint stores. The majority of homes in the United States now need painting and the interiors need decorating too. Recent surveys show that many home owners are doing a considerable amount of this work themselves. Besides the painting and decorating of homes already built, there is a tremendous demand for paint, wallpaper and glass for the new homes being constructed.

Experience in the paint field is important. A retired painter or builder can pass along much practical information and many helpful hints to customers and will very likely be able to sell a great deal more paint and accessories than those who handle paint as a side line.

A small retail paint store owner should figure on doing a minimum annual sales business of about $25,000 to allow sufficient net profit to pay himself a reasonable salary and to provide a small balance for expansion. It is not implied, however, that total sales of $25,000 are necessary at the start. The gross profit in the average successful paint store is about 36 per cent. An analysis of profitable retail paint stores doing about $19,000 annual sales volume showed that the owners averaged $2,100 in salary and had left over for profit dividends and future expansion a net profit of $972.

Select a progressive area that shows good growth possibilities and select merchandise to fit the community needs. A book that gives a home-study course in painting techniques is *The Practical Paint Course,* published by the American Paint Journal, 3713 Washington Avenue, St. Louis 3, Missouri. The many publications in the "Establishing and Operating Your Own Business" series published by the United States Department of Commerce will help you on sales and merchandising.

Sporting-goods Store. Experienced fishermen and hunters, former athletes and coaches, and handymen who can repair rods, reels, guns, restring tennis rackets, fix bicycles and do hundreds of little jobs can start a small sporting-goods store and make a fair living doing something they really enjoy.

The proprietor's earnings, covering the owner's salary and net profits, run from 10 to 15 per cent of sales in well-managed sporting-goods stores. A store doing an annual business of $20,000 might be expected to provide an income of from $2,000 to $3,000 for a sole owner in a reasonably good year.

This type of business can be operated successfully in a small town, especially in resort and vacation areas. A sporting-goods store has the best chance of success in an area that is active, progressive, likes sports and has a good recreational program. The area should permit the operation of some kind of sports activity twelve months of the year. In some small towns, the line of sporting goods is combined with phonograph and radio equipment, flashlights, books and other items. Repair service on sporting items is a good source of revenue.

Bookkeeping, Accounting and Tax Service. This might consist of only one individual and an assistant, or a larger organization employing five to ten people. Gross receipts might range from $3,000 a year for a newcomer to around $40,000 for a larger well-established firm. This type of business can be located either in a large city or a small community. Clients may be small business men, professional men or private individuals with income tax problems.

The increasing need for records and reports because of tax laws, and the growing awareness of the value of accurate record keeping for good business management, all point to a long-term demand for small bookkeeping and tax firms. Obviously, a person interested in starting a small bookkeeping firm needs to have a technical background and training in accounting and related subjects. He should also have some knowledge of finance and insurance. In this business you can work at home and either do your own typing or have it done on a part-time basis. Or you may rent desk space in an office. It is not necessary to be a C.P.A., but it helps. Some state laws require an annual registration and license fee before you can practice public accounting. You should investigate the matter thoroughly before taking up residence in a state. The size of the city or town will affect your dollar income. Since living and business expenses are higher in the larger cities, a greater dollar income may not be worth more in terms of real income than a somewhat lesser income in a smaller community.

In rural communities you can operate a traveling (truck-mounted) office, with farmers and rural business men as clients.

Fees for work performed are usually figured on an hourly basis, though some small bookkeeping firms charge a flat fee for monthly services. Fees are based on the average number of hours required to do the work multiplied by a basic rate such as $3 or $5 per hour.

Automatic Merchandising. In this type of business, coin-operated machines are used to sell merchandise, such as packaged candy bars, soft drinks, cigarettes, ice, wood, sandwiches, frozen foods—and many other packaged goods.

Your route and the location of your machines are the keys to successful volume in sales. Places most frequented by large numbers of people are the most profitable locations. The nature of available locations and the amount of capital you have determines the kind of route to establish. This is the kind of business that can be started with a few machines and operated on a part-time basis. You can gradually add to the number of machines until your work becomes full time. Capital requirements depend upon the size and kind of route you wish to establish. Reputable operators estimate that for one man to begin a full-time business requires $5,000. Avoid going into this business by making only a small down payment for machines. You should preferably have sufficient money to buy the machines outright.

Automatic vending is primarily a five-and-dime business, and the profit is in pennies or fraction of pennies. The amount of profit depends on the volume of sales. In order to obtain substantial earnings you must have many coin-operated machines in good locations.

The business can be operated from your home. A large route calls for a good deal of traveling and long hours of work. There is evidence that this type of business will grow considerably in the next few years, as new territories are opened up, machines improve and new fields open up for merchandising new items. Choose the machine that, in terms of operation, appearance and size, suits your route and locations. Whatever the merchandise you choose to sell, never fail to obtain the highest quality. Nationally advertised products sell more easily through automatic merchandisers than unknown products.

Mail Order Is a Good Business if You Have a Good Item

The mail-order business offers income-making opportunities for many retired persons who are looking forward to an independent business of their own. It appeals to older people who have a keen desire to pursue a hobby, craft or an avocation.

Broad experience is not a prime essential for success in the mail-order business. Much of the success depends on your product, the market in which it is sold, the method of presentation and your approach. You can pick up knowledge and experience as you go along. Of course, to be successful, some know-how is essential. You can secure much of the specialized information you need from several how-to-do-it books now on the market.

The type of mail-order business referred to here is not the large, general mail-order house carrying a complete line of consumer goods. What we have in mind is a small specialty mail-order operation carrying one good article or a narrow line of goods for sale by mail.

To get an idea of the scope of specialty mail-order houses, look through the advertising sections of popular and craft magazines and farm magazines, and the mail-order sections of large metropolitan Sunday newspapers. Notice the variety of mail-order propositions offered. Some of the advertisers are manufacturers, growers or distributors. Others are one-man mail-order specialty businesses. Some are operated only during seasonal periods. A number never get beyond the part-time stage.

Stock propositions, consisting of a supply of merchandise and imprinted literature offered by some manufacturers are, as a rule, not good money-making propositions. Staple merchandise that is commonly sold in stores will not be highly profitable when sold by mail. Specialty items, office supplies, home gadgets, household specialties, novelties, curios, unusual jewelry, craft items, hand-woven rugs, garden furniture, fruit-and-nut gift baskets and packages, unusual articles made at home or in a small workship—these are the types of articles that offer the best prospects for a profitable mail-order business.

How-to-do-it books, "information" instruction and correspondence courses, equipment and supplies for home craftsmen, are also good items for mail-order selling. Many mail-order operators do not have the facilities or equipment to make the products they sell. They have the items manufactured for them on a contract basis.

It requires some working capital—not so much as is needed to operate many other businesses—to establish and operate a successful mail-order business.

Small mail-order operators earn from a few dollars to several hundred dollars every month by devoting spare hours to their mail-selling enterprises. Some part-time operators are adding $1,000 to $2,000 a year to supplement their regular income. There are a large number of one-man, full-time mail-order enterprises in this country that are paying their owners $3,000 to $5,000 and more a year.

A small mail-order project can be started in your spare time without interfering with your regular work. It is the type of business that can be started and developed before you retire. In fact, to build a good mail-order business you should start small and proceed slowly while you test your proposition. When you're convinced you have a profitable product, you can strike out with a considerable amount of capital.

According to research surveys, 30 per cent of all mail-order businesses were started with a capital of less than $500, while another 30 per cent began with $500 to $3,000. Much depends upon the individual, his manner of working and the cost of the products he sells by mail.

Here are four elements usually present in successful direct-by-mail selling: (1) a letter that sells; (2) a circular that supplements the letter, describes and illustrates the product and has testimonials; (3) an easy-to-order business reply card, order form or self-addressed envelope; (4) a good mailing list. Seventy-five per cent of the success or failure of direct mail campaigns is said to depend on the type and quality of the mailing list.

The mailing list can be built up from replies to advertising placed in newspapers and magazines and from radio and television advertising. Or you can buy or rent a specific mailing list from a list broker or list compiler.

The mail-order beginner should check the legal aspects that might apply to his operation. Foods, drugs, drug devices and cosmetics are subject to the Federal Food and Cosmetic Act.

Developing New Products

Retired engineers, mechanics, draftsmen, professional men, salesmen—almost anybody with a fertile imagination and a gift for recognizing practical possibilities might use some of their retirement time for the development of new products.

An executive's wife had an idea that started a meat packer in the canned onion soup business; a salesman thought up an idea for a canned chicken product; the president of a company had the idea for a golf bag "toter"; the list of government-owned patents available for sale was the idea source for a kitchen gadget and for an insecticide; a food broker thought up the idea for canned apple juice; a museum exhibit resulted in a new vase for a pottery manufacturer; a doctor's hobby of experimenting with wheat germs resulted in his bringing out a new line of health foods; a mechanic watching his wife having difficulties holding material while sewing got the idea for a simple clamp device.

There are so many possibilities in new products that no hard and fast rule can be laid down about the types of products to look for. Manufacturing companies are always on the lookout for new products that can be made by their present labor force with existing equipment and sold by the sales force to their customers. Some companies like to add new products to diversify their lines.

Large companies generally use their own research and development laboratories and market research personnel to develop new products. Smaller firms not in a position to organize for large-scale new-product development are good prospects for privately developed new products. Some new-product developers start their own small businesses to manufacture and sell practical new products that have profitable market potentials. Others have the products made for them on contract and do their own selling by mail order, or to jobbers and retail outlets or through manufacturers' representatives.

Before investing money in the development of a new product, it is wise to assemble and compare several good ideas and select the best. You should make a market and consumer survey to avoid putting too many dollars and too much time into an item that has limited profit possibilities. Design and develop a product fitted to consumer needs and desires—not just something *you* like. Test the product carefully under actual use conditions before placing it on the market. Have a patent search made before making your final design and tooling up for production.

Other important factors in marketing, in addition to selling, are price, package design, a good product name (be careful not to infringe on registered trade-marks), advertising and sales promotion. Keep a precise record-history of the inception and development of a new product. You might need it for patent application or protection in case of being cited for patent infringement. Be sure to read the United States Department of Commerce publication, *Developing and Selling New Products.*

Opportunities in Selling

The opportunities and possibilities in selling are vast. You can adapt your talents and skills to that branch of salesmanship which gives you the most working pleasure.

You can sell a product or a line of products to substantially the same people. The route salesman who calls at the home selling milk, eggs and butter is in this classification. So is the salesman who calls regularly on an established list of dealers, wholesalers or manufacturers in a selected city, county or state.

You can sell tangible nontechnical products like clothing or apparel, technical products like electronic devices or intangible services like insurance or advertising space. There are salesmen who specialize in selling to manufacturers, others who sell to distributors and dealers and still others who sell to ultimate consumers. Further breakdowns in the specialization of selling are manufacturers' salesman, sales engineers, manufacturers' representatives, wholesale salesmen, retail-store salesmen and clerks, and house-to-house salesmen. Some salesmen are paid a straight salary. Others work on a straight commission basis. There are many variations and combinations of these two basic compensation plans.

Retired salesmen and sales managers, advertising men and women, business people, engineers and others with qualifications for making a success at selling should consider some type of selling as an opportunity to supplement retirement income. Try to pick a product you have a liking for. Your regular workday experience will probably help you in making a choice. Be sure the physical demands of selling are not greater than you should undertake and that you are well fitted for the task.

A good salesman is always needed. The man or woman who knows what kind of merchandise he or she would like to sell and the type of selling he or she would like to engage in has an excellent opportunity to secure profitable, satisfying work. No hard and fast figures can be given on earnings in so variable an occupation as selling. The good salesman, no matter what line he sells, always does well. Salary income ranges from the wages of a sales clerk to $10,000 and more for salesmen with unusual ability and managerial skill.

The Real Estate Business

This covers selling or leasing property, placing mortgages, collecting rents and performing other services on a commission basis. It is a popular retirement occupation and is likely to be overcrowded in some localities.

In the real estate business, your time is your primary asset. You must be willing to serve customers at all times, at night and over week ends. The amount of money a broker makes depends on the number of transactions he closes. This is governed by his energy, ability and initiative. The commission on individual transactions may be fixed by agreement between the broker and the person he represents. However, the real estate boards in key cities have set up schedules of minimum rates which board members are requested to observe. This is usually 5 per cent of the base amount of the sale price for city property. The commission rate specified by some real estate boards for the sale of farm and village properties is 10 per cent of the sale price.

To protect the public as well as the honest and competent brokers, the majority of states have license laws which regulate real estate brokerage. Almost every city has a local real estate board which is interested in promoting and protecting local business. Local boards are usually members of the National Association of Real Estate Boards. State boards usually conduct classes to train real estate salesmen.

If you would like to know more about preparing yourself for a career in real estate, write to The National Association of Real Estate Boards, 22 West Monroe Street, Chicago, Illinois. Ask for a free copy of *Preparing for the Real Estate Business.*

Property Management

Managing income property for the owner is a specialized business. You can hardly expect the owner of important property, such as an apartment house or office building, to allow you to operate it until you have experience in this type of business. If you have no experience, you might start by managing a small property which yields fees too small to interest seasoned managers of larger properties. You might, also, take care of vacation cottages for owners during the months they are empty. You could act as renting agent too. In this way you can acquire property-management experience.

There is a good deal more to managing income-producing property than collecting rents and attending to tenant complaints. Duties fall into three classifications—those pertaining to tenants, such as service and rent collecting; operating duties, such as inspection and maintenance of the building; managerial duties, such as keeping records, providing statements to owner, tax and financial problems and budgeting expenses. While practical experience is necessary, knowledge may be acquired from special courses offered by the National Association of Housing Officials, Washington, D.C., and the National Association of Real Estate Boards course at the University of Chicago. Local real estate boards in a great many cities have set fees for managing properties. These fees vary among communities.

The Motel Business

The growth in the number of motels and motor courts along the highways is evidence of their popularity and of their profit-making possibilities. While operating a successful motel is not so easy as it looks, there are many opportunities for retirees with initiative, business ability and a willingness to tackle a variety of odd jobs.

The average motel has approximately twenty-five units to a court. Authorities in the motor-court industry advise that it is impractical to start a motor court with less than ten units or rooms. The larger motels or motor courts have from thirty-five to fifty units, some as many as one hundred units.

If you have the idea you can run a motel on a semiretired basis without hired help, you are mistaken. If you and your wife try to do most of the work yourselves, you will find that you are working harder than ever. More difficult than the work is the confinement. If a husband and wife run the motel, one or the other must be on hand throughout the day and night. Should the court have less than ten units, it cannot afford more than the services of one maid.

Capital requirements will vary depending upon the size of the court or motel, location, land costs, type of building and many other factors. Costs will vary from $3,000 to $12,-000 per unit, a unit being a single cabin or room. The average cost of a new motel is $35,000 to $50,000. A high rate of occupancy is the difference between substantial profits and mediocre returns or even loss. Experts in the industry state that the average earnings of all motel owners are about 30 per cent after taxes. Roughly, a motel doing an annual business of $20,000 brings in a net profit of around $6,000 and one doing $40,000, a profit of $12,000. Some amateurs in the business do not know how to keep books, operate on insufficient capital, lack business ability, fail to keep units modernized—and as a result lose money.

Success or failure in the motel business depends upon the owner's own efforts and abilities, routing or rerouting of the main traffic highway, legislation affecting roadside businesses, change of neighborhood, competition, economic conditions of prosperity or depression, sufficient capital invested in the business. Florida State University, the University of California and the University of Houston (Texas) offer courses in the operation and management of motels.

Other Types of Businesses in the Same General Classification

Vacation cabins and trailer parks in resort areas are rented by the week or month. You can rent out rooms in a large house to tourists or vacationists. Since large houses are a drug on the market nowadays, it is often possible to buy one at a low price. With a little remodeling a large house can be converted into an attractive tourist home. Location, parking and garage facilities are important factors in the successful operation of a tourist home. If located in a college town, you can rent rooms to students.

Vacation Camp and Cabins

At an open-all-year camp, operated by a retired man and his wife on the shore of a lake in Southern California, there are thirty-five cabins available for renting at $3 to $5 per night per couple. Cabins at the $3 rate have furnished kitchen and bedroom. If bedding is desired the charge is 50 cents per bed extra. The adobe cabins renting at $5 per night include bathroom with shower, all-electric kitchen, double beds and electric heat.

Trailer and tent camping space is provided at 50 cents per night, $3.50 per week or $14 per month. Fishing privileges cost 50 cents per day per person. This camp serves meals, light lunches, beer and soda. A grocery department carries everything but fresh meat. Fishing tackle is rented or sold.

Brains and Experience Advisory Services

Here are a few case histories of management men retired from business who have formed groups and offer their pooled talents for consultation and seasoned advice.

Retired engineers and draftsmen from the General Electric Company and American Locomotive Works, Schenectady, New York, formed the Mohawk Development Service. Here more than a dozen oldsters, from sixty-six to seventy-four years of age, provide engineering, drafting service and consultation on electrical and mechanical problems. They draw the same rate of pay as General Electric pays for comparable work.

In El Paso, Texas, a group of retired experts in various fields have organized Consultants, Inc. to furnish counsel to a list of clients.

Management Counselors, Inc., New York City, offers a panel of forty experts in thirty-four industrial lines, as well as banking and finance. They give seasoned advice for a moderate fee.

A group of thirty retired executives of large and small industries in Wilmington, Delaware, offer business advice free to widows and small businessmen.

This idea can be expanded. A movement in this direction is the formation of Senior Achievement Groups, similar to the popular Junior Achievement programs. Retired persons organize themselves into groups. They establish their own managerial, supervisory and production groups, and market their own products.

The Senior Achievement movement also could easily expand in another direction. A local association could be formed for the purpose of making members self-sufficient by applying the homely principles of the early New England colonists. This would take the form of pooling the knowledge, skills and labor of each of the membership for the benefit of all.

The plan in a modified form would cover swapping work projects among members. Each member would file a list of his skills in such jobs as house painting, paper hanging, carpentry and alterations, reconditioning furniture, landscape gardening and similar work. The skills of the womenfolk could be catalogued for homemaking specialties. At regular get-togethers, assignments would be made on a group project. The member most experienced in, say, house painting, could act as supervisor on projects calling for this type of work. In this way what one member could not do alone, the group could. It would provide a type of economic security for the membership. Since the work would not be in the line of regular full-time employment for wages, there would be no compulsion to complete the project on a deadline schedule.

If the group should run out of projects for the association membership, they could take on community projects like constructing a shuffleboard court or building and installing picnic tables or fireplaces in the community park or recreational area. While every community wants things like this done, the community, somehow, seldom finds the time or the manpower.

There's a wide variety of useful and cooperative jobs that such a Senior Achievement group could do in its spare time.

By helping themselves and others intelligently they would create active and worthwhile careers for themselves.

Baby or Invalid Sitting Service

This is an ideal way for a retired woman to earn a supplementary income. It also provides a means of combating loneliness. You can engage in baby sitting or invalid sitting by offering your own services. Or you can establish and manage a group of sitters by setting yourself up as a sitting agency service.

To operate as an agency you need a group of older women or men or teenagers on whom you can absolutely depend, a telephone and a system for keeping records of sitters and clients. You can operate the service from your home. You will need to advertise your service by inserting a small advertisement in local newspapers, mailing postal cards to a list of neighborhood parents, church groups and clubs, listing your service in the yellow pages of the local telephone book. Consult the town clerk to learn whether you need a license to operate a sitting agency service in your locality.

If you operate a sitting agency you will find that about forty sitters is all you can take care of. Rates for individual sitters are about $1.50 for the first three hours plus 35 to 50 cents for each additional hour. As the operator-manager of the agency service you should collect 20 to 40 per cent of the fee.

Those interested in this as an occupation should send for a copy of *Baby Sitter's Handbook*. Write to Science Research Associates, 57 W. Grand Avenue, Chicago, Illinois. The price is 40 cents.

Products Tailor-made to Customer Taste

Making cigars to order is the profitable small business enterprise of a salesman teamed up with a cigar maker. A sample cigar is handmade to a controlled formula in wrapper and filler. This test-it-yourself sample is given to customers to determine their preferences. The reaction of the customer to the sample cigar is recorded. Boxes of the cigars are then handmade to suit the customer's taste. Customers like this special service and a thriving business is being developed.

This idea has also been used successfully in the merchandising of pipe tobacco and perfume. A small, profitable business could be developed also for a number of products in which one of the major selling features is personal taste enjoyment. The blending and selling of coffee to suit personal preferences is one possibility. Products that have a rapid rate of consumption and are purchased frequently offer the best possibilities for a part-time or full-time small business enterprise, in the made-to-your-personal-liking field.

There's Money in Worms

A Californian does an annual business of $50,000 raising and selling earthworms. A woman in the earthworm business started with $10 invested in worms and in three years had her earthworm sales up to $4,000. A poultry farmer started raising earthworms as a side line and in four years made more money from the sale of worms than from his poultry hatchery.

The principal uses for earthworms are for soil building for farms and gardens; for fish bait; for zoos, laboratories, aquariums and game breeders; for breeding stock sold to earthworm raisers.

With as little as $10 to $20 you can get started on an earthworm breeding project. For about $100 you can buy ten thousand fine breeding earthworm stock. In about a year you should have enough worms to start selling on a regular, businesslike scale. Earthworm raising offers good prospects for a retirement business either as a part-time or full-time operation. With good breeding stock started, experts in the business say, you should be able in about three hours work a day to pack and ship about $9 worth of worms. Working a full day or with one helper, you should be able to ship about $20 worth a day.

There are over one thousand species of worms to choose from. You will find many breeders of worms listed in gardening and hobby magazines. Write to several asking for literature on the species they raise. The state agricultural college can help you in selecting the best type to specialize in. One of the best booklets on the subject is *Raising Hybrid Earthworms for Profit*, by Earl B. Shields, Earl B. Shields, 107 West Wacker, Chicago 1, Illinois, postpaid $1. Also by the same author-publisher, *A Directory of Earthworm Hatcheries*. Postpaid 50 cents.

Animal Sitter

There's a woman in a suburb of Los Angeles who is building up a thriving business as an animal sitter. Traveling about in a light truck, she visits about six "clients" a day. These vary from goats to goldfish. Her specialty is feeding and taking care of animals and pets in their own homes, while folks are away on vacation, in the hospital, etc. Her prices vary according to the animal or pet. Goldfish care costs $1 per day; cats and dogs, two visits a day, $2.75. Visits with goats and horses cost $2 each. Goats must be milked and horses exercised.

"Hotel" for Pets

Many dog owners would welcome a place to board their pets while they are away from home. They hesitate to leave their pets caged up in the small areas provided by veterinarians. One woman solved this problem by building a series of pens ten feet square in a barn with a cement floor. Long runs were built outside under trees so that the dogs could get exercise. During the vacation season there is a waiting list for available pens. The charge is $1 a day for room and board. A bath costs $1. Veterinarians and pet shops refer dog owners to her. She also runs small advertisements in the classified section of the local newspaper. This activity could be expanded to include obedience lessons and the selling of pet-shop accessories, such as dog baskets, blankets, harnesses, etc. Good opportunities exist for this type of service in locations adjacent to city areas.

Small Animal Breeding for Pleasure and Profit

While there are about 150,000 chinchillas in the United States and Canada, the industry has not yet reached the stage where pelting is possible for profit. It has been estimated that the national herd will have to be in excess of a million chinchillas before ranches reach the stage of profits in pelts. It takes up to 150 pelts to make a coat. Breeders say that they make money selling pelts at $25 each. This means $3,750 for raw materials for a coat. It is doubtful that the chinchilla coat market is big enough to provide large volume at such high prices. The money being made today is in the sale of breeding stock. Chinchillas sell for $800 to $2,500 a pair. Some ranchers make $200 and more a month selling breeding stock. Those who get out and hustle seem to do all right. However, this seems to be a luxury industry and when we get into a tight money era it will face tough going. There are quite a number of retired persons making money in the business of selling breeding stock. But the chinchilla industry faces a lot of ifs when it comes to the fur market.

Many retired men and women make a comfortable living raising and selling small animals and birds. The secret of success is to specialize in something for which there is a demand and not too much competition. If raising dogs, pheasants, goats, rabbits, singing canaries or rare birds appeals to you, look into the market possibilities for selling your stock. Research organizations and hospitals buy mice, guinea pigs, rabbits and other animals for medical research projects. Hotels, clubs, restaurants, shooting clubs, private game preserves and other sporting organizations buy many thousands of pheasants each year. Rabbit meat is popular in some areas as a food item. Goat milk finds a good market in some localities. There is always a good market for select breeding stock of small animals and pets of all kinds.

Some states require licenses for raising fur animals in captivity. Information on this matter can be obtained from your state game commission. Some towns also have restrictive ordinances.

Boats for Hire

A retired man at a vacation spot in California has 150 boats available for hire at $1 per day for one to three passengers, $2 a day for four to eight passengers. Outboard motors rent for $3.50 per day. Half-day rates start after twelve noon.

Additional "for hire" businesses include folding chairs sold, rented for all occasions, including banquets; wheel chairs rented; bicycles for sale, rented, repaired; typewriters rented, for sale, repaired; fishing tackle rented, bait for sale.

Parcel Delivery Service

One retired man I know bought a light secondhand delivery truck and had an attractive paint job done on it. He has a contract service with several retail stores to make parcel deliveries. He charges from 10 cents to 50 cents per parcel, depending upon the size of the parcel and the delivery distance. He makes store pick-ups once in the morning and once during the afternoon.

Investing in an Established Business

You may be offered the opportunity to buy an established business. Perhaps you can buy it at a good price if the owner is anxious to sell. Don't, however, approach the subject of buying a business at a bargain. Under normal conditions there are no bargains or "steals." Take plenty of time to make a careful analysis and appraisal of the business.

Try to find out the owner's reason for selling. It may be entirely different from what he tells you. He may be trying to unload a sick or dying business, a "white elephant" on an unsuspecting prospect. Here are some legitimate reasons why owners sell established businesses: desire to retire from active participation in the business, bad health, plans for moving to another region, need to settle an estate, disagreement among partners, marital differences, business not suited to their temperament. But watch out for these factors: location of business on the downgrade, main highway being relocated, new zoning laws which threaten future of the business, no demand for products or services in the area, the franchise to sell principal line is being lost, too much competition, lease expiring and landlord refusing to renew it.

Wisdom demands that you investigate the business proposition as thoroughly as possible before you get too deeply involved. Don't let the owner or his agent push you into buying a business before you complete your investigation. Ask the owner for copies of his business records, and also his income tax returns since he has operated the business he wants to sell. Find out when the business was originally established, how many times it has changed hands and if it has been consistently profitable. If you decide to buy, appraise each of the assets separately to determine what price you should pay. What is the value of the equipment and the stock on hand? Check every item. Unless you do so, you may find it necessary to discard a lot of material that you took for granted was in good condition. It might be a good idea to have an accountant check the financial records and make an evaluation of the business. Compare the business in its present state and the price asked for it with one you could start and develop yourself. Sometimes when a business is sold, the former owner wants to sell his receivables. These are accounts of customers who owe him money. If you take over these accounts, be sure that you are actually buying customers and not bad debts. Check the list of customer accounts receivable with the local retail credit association or banker. Engage a competent lawyer to draw up the purchase agreement.

Five Steps in Establishing a Retirement Business

1. *Early Start in Preparation.* Find out as early as possible the type of business you would like to establish and operate in your retirement years. Your aptitude, interest and health are vital factors in determining whether or not you should engage in a particular business. Your knowledge of the business, practical experience in it and financial status are essential factors in determining the type of business you are likely to make a success of.

Most businesses fail because of the owner's lack of business capacity and lack of capital. An early start in planning will enable you to acquire by reading and studying, by part-time practical experience, the necessary business capacity to establish and operate the business of your choice. A carefully planned savings, investment and income-producing program, started early, will provide you with the capital needed to open or buy your business. By planning and organizing your spare time, you can make an interesting hobby out of preparing to establish a profitable business of your own when you retire. In doing this you will be storing up understanding and knowledge that you will need when you make the big plunge on your own.

2. *Studying for Business Operation.* You cannot have too much knowledge about the business you propose to engage in. Gaining more knowledge is a continuous process.

Government Helps. The publications of the United States Government are prepared in the form of leaflets, pamphlets, bulletins and books by the various agencies. The Department of Commerce publications include *Small Business Aids*— over five hundred titles covering such subjects as financing, selling, advertising, insurance and record-keeping; *Establishing and Operating Series*—mostly on retail and service trades. This series includes over forty books that thoroughly discuss the major problems of a particular type of business. Types of businesses covered range from small woodworking shop to service station, from restaurant to jewelry store; *Basic Information Series*—bulletins which are listings of governmental and nongovernmental publications, directories, trade papers and trade associations for various fields of business. Questions or problems which arise on which no publication has been prepared will be answered by specialists in the Department of Commerce. Address your letter to Bureau of Information, Department of Commerce, Washington 25, D.C. Published information is for sale by Superintendent of Documents, United States Government Printing Office, Washington 25, D.C.

Books on Your Specialty. Visit your public library every so often and take out how-to-do-it books on the subject of your business interests.

Trade Papers. Numerous general business magazines are published by each type of trade and business. Subscribe to the leading trade magazine of the business field you plan to enter. Reading these magazines will keep you in touch with what is happening in the business and keep you up-to-date on new products and new applications. Keep a clipping file of articles that are of particular interest to you.

Trade Associations. Many businesses and industries have active trade associations of their own. You can pick up a great deal of helpful information attending national and state conventions and trade shows. Watch local newspapers and trade journals for notices of conventions in your locality.

Manufacturers' Catalogs and Booklets often are textbooks on their lines of products. A study of their sales and instruction literature is well worth while. Manufacturers also prepare sales manuals on store layouts and sales techniques covering their products.

Schools and Correspondence Courses. Check with local public and private school and college administrators regarding classes available. Many courses, conducted at night, cover a wide range of vocational subjects and occupations. Enrollment in one or more of these courses may develop your skill, talents and technical training for a retirement occupation or business. Many a person has developed a successful new career by studying selected occupations by the correspondence method. Accredited correspondence schools train you, in your spare time, by regular lessons which are informative and practical.

3. *Getting Practical Training.* The records of those who have succeeded and those who have failed in business prove beyond a doubt that practical experience is one of the most important assets you can possess. Therefore, if you have never worked in the type of business you plan to establish when you retire, you will be wise to take a part-time job on week ends or during some of your vacations in such a business. You could, of course, wait until you retire and then work for six months or a year getting on-the-job practical training and experience in a well-established and successful business.

4. *Getting Occupational Tools and Equipment.* In some types of businesses, a woodworking shop, for example, you can begin to collect much of the necessary tools and equipment while you are still working on your regular job. You may be able to pick up bargains as they become available or buy new tools and equipment out of savings from your regular salary or wages. It is important to have good judgment in buying these things in advance, so that you don't load yourself with a lot of obsolete equipment.

5. *Selecting a Location.* Decide in which region of the country you wish to establish your business. Begin a study of the various towns and communities in the region. Find out which offer the best opportunities. Visit the area selected during your vacations for a personal checkup of general business conditions. Study it carefully. Is the city or town lively, progressive, growing? How about competition? Is there any? What is the rent situation? What about sources for obtaining merchandise? Is there really a potential market for your proposed products or services? Study both sides of the picture—the disadvantages as well as the advantages.

Bibliography

Names and addresses of various trade papers devoted to selected businesses:

Radio & Television Retailing, 480 Lexington Ave., New York 17, N.Y.
Radio & Television News, 366 Madison Ave., New York 17, N.Y.
Electrical Merchandising, 330 W. 42nd St., New York 18, N.Y.
Electrical Construction & Maintenance, 330 W. 42nd St., New York 18, N.Y.
Air Conditioning & Refrigeration News, 540 W. Fort St., Detroit 26, Mich.
Gift & Art Buyer, 212 Fifth Ave., New York 10, N.Y.
Giftwares & Home Fashions, 1170 Broadway, New York 1, N.Y.
Antiques Dealer, 15, E. 26th St., New York 10, N.Y.

Retail Bookseller, Hillsdale, N.J.

Book Review Digest, 950 University Ave., New York 52, N.Y.

Publishers' Weekly, 62 W. 45th St., New York 36, N.Y.

Retail Tobacconist, 1860 Broadway, New York 23, N.Y.

Soda & Confection Retailer, 139 W. 72nd St., New York 23, N.Y.

The Woodworker, 2232 N. Meridan St., Indianapolis, Ind.

Woodworking Digest, 222 E. Willow Ave., Wheaton, Ill.

Machine & Tool Blue Book, 22 E. Willow Ave., Wheaton, Ill.

Modern Machine Shop, 431 Main St., Cincinnati 2, Ohio

American Machinist, 330 W. 42nd St., New York 18, N.Y.

The Post, 18652 Fairfield Ave., Detroit 21, Mich.

American Paint & Oil Dealer, 3713 Washington Ave., St. Louis, Mo.

Sporting Goods Dealer, 2018 Washington Ave., St. Louis 3, Mo.

Journal of Accountancy, 270 Madison Ave., New York 16, N.Y.

Vend, W. Randolph St., Chicago 1, Ill.

Reporter of Direct Mail Advertising, 17 E. 42nd St., New York 17, N.Y.

National Real Estate Journal, 427 Sixth Ave., S.E. Cedar Rapids, Iowa.

American Motel Journal, 5 S. Wabash Ave., Chicago 3, Ill.

Resort Management, 135 W. Wells St., Milwaukee 3, Wis.

American Restaurant, 5 S. Wabash Ave., Chicago 3, Ill.

Drive-in & Highway Cafe, 1850 S. Manhattan Place, Los Angeles 6, Calif.

Florists Review, 343 S. Dearborn St., Chicago 4, Ill.

Women's Wear Daily, 7 E. 12th St., New York 3, N.Y.

For a complete list of trade papers in all classifications, see *Standard Rate and Data.* Your public library probably has a copy.

U. S. Department of Commerce Publications. Write to Superintendent of Documents, U.S. Government Printing Office, Washington 25, D.C.

Domestic Commerce Publications Price List, PI 62. Free.

Establishing and Operating—

    Your Own Business. 25 cents.

    Air Conditioning & Refrigeration Business. 25 cents.

    Automatic Merchandising Business. 20 cents.

    Beauty Shop. 30 cents.

Book Store. 15 cents.
Bookkeeping Service. 15 cents.
Confectionery-Tobacco Store. 20 cents.
Electrical Appliance & Radio Shop. 45 cents.
Flower Shop. 20 cents.
Gift & Art Shop. 20 cents.
Letter Shop. 15 cents.
Mail-Order Business. 30 cents.
Metal Working Shop. 45 cents.
Paint, Glass & Wallpaper Store. 15 cents.
Real Estate & Insurance Business, 40 cents.
Restaurant. 75 cents.
Retail Bakery. 35 cents.
Service Station. 40 cents.
Small Woodworking Shop. 15 cents.
Sporting Goods Store. 15 cents.
Year-Round Motor Court. 30 cents.
Opportunities in Selling. 25 cents.
Small Business Problems—
Selecting a Store Location. 20 cents.
Financing a New Business. 25 cents.
Record Keeping for Retail Stores. 15 cents.
Basic Industrial Location Factors. 25 cents.
Check List to Help Introduce Your New Industrial Product, Cat.
No. C18:206:53. 10 cents.
New Product Opportunities, Cat. No. C18:271:6. 25 cents.
Woodworking & Furniture Repair, Cat. No. C18:271:6. 25 cents.
Practical Nursing, Cat. No. FS2.8:149. 65 cents.
Underwriting Manual, Cat. No. NHA2.6:UN2/947. $2.
Opportunities in Selling, Ind. Series No. 65. 30 cents.
Developing & Selling New Products. 35 cents.
Government Information on Retailing. 15 cents.
The Outlook for Women as Physical Therapists. 20 cents.
Chinchilla Raising, Cat. No. A1.35:266. 5 cents.
Guinea Pigs, Cat. No. A1.35:252. 5 cents.
Hamster Raising, Cat. No. A1.35:250. 5 cents.
Mink Raising, Cat. No. A1.4/2:801. 15 cents.
Angora Rabbit Wool Production, Cat. No. A1.4/2:785. 10 cents.

CHAPTER VII

If You Would Like to Retire to a Farm

The Farm Today

Thirty years ago most farms in the United States used kerosene lamps for home lighting and lanterns in barns. Wood-burning stoves were used for cooking and heating. There were no refrigerators, no indoor running water, no indoor plumbing facilities. Working the farm and doing the chores were backbreaking jobs. There was little or no power-driven mechanized farm machinery.

The farm today is vastly different. There has been a power and laborsaving revolution on the farm. Farmers now have the best in electrified home and farmyard lighting and electrical home appliances. They have motor-powered tools, tractor-driven farm machinery and electrified water pumping systems. Cooking is now done by electricity. Homes and water are heated by liquefied petroleum gas. Hoists eliminate lifting. Hand trucks, conveyors and automatic feeders eliminate carrying heavy loads. Yes, new ways of living and doing things have come to the farm. Many a farm home is now as comfortable and as modern as a city or suburban home.

The trends in the use of farm land have changed, too. The change in consumer preference has affected the demand for different types of agricultural products. Fruits, vegetables, meat and poultry have increased in per capita consumption, while sugar, sirups, fats, oils, potatoes, flour and grain products have declined. Also, public acceptance of rayon, nylon and other synthetic fibers have influenced the demand for farm-produced fibers, cotton and wool.

Farming now is a well-paid occupation with excellent opportunities for you to live better and find economic independence. Anyone who has the knowledge and experience to produce farm products, or is willing to obtain it, and has the necessary capital to get started can find unusual opportunities to make a good living from the land.

Here is some interesting data from the United States Department of Agriculture, Miscellaneous Publication No. 699, *Farm Land Ownership in the United States.* "Age does not appear to be a serious factor in farm ownership. Twenty-four per cent of all farm owners are in the age group 55 to 64 and 18 per cent are 65 to 74 years old. As to the occupations of farm owners: 65 per cent are active farmers; 14 per cent are engaged in clerical work and in skilled and unskilled trades; 10 per cent are in the business and professional group both active and retired; 8 per cent are retired farmers; and 3 per cent are housewives. Almost 82 per cent of farm-land owners live on a farm. The majority of retired farmers, business and professional men, and housewives who own farms do so in the capacity of landlord rather than actively operating the farm land themselves. Some 45 percent of the farm owners who rent out land depend upon that land for their principal source of income."

Acquiring a Farm Before Retirement

You don't necessarily have to wait until you retire before acquiring farm property. It is a good idea to be on the lookout for a suitable farm or ranch some years prior to your tentative retirement date. If you come across property that meets your requirements, buy it—if the location, the time, and the price are right. If you have to take out a mortgage to buy the property, you can use some of your savings while working at your regular job to reduce or pay it off. By the time your retirement date rolls around, you will probably own the property without substantial encumbrances against it.

If you acquire farm property at a location that is too far away from your present employment, you can lease the property to a reliable tenant and use the rent income to help pay off the mortgage obligations. Or you can engage a renter to operate and maintain the farm or ranch on a share-the-income basis, during the years of your absentee ownership.

Be sure to select a renter who is experienced, industrious and conscientious. The owner, in addition to furnishing the land and buildings, pays the taxes, insurance and repairs on buildings. A renter usually owns his own machinery and sometimes half the livestock. Each stands half the cost of seed, fertilizer and hired operating expenses. Both owner and renter divide cash sales of farm production and normal increases in livestock on a monthly or yearly basis. Have a contract in writing, setting forth the duties of each party and the division of the income. If you expect a good renter to stay and work on your farm, he must receive a fair return for his time and labor. Working together you can make your farm more livable, more productive and more profitable.

Best Time to Buy

Usually the best time to buy a farm is when the price of land is relatively low and there is likely to be a rise in the market value of agricultural products. All records show that the prices of farm products rise during a war period and fall after the war. The price of farm land fluctuates similarly.

If you are planning your retirement on a long-range basis, you can wait for the price of farm land to decline. Those approaching retirement would do well to buy a farm home as early as possible even though prices are high. It is good business to buy the farm outright so that you can go into retirement without the load of a mortgage debt. If you can't afford to buy a farm outright, you should have enough cash to make a substantial down payment and provide for mortgage payments to be extended over a long period. In this way you protect yourself during years of low income when prices of farm products are declining.

Don't Try to Be a Pioneer

In any community, your success depends upon your choice of a farm. Other important factors are your knowledge of soils, crops, livestock and the use of farm machinery. Don't try to be a pioneer at retirement age. The hardships that are part of the settling of new lands should be left to the younger generation. Your best chance for success and happiness is in an established agricultural community. There you will find those facilities that make a desirable place to live and neighboring farm families to aid you in making adjustments to the community life pattern. Congenial surroundings are essential to a happy and profitable farm life.

Remember a farm home is a way of life. Be sure you want it before you start. Location with respect to good roads is important. So are churches, schools, hospitals and other services. The availability of electricity, telephone service, RFD, water supply, radio and television service, all should be looked into.

If you are not familiar with farm values in the community, have an appraisal of the property made by a qualified appraiser before you buy. He will test the soil texture and other factors influencing productivity and will estimate the net earning capacity of the land.

You Can Start with a Half Acre to an Acre

A small farm home can provide a satisfying way of life and reduce the cost of the family food budget, if carefully planned and properly managed.

In most localities, a half acre to an acre has been found to be adequate for a small farm home. A half acre is a little more than one hundred by two hundred feet. That is about all the land that can usually be cared for by elderly persons, or by one person in his spare time. The California Agricultural Extension Service says: "A half-acre will provide space for a house, an outdoor living or recreational area, garage and tool shed, vegetable garden, berry patch, 10 to 20 fruit trees, and an area for a few chickens and rabbits."

The average rural resident on a small farm home of this size will have some difficulty marketing his surplus products. Commercial packing plants and produce agents will not handle the small quantity of produce that can be raised on an acre. Surplus may be sold to or traded with neighbors, sold to roadside stand operators or retail market stores or stored in a frozen food locker. An acre is not enough to provide financial independence. But it is the best kind of insurance against poverty. It is more desirable to have a few acres of good land on an improved road with improved community services than to have larger acreage in a poor location, especially when excess acreage cannot be operated efficiently.

Larger-size Farm Needed to Produce Income

If you want your farm to produce the income you need for family living, a larger farm will be required. The actual acreage needed will depend upon the type of farming you undertake, the productivity of the soil and the region in which the farm is located. Family-size farms are usually the most economically operated and in the long run the safest, particularly for those lacking experience in the operation of large-farm business.

What to Grow

Some crops require more labor and capital investment than others. In general, crops that cost more to produce bring in a greater return per acre, although they are more hazardous. Intensive crops, such as vegetables and fruit, require added labor, and higher expenses for seed and fertilizer. There are additional costs to harvest such crops. Good markets are essential.

Cotton, corn, soybeans and peanuts require smaller expenditures for labor and supplies, but larger acreage. Cattle or sheep ranching requires the most extensive acreage.

Dairying calls for more constant attention than any other type of farming. Cows need to be milked morning and afternoon seven days a week. Dairy cows require 140 hours per cow per year of labor as compared to 40 hours for beef cattle. Lifting filled milk cans and seeing to the continuous sanitary housekeeping around the barns are usually too strenuous for retired persons.

Other things being equal, more capital is required to finance orchards than truck crops, and truck crops than field crops.

Some crops can be sold to canneries or to packers on the vines or on the trees. Of course you will not make as much money from your crops selling in this way. On the other hand, you will not have the bother of a harvesting problem.

Other than growing your own food supplies, you should not carry on too many different kinds of farming. You will find it more profitable to concentrate on a major specialty farm product. It should be a quality product to bring in top prices.

Truck Crops

Early market and high quality bring in highest returns. Melons, cantaloupes, sweet corn, tomatoes, radishes, carrots, celery and asparagus are a few of the cash crops that lend themselves to specialization. Truck farms from twenty to fifty acres provide opportunities for a good income.

Berries bring in high returns from relatively small acreage devoted to their cultivation. Strawberries, raspberries, blackberries, blueberries and cranberries provide a good living on five to ten acres. Knowledge of timing, fertilizing, irrigating, spraying and harvesting operations is essential for success. Marketing is usually done through an association of growers.

Orchards

The quickest and easiest way to become an orchardist is to purchase an established orchard. The other way is to start with small trees called whips. It takes five to ten years, depending upon the kind of fruit, to bring whips into commercial production. If you buy a mature orchard, check on the age and condition of the trees as well as the market potential for the fruit. Orchards require several sprays a year, as well as pruning and harvesting. About ten pickers are needed at harvest time to pick the fruit that one man can care for during the rest of the year. Some fruits are bought on the tree.

Mild climate, soil fertility and irrigation or rainfall are important factors for orchardists. Bees are necessary for pollinization. Net income or earnings per acre from fruit have been good during the past several years compared with other farm products. Most commercial orchards run from ten acres upwards. You can specialize in citrus fruits, papayas, avocados, guavas, figs, pears, peaches, apples, almonds, walnuts, etc., depending upon the climate, soil and frost conditions. Write to the college of agriculture in the state you plan to settle in for detailed information on full-scale fruit farming in the state.

Nursery Stock

With specialized nursery stock, planted twenty-four inches apart on forty-two-inch rows, you can grow over six thousand plants to the acre. In central and southern Florida, from seven thousand to ten thousand rose plants are planted to the acre. Fifty to seventy-five saleable cut roses per plant can be grown each year, depending on the variety of rose and general conditions. Ferns provide a good source of revenue in Florida. Ferns and other foliage plants are potted and sent to department and five-and-ten-cent stores in all parts of the country, where they are sold.

A few acres of flowering shrubs, though they take four or five years to reach market size, will bring you high return per acre. A rotation system of harvesting and planting new seedlings can produce a perpetual source of income.

Christmas Trees

Since good returns can normally be expected from the sale of Christmas trees in eight to ten years after planting, a number of persons in their fifties are planting them on their farms now so that the trees will be ready to harvest when they retire.

If the tree seedlings are spaced 4 feet apart with four feet between rows, you can plant 2,720 Christmas trees to the acre. The tree sizes most in demand by the Christmas trade are those between five and eight feet high. Planting stock is usually obtained from public or private nurseries. Names and addresses can be obtained from the Forest Service, United States Department of Agriculture, Washington 25, D.C.

A Christmas tree grower in New York State has had an average yearly harvest of 600 trees from a fifteen-acre tract over a period of fifteen years. He has grossed $7,000 on a combination retail and wholesale selling basis. This grower estimates it costs him 30 cents per tree to plant, prune, harvest and market, or a total of $2,700, leaving a net return of $4,300.

Mushroom Sales on the Increase

Cultivated mushroom growing is not a seasonal activity, they can be grown the year round. By rotating the plantings in mushroom beds, you can have three plantings a year in the same mushroom beds. The normal crop from each planting is about two pounds from each square foot planted. Beds come to bearing in four to eight weeks after the spawn is planted, and bear mushrooms over two months from each planting. Mushrooms need plenty of fresh air and an even temperature. For optimum growth fifty-eight to sixty-two degree temperature is essential. In some parts of the country this means summer cooling and winter heating. Mushrooms grow best in poorly lighted or dark places. That is why mushrooms are often grown in caves and abandoned mines. They can be grown commercially in beds located in sheds, stables or barns. You can build mushroom houses of cinder blocks, with solid walls and no windows. Mushrooms can be shipped fresh or dried. However, fresh mushrooms are the better profit-makers. As a rule, the larger the mushroom, the more it brings. Because they weigh so little, there are several dozen mushrooms in the ventilated pound and half-pound boxes in which they are shipped to hotels, groceries and restaurants. Prices are fairly stable at 45 to 50 cents a pound. They can also be sold to roadside stands, produce wholesalers and canneries. Figures from the latest United States Department of Agriculture census show that sixty million pounds of mushrooms were grown in the United States in one year.

You Can Make Money Selling Honey

Beekeeping is a practical and money-making specialized activity. Few occupations require so little capital. Many hobbyists and back-lot beekeepers get considerable pleasure and relaxation from a few hives of bees. In addition to direct returns from the sale of honey, the beekeeper has some monetary return from the sale of beeswax. There are some fifty-four crops that are dependent upon the honeybee for pollination. Many beekeepers truck colonies of bees to orchards where substantial fees are collected for their pollinization work. About fifty million pounds of honey are used each year by the baking industry. Other large quantity users are manufacturers of confectionery, ice cream, beverages and similar products.

In San Diego County, California, there are over one thousand registered apiaries with forty-five thousand colonies of bees. At Rutherfordton, North Carolina, there is an apiarist who has thirty-four colonies of bees. From these colonies he harvests five hundred pounds of de luxe sourwood honey and three thousand additional pounds of tulip poplar and clover honey. He sells his sourwood honey for $1.50 a quart; his mixed kinds for $1.25; and the tulip poplar honey for $1.00 a quart. These prices pay him well for his time and interest.

In Massachusetts, farmers pay $10 each to rent hives for one or two days in the blossom season. One hive is required for about every fifty fruit trees. During the blossom season which may last from a few days to a month, depending upon the locality, hives may be rented to five or six fruit growers at $10 each. With fifty hives, for example, a quick profit of at least $2,000 can be realized in a short time, with careful timing. The more moves made at blossom time, the more money can be made. Scheduling the moves ahead of time is essential.

The initial cost in beekeeping is about $21. This includes the cost of one hive, the bees, a queen, mask, bee smoker and a hive tool for withdrawing the honey combs. Beginners seeking information should write to Bureau of Entomology, United States Department of Agriculture, Washington, D.C., or ask for all available free publications on beekeeping, as well as a list of those which may be purchased. Several of the state agricultural colleges have specific bulletins applying to beekeeping in their particular areas. A recognized "bible" in the field is *The A,B,C and X,Y,Z of Bee Culture* published by A. I. Root, Medina, Ohio. Price, $3.95 a copy.

Poultry Pays Off

There's money in poultry, if you give the birds the right kind of care. You can specialize in layers and sell eggs. The average pullet now lays about 165 eggs a year. You can specialize in raising broilers. Improved breeding, high-efficiency feeds and mass production methods make it possible to raise three or four broods per year. With present-day equipment, one man can handle up to eighteen thousand broilers at a time. A building sixty by twenty-five feet is capable of brooding eighteen thousand broilers.

Poultry raising requires less heavy work than other types of farm enterprises. Automatic waterers and feeders cut manual labor to the bone. Poultry raising is well adapted to small farms. Newcomers are urged to begin small and grow to desired capacity as experience and profits justify. Existing buildings can often be used at the start.

Poultry raising is less seasonal than other types of farm production. However, eggs and broilers run in fairly well-defined cycles of high and low prices. Intelligent management calls for planning production so as not to overproduce in periods of low prices. Eggs bring highest prices during the summer months. Broilers usually bring good prices in winter and holiday months because most poultry raisers unload their flocks in late spring or early summer.

In some localities turkey raising and turkey egg production are important farm activities. Young turkeys require particularly close attention. Most states do not produce enough turkeys for local consumption.

Where can you sell quality poultry products at good prices? Neighbors are good prospects. They are easy to serve and dependable customers. At home or at the roadside you can attract customers by using an attractive roadside sign. Also, stores and roadside stand operators want a good source of quality eggs. They'll be glad to buy yours in clean, fresh, attractive cartons. A good egg business can be built up this way. The same goes for hotels and restaurants which make a specialty of serving eggs with uniform yolks. You can run an egg route. Housewives like to buy eggs at the kitchen door.

Some feed companies with nationwide distribution, as well as local feed dealers, operate egg-marketing services to help poultrymen sell their eggs. Such services include attractive roadside signs, jumbo advertising postcards to send to customers or to prospective customers, advertising mats for local newspapers, name stamps for egg cartons. They also provide colorful cartons with magnetic sales appeal.

Homemakers will pay ten, fifteen or even twenty-five cents per dozen more than the wholesale price for eggs, if they are top quality and attractively presented. Quality and freshness are the most important factors in marketing eggs, followed by price and size.

Pig Hatcheries—A New Business with a Big Future

A recent scientific discovery is expected to revolutionize pig raising. By this new system, the little pigs are taken from the sow before they are twenty-four hours old and put in wire brooders somewhat like those for chicks. After the pigs have had some colostrum, they are fed a new synthetic milk called Terralac. Under this system of feeding, piglets which weigh under three pounds at birth reach a weight of forty pounds in eight weeks. After about four weeks on the synthetic milk, dry pig starter is added to their menu. By the time they are six weeks old they are completely on solid feed.

This new system offers attractive prospects to farmers who want to specialize in pig raising since it promises to enable them to raise large numbers of pigs in hatcheries. This new idea seems destined to bring about as great a change in the hog industry as the incubator brought about in the raising of poultry. The pig hatchery as a business is about at the stage where the chicken hatchery was fifteen or twenty years ago. In the poultry business, hatcherymen specialize in turning out baby chicks and poults; feeder poultrymen convert them into broilers, egg layers and turkeys. Hog raising isn't that well organized yet—but signs point to its rapid development.

The biggest hazard in the pig hatchery business is disease. Time and research will solve this problem as they have other agricultural problems. If you want to get into a new agricultural enterprise in its pioneering stages and grow with it, running pig hatcheries is the business for you. Check with the state agricultural college in the state where you plan to locate for the latest developments in raising pigs without sows.

A Private Fish Pond

Hundreds of farm families in the South have fish ponds where they can catch fish almost any day of the year. These fish ponds provide outdoor recreation for all members of the family and their friends.

In most states soil conservation technicians will aid in planning and locating a good fish pond site. The United States Fish and Wildlife Service, as well as state fish and game departments, will furnish fish to stock the pond *free* for the asking. Some states charge a small fee for delivering the fish.

The pond must be fertilized at about four-week intervals, after it is stocked with hatchery fish. The fertilizer is not for the fish but to aid the growth of green microscopic plants in the pond water. Thousands of small insects feed on the green plants. Bluegills feed on these small insects, while bass in turn feed on the small bluegills. From an acre of fish pond you should catch from one hundred to two hundred pounds of fish each year. Also, a well-landscaped fish pond can be a source of great enjoyment and an asset in increasing property values.

Soilless Gardening

If you want to get into a new and fascinating branch of gardening that is destined for a bright and expanding future, try hydroponics—the culture of plants without soil.

You can engage in hydroponics as a pure experimentalist and amateur botanist, a spare-time hobbyist or a commercial farmer. Hydroponics is agriculture's first real competitor. It outyields traditional soil farming in a number of crops. It can produce crops where soil fertility is lacking, or water is scarce as in some regions of Florida, Arizona and New Mexico. The basic equipment for soilless gardening is a basin to hold the nutrient solution. This can be a small tank made of sheet metal, concrete or wood. A common five-gallon can found at filling stations can easily be converted and adapted into a serviceable tank, as a first step. Regular basins or tanks, for amateurs, are five to seven inches deep, two to four feet wide and six to twelve feet long. Commercial operators use basins that run the entire length of their greenhouses.

The seedbed for plants, which rests on top of the basin, is made of a simple, open, six-inch wide wood frame with a fine mesh chicken wire fastened over the bottom side. Coarse materials, such as straw or excelsior, are mixed with fine materials such as wood sawdust, sphagnum moss or glass wool, and placed within the frame.

The nutrient solution can be purchased at seed stores or you can prepare your own from standard formulas. The basin or tank is filled with the nutrient solution to within one and a half inches from the bottom of the seedbed. Some of the popular plants adaptable to hydroponics are vine crops, such as tomatoes, cantaloupes, cucumbers, watermelons and squashes; potatoes; root vegetables, such as carrots, radishes, beets, and parsnips; leafy vegetables, such as lettuce, cabbage, and celery; field crops, such as tobacco, barley, rye, oats, rice, etc.; herbaceous annual flowers; flowers from bulbs, corns, tubers and rhizomes; roses, gardenias, and fuchsias. Yields claimed for hydroponics are from four to ten times the average yield from soil.

For further information, read *The Complete Guide to Soilless Gardening* by William F. Gericke (Prentice-Hall, New York). Also write New Jersey Agricultural Extension Station, Rutgers University, New Brunswick, New Jersey. Ask for Bulletin No. 636, *Methods of Growing Plants in Solution and Sand Cultures.*

Grassland Farming—The Big Opportunity

Grassland farming, especially for the production of beef cattle, is becoming a popular and prosperous agricultural enterprise for those who have the capital to invest. It involves fertilizing the soil, sowing grasses and legumes for pasture grazing, for hay and for silage, and the conversion of this feed into livestock products. When properly limed, fertilized, seeded and managed, an acre of grassland pasture will produce three times as many feeding units as an average acre of corn.

Beef cattle, dairy cows, sheep, horses, swine, poultry and goats depend for food upon grasses and legumes. They can feed on the grasses right off the ground and return much of the fertility back to the soil. Grasses furnish almost the entire feed supply of beef cattle for at least half the area of the United States. Grasses furnish grazing pastures for the entire year in many areas of the southern states, and along the coastal area and Central Valley of California.

The South offers greater potentialities for grassland farming than any other area in the nation. Land resources are ample, comparatively cheap and located within twenty-four-freight hours of the big beef-consuming markets of the great industrial East. Cattlemen of the South claim that they can put more weight on cattle in pasture in the winter months than some northern farmers can all year, and on land costing one-tenth as much. The South has the soils, the rainfall, the year-round climate under which pasture grasses thrive best. There, livestock can graze eleven to twelve months of the year.

The opportunities in grassland farming for beef-cattle production are: (1) As a breeder, you sell purebred cattle to farmers who want to improve their herds, or young range stock to feeders; (2) As a feeder, you buy calves and yearlings to fatten and finish out to a weight of one thousand to twelve hundred pounds and sell them to a packing house or to a livestock marketing organization.

You don't have to search far for evidence of successful beef-cattle raising in the South. The entire area abounds with amazing examples of what is being done. One illustration will suffice to make the point. One of the leading citizens of Cleveland, Alabama, has about one thousand acres in grassland pasture. He uses a supplementary concentrated feeding system to finish off cattle for marketing. His pastures usually have over three thousand head of cattle grazing on them. This cattleman buys yearling steers and doubles their weight in less than a year. He puts about three hundred pounds on older steers in four months. About five thousand head of beef cattle are sold off his place each year. He is reputed to gross about a million dollars a year from his beef-cattle raising. Though he is sixty-nine years old, he is very active in running his business.

The cattle business, like other agricultural enterprises, has its ups and downs. But cattlemen who keep their herds young, have plenty of feed (especially grassland pastures) and avoid overborrowing make excellent returns on their investments over the years.

Despite the growth in the livestock business over the past twenty years, the need as well as the incentive for further expansion still exists. Beef production on grasslands gives better returns for capital, labor and management than most farm crops. Sheep raising is similar to cattle raising. Both sheep and cattle are less specialized and are not so intensive or arduous as dairy farming. Dairy farming also involves a greater outlay per animal than range raising of beef cattle, sheep or hogs. The old cotton fields, from North Carolina to Mississippi, can be bought cheaply. They can be made into pastures of "green gold."

Your first step is to decide whether you want to be a breeder or a feeder. Cattle ranches vary widely in location, type of livestock, size of herd and acreage. Usually from five hundred to two thousand acres are needed for year-round pasture grazing. With acreage costing from $20 up an acre, the investment in land runs into a considerable sum.

Hickory-smoked Meats Sold by Mail Order

Many country residents who have developed specialized skills have turned their skills into profits. One example is selling hickory-smoked meats by mail order. High-quality steers and hogs are butchered and cured country style in a preparation that includes special seasonings. The meat then goes into an old-fashioned smokehouse where it is kept until proper tenderness is achieved in an atmosphere of hickory smoke.

One such producer sells his hickory-smoked bacon in 6-, 7-, and 8-pound slabs at $1.10 per pound. Paper-thin slices of dried beef, processed over hickory embers and packed in cellophane bags, bring $2.00 a pound. Hickory-smoked hams, boned and baked, then coated with gelatin to seal in the spicy flavor, sell for $1.60 a pound and weigh from 10 to 14 pounds. Ready-to-bake smoked hams are $1.10 per pound. Specialized products like these are advertised in small space in magazines, reaching homemakers with high incomes who do considerable entertaining, as well as those who like to serve unusual dishes.

If you can produce a specialized farm product that is better than the average on the market, package it attractively, tell people about it and offer it for sale at a reasonable price that assures you a profit, you can usually make a good living from your efforts.

Farm Home–Restaurant Business

City residents and travelers appreciate the pleasures of a home-cooked meal in farm surroundings, prepared with freshly killed poultry and farm-grown vegetables. Old-fashioned home cooking is so scarce in restaurants today that people will drive miles out of their way to patronize places offering real, on-the-farm meals. Meals should be cooked with skill and served the way "mother used to do it." A farm operator strategically located on a much traveled highway, with an attractive roadside sign out front, can make a good supplementary income serving meals from products of the farm. A small farm home–restaurant can serve meals in one or two front rooms as a start and expand as the business grows.

Farm or Ranch Vacation-resort Home

Many city folk, as well as artists and writers, enjoy spending a few weeks resting quietly "back on the farm." If you have a few spare bedrooms, you can probably build up a clientele of paying guests during the vacation season. You can offer horseback riding, fishing, swimming and hay rides. A farm or ranch located on a lake or brook, near a national or state park, near the seashore, mountains or summer theater colony, provides additional recreational facilities. You can, if you prefer, build small sleeping cabins on the property and have your guests come up to the main house for meals. Small advertisements in city newspapers would help to keep your rooms or cabins rented for the season. A reputation for providing good accommodations, as well as good farm meals from home-grown food, are essential for success. You can also arrange with nearby motels and tourist courts to take overflow guests. Many country homes with spare rooms offer board and lodging to persons without established homes such as school teachers, nurses and others residing temporarily in the area.

Sell Farm Products at Retail

Many farmers sell a good percentage of their farm products at retail. If you are on a road with a good volume of automobile traffic, you might want to set up your own roadside stand close to your home. To be successful, a roadside stand must be visible some distance ahead and must provide adequate parking space for customers.

Fruits and berries can be sold as fresh products or marketed as jams, jellies or preserves. Direct-to-the-home selling is often profitable if you don't have to travel too far. You can do a week-end business selling farm products by advertising in nearby town newspapers or mailing postcards to a list of selected people. It is also possible to build up a steady business selling farm products to city people, shipping by parcel post. Smoked hams and turkeys, fruit gift baskets, honey and similar products are ideal for mail order selling. Be sure to grade and ship only high-quality products so that your customers will reorder.

An attractive businesslike sign in front of your home is an asset. It can help you sell breeding stock, honey, eggs, poultry, vegetables, fruit, special services and side lines. A distinctive name for your farm or roadside stand is a great help in advertising your enterprise.

Farm Caretaker

A retired man and wife, who once operated their own farm, act as caretakers while the farm owners take a vacation. They move out to a farm and run it for the owner while he and his wife are away. This retired couple even take care of the owner's children. Because they are trustworthy and dependable, they are paid well for their services.

Personal-service Job Opportunities in Farm Communities

One of the greatest opportunities for achieving lower production costs in farming is through the use of specialized farm implements and services. It is estimated that 50 per cent of all farm work is still done by hand. Through mechanization, much farm work can be simplified and time made available for other activities.

"In almost every farming community there are various jobs and services which farmers want done and are willing to pay for. Such jobs can sometimes be combined well with a small, part-time farm, or can be done to piece out the income of a man living in a village."

This quotation, and the suggested farm service jobs that follow, from the United States Department of Labor in *Occupational Outlook Handbook,* point up the opportunities open for enterprising persons to earn supplementary income from personal services associated with farming.

Custom Farm Mechanization Work. Threshing, combining, tractor plowing, potato digging, hay and straw baling, etc., provide part-time work for a man who owns (sometimes rents) specialized farm implements. Ordinarily, the owner of the equipment will go from farm to farm doing the job on a custom-work contract, usually having a list of jobs scheduled ahead.

Livestock Trucking. A specialized job that requires a truck with a body especially fitted to handle animals, it provides virtually a year-round job in certain regions.

Whitewashing Service. In the dairy and poultry regions, a man with a whitewashing outfit can keep busy the year round. This necessitates a light truck with spray rig large enough to do this kind of work. A man offering such a service usually has a regular route, which covers a large number of farms, and goes back over the same route perhaps once every three months. Ordinarily the farmer pays a flat fee for the job, possibly $5 to $20, depending upon the size of the buildings. A whitewashing outfit can usually do several jobs a day.

Fruit Spraying Service. In the orchard sections, tree spraying will usually occupy a man with a mobile spraying outfit several months of the year. The equipment is usually a light truck with a good spray rig which will reach to the height of fruit trees. Charges are either by the job, by the tree or, in some cases, a flat rate by the season to keep the orchard properly sprayed.

Mobile Repair Shop. The outfit usually consists of a covered truck, its interior equipped with tools for both metalwork and woodwork. It must have a forge as well as ordinary bench equipment and supplies. The mobile repair truck stops at farms or comes on call to fix anything from a broken plow handle to a heavy tractor. Some outfits furnish a good income to the owner, but an investment of $1,000 to $3,000 is necessary for the essential equipment.

Variations are the mobile welding outfit and the mobile blacksmith shop, operated as separate businesses or connected with shops in town.

Electrical and Carpenter Services. Electricians and carpenters are in great demand in rural areas. Such services require a car or a light truck and usually a small workshop at home. Carpenters in slack seasons usually turn out such products as ladders, potato crates, fruit baskets, etc.

Artificial Insemination. Here is a comparatively new field that has opened up new jobs in dairy regions. Usually, a group of owners of a particular breed of cows organize an association and buy one or more purebred bulls of that breed. The bull is kept in some central place. When a cow belonging to one of the members is to be bred, the inseminator takes semen to the farm and the cow is artificially bred. Handling the bull and the breeding operations involved were formerly done by veterinarians, but now much of the work is done by men who have had a short training for the job. It is a steady, salaried job, and pays a comfortable living.

Well Drilling. This is a part-time job in many farm regions that may keep a man busy eight or nine months a year. It requires some knowledge and experience. For deep wells, the equipment needed includes a tractor and a derrick or drilling rig, plus tools and supplies. Ordinarily, the driller charges a fixed rate per foot for drilling.

Mobile Grocery Store. Another established institution in many farm sections, providing a good year-round income for the merchant. This enterprise requires a covered truck, often containing a refrigerator, and equipped for carrying all kinds of groceries. Some kind of store or warehouse building in town is necessary to serve as a base of operations. The traveling store covers a fixed route each day, sometimes covering the same route twice a week.

Trader and Buyer. Opportunities exist for men who specialize in buying and selling poultry and similar products. Wise livestock traders often do well financially but must have facilities for handling stock and must be experienced in judging animals, values and market conditions. Native products, such as wood, honey, maple syrup, etc., also offer good opportunities to the trader.

Recreation Jobs. In areas offering recreation facilities, there are seasonal jobs as guides, camping experts and recreation leaders. Many men are so employed from the beginning of the spring fishing season to the close of fall hunting. Some of these are part-time farmers or ranchers. For these jobs a man often needs nothing more than an expert knowledge of the region and skill in outdoor matters; in some cases, he may own or lease considerable equipment, including boats, horses, guns, fishing tackle.

Get to Know the County Agent

The county agent is a public employee selected and paid jointly by the United States Department of Agriculture and the state agricultural college and county board of control. He is the local fountainhead of agricultural information, the farmer's counselor and trouble shooter. The county agent's headquarters is usually at the county courthouse. The county agent can help you a great deal in getting established in farming in his county.

The agricultural extension services of the state agricultural colleges, as well as experimental farms, also provide valuable practical information on the types of agricultural products best suited to local areas. Many state school systems offer vocational agricultural classes. The United States Department of Agriculture, Washington, D.C., publishes hundreds of pamphlets on all phases of agricultural living.

Seeking the Farm You Want

Build up a mental image of the farm you'd like to own, and then look for one that meets your specifications. Study the offerings of farms for sale with an open mind. You may have to examine many farms of the desired type, size and locality before you find one that approaches the specifications you have in mind. Seeking a farm calls for much inquiry, traveling and patience. It is rarely possible to find on any particular farm all the desirable features you are looking for. Weigh the advantages and disadvantages of the farms for sale and select the farm that most appeals to you.

Correspond with, or interview, those familiar with farm real estate in the locality to which you plan to move. Friends living there, bank officials having foreclosed properties, real estate agents, secretaries of farm loan associations, staffs of agricultural colleges, county agents—all are good sources of information. Subscribe to the leading local newspaper and study real estate listings. If you do not know the name of a reliable real estate agent, ask the chamber of commerce or a local bank to recommend one.

Before making a definite decision as to the type of farming you should undertake, visit the region of the country which you prefer for retirement living. See for yourself what each area of the region has to offer. Consult the county agents. Talk to farmers who have already settled there. Visit the nearest agricultural experimental stations in the regions under investigation. Check the chamber of commerce or realty boards for land prices, information about living conditions, taxes, climate and other general information.

After the decision has been made to purchase a particular farm, it is important to know the legal status of the property and to make sure the title is clear. Have a lawyer check on these points for you. Don't buy farm property without personally inspecting it.

Best Areas for Retired Persons to Operate a Farm

The 1950 census reveals that the fastest growing regions of the United States are the Pacific Coast, mountain and Southern states. The indications are that these sections of the country will continue to grow in population faster than the rest of the country. From the standpoint of climate, length of growing season, outdoor living conditions and opportunities in agricultural production, the Southern states and California offer the best advantages for persons who wish to retire to a farm.

Opportunities in California

One-family Commercial Farms. Since the plane of living in California is rather high, an average net income from $2,500 to $3,000 is desirable for successful farm living. This sum, however, varies from $1,800 to $5,000 according to the needs of the farm family. Many one-family farms are too small to provide this income from commercial farming alone.

The size of farm needed to produce a $3,000-a-year income varies according to the type of farm and the locality. With a citrus orchard, a $45,000 investment in fifteen to twenty-five acres can, over the years, produce an average return of 5 per cent or $2,250. The operator's labor would perhaps add another $700. With poultry, an investment of $20,000 on two to five acres, with fifteen hundred to two thousand hens, should return $1,000, while twenty-five hundred hours of labor would bring $2,000—a total of $3,000. The proper size for a family farm in California for raising peaches, pears, apricots, prunes, plums, apples, walnuts and other deciduous fruits is from fifteen to thirty acres on irrigated land, but somewhat larger on poorer soils or land without irrigation. An adequate deciduous fruit farm costs from $20,000 to $50,000.

Vegetable farming is highly specialized with much of the activity conducted by large commercial growers on rented land. Two crops a year are obtained in some localities. Twenty acres of farm land is about the minimum for a family farm. A twenty- to thirty-cow dairy farm, with thirty to forty acres to produce the needed forage, would bring in an average net income of $3,000. Livestock raising takes considerable investment in California. There are two main types: the range-stock ranch, and the general farm where livestock is raised and fed in connection with crop production. Usually one hundred breeding cows are necessary, with sufficient owned or rented range land, and enough crop land to produce the required hay for supplementary feeding. Between five hundred and five thousand acres are required for a herd of this size, with an investment of about $40,000 for the range alone. Sheep ranches are similar to cattle ranches in acreage required, but need six hundred to one thousand breeding ewes in place of one hundred breeding cows.

Small Farm Homes for Better Living. California offers numerous small farm homes intended to cut the cost of living, but not as a commercial undertaking for family cash income. These are actually homes in the suburbs or in the open country, with agricultural production limited to food for family use. These homes are usually selected because of their desirable location or climate and to reduce living costs and enjoy better living on a farm.

The Southern California Area. This region occupies the southern quarter of the state. The coastal zone extends inland a few miles at Santa Barbara to about seventy miles east of Los Angeles and south to the Mexican border. The chief crops of the area are oranges, lemons, walnuts, avocados, berries, a variety of vegetables and a few field crops. This is the major citrus area of the state. There is also an intense local poultry industry. Land values are among the highest in the United States, bare land costing $300 to $2,000 an acre and good citrus orchards costing as high as $5,000 an acre.

The mountain and desert regions of Southern California are not important from an agricultural standpoint. Farming is possible only in irrigated valleys. Imperial Valley is a large and important agricultural area. Irrigated field and truck crops cover most of the acreage. The citrus fruits, grapes and dates are of minor importance. Coachella Valley, irrigated by deep wells, produces dates, grapefruit, cotton, alfalfa and out-of-season vegetables. The length of the growing season in Southern California is 365 days on the coast to 270 days in the interior.

The Central Coast Area. This region extends from about 80 miles north of San Francisco to about 260 miles to the south. The region is largely one of family-size farms and large commercial farms. Only near the cities are there many small and part-time farms. Considerable livestock is produced on the grassland and range pastures. In the valleys and on some hill slopes, production is in grain, dairying, poultry, berries, fruits and vegetables. Good opportunities are open in Salinas Valley (Montgomery County), where large acreage will come under irrigation when a large dam now under construction is completed. The length of the growing season is 204 to 310 days.

The San Joaquin Valley Area. This area is bounded on the east by the Sierra Nevada Mountains and on the west by the Coast Range, joins the Sacramento Valley on the north and borders Southern California on the south. This is the largest agricultural region in California. Here are grown grapes, deciduous fruits, citrus fruits, figs and olives. Field crops, however, occupy most of the land. The region is the most important dairy district of the state. Poultry raising is scattered throughout the area. Livestock is produced in the Valley, some being pastured on the ranges and national forests.

The Central Valley Water Project is expected to make possible about ten thousand more irrigated farms, mostly in the San Joaquin Valley. This region offers more opportunities for additional farms than any other part of the state. The growing season averages 274 days in the southern section and 299 in the northern section.

The Sacramento Valley. This is the northern half of the Great Valley of California. Being north of the San Joaquin Valley, it is colder and has more rainfall. The region is largely devoted to field crops and general farming with some dairying. It also contains several important fruit districts producing peaches, prunes, almonds, pears, walnuts, olives and some citrus fruit. Commercial poultry farms are found in several localities. Livestock, both cattle and sheep, are wintered in the Sacramento Valley to be pastured in private range lands and national forests in the mountains during the summer. Considerable opportunities exist for new farms in this region and for increasing the production of existing dry-farms when irrigation is developed. In the foothills to the east are fruit and other farms too small for adequate commercial farming which make ideal farm homes for those with assured outside incomes. The growing season in the region averages 250 to 270 days.

The North Coast Area. This region runs up to the Oregon line and is largely occupied by the Coast Range. The mountainous area is covered with forest or brush. Farming is limited to the valleys and a narrow shelf along portions of the coast. Beef cattle and sheep ranches occupy most of the country that is open to grazing. Most of the good farm land is fully utilized. Growing season is 210 to 277 days.

The East Mountain Area. This area is cold in winter, moderately warm in summer with low annual rainfall. Farming activities are largely in the production of hay and grain. Cattle and sheep are grazed by permit in the national forests. To obtain grazing rights, a newcomer has to buy or rent an established ranch. Opportunities for newcomers in this area are limited.

Opportunities in Florida

Florida has about twenty million acres of land that can be made adaptable to rich agricultural production. Only about two million acres are under cultivation. There is, however, one important limitation. That is the soil. Florida soil conditions vary greatly among the different areas of the state. The state has three different zones of climate with a different type of farming in each zone. The sixty-five thousand farms in Florida are almost equally divided among the northern, the central and the southern zones. The average size of farms is two hundred ninety acres, with land and buildings valued at $15,000 per farm. There are twenty-nine distinct types of farming areas. Within each of these areas there are many variations.

One-family Commercial Farms. No state-wide standards can be set down for the most desirable size of farms on which to make a good living. Reports from the College of Agriculture, University of Florida, indicate that one needs at least fifteen hundred to two thousand good hens to make a fair living from poultry. At least one hundred good beef cattle are needed to make a fair living from raising livestock, fifteen to twenty cows from dairying, thirty acres from citrus fruits, fifty to one hundred cultivated acres of general farming depending on the nature of the crops. Ten good acres of truck land may be enough for some vegetable production, while other vegetables may require twenty or more acres. However, a man and wife alone can't produce ten acres of vegetables and hired help is necessary to make a good living at truck farming.

It costs less to buy farm land capable of producing a specified net income in Florida than it does in California. The price of land in Florida ranges from $7 to $2,000 per acre, depending upon location, improvements and soil productivity. Most farm dwellings are inadequate, according to the standards and needs of northern people. Many truck and citrus farms have no dwelling at all—the owners living either in nearby cities or towns or in the north.

Some of the improved Florida pasture will support a head per acre for cattle raising. The average on improved pasture is one head to three acres. A new grass coming into use promises to support as high as four head to the acre. Cattle raising in Florida does not require the heavy investment in buildings necessary in other areas. Florida's poultry industry with a production of twenty-two million chickens does not take care of the demand for local consumption.

Small Farm Homes for Greater Security. An important and growing group of residents of Florida live on small farms that contribute some subsistence but little or no cash income. If these farms are carefully selected, retired persons can supplement retirement benefits by raising home-grown food for the family. The optimum size of such an undertaking for elderly persons appears to be about one-half acre. In most cases, they should limit their efforts to producing vegetables and poultry. The retail value of the vegetables produced annually is about $100 per person and of eggs and poultry about $20. In selecting a farm, investment should be kept low in order to maintain as much of the accumulated savings of the family as possible.

A well-managed part-time farm offers a means of supplementing the incomes of retired persons, and of those who live on a farm but whose major employment is off the farm. They should have no physical handicaps or medical ailments, or be too elderly for the strenuous work needed to make the farm productive. To be successful, adequate family labor or hired labor must be available when the farm needs attention. The type of farming followed should be that of the area where the farm is located. In a study of thirty-one broiler farms in the Palatka Area, conducted by the Florida Department of Agriculture, it was found that one-fourth of the producers had retired from other occupations. It is easy to overinvest in a part-time farm. Care should be exercised lest the extra investment be too great for the returns. The majority of retired persons, however, who desire to engage in farming in a small way should approach it as an opportunity for rural living and limit their efforts to the production of food for the family.

The Northern Florida Zone. The chief farm produce here is tobacco, cotton, peanuts, oats, watermelons, berries, tung nuts, pecans, livestock and poultry. There is also some production of various legumes and feed crops. Turpentine and resin are obtained from the pine forests. Extensive citrus groves are found in the southern districts of the zone. Nursery stock for transplanting is produced in the section. The growing season is 300 to 320 days.

The Central Florida Zone. A good portion of the land is planted in citrus groves. This is the orange, grapefruit and tangerine belt of Florida—the location of the largest packing houses, juice canneries and frozen concentrate plants. Polk County is the second ranking county in the country in number of citrus trees planted. Many farms specialize in truck crops. Celery, cabbage, field peas, tomatoes, strawberries and watermelons are the favorites. Nurseries of flowers, plants and ornamental shrubs are numerous throughout the area. Beef cattle, dairy cattle and poultry are raised extensively. The growing season averages 320 days.

The Southern Florida Zone. The climate is much warmer in this zone during the winter months. Occasionally frost occurs in the northern part of the zone. For the most part, this is the subtropical part of Florida. Winter vegetables are the big crops. They include cabbage, beans, celery, peppers and tomatoes. Palm Beach County ranks first of all counties in the nation in acreage of vegetables harvested for sale. Some citrus, tropical fruits, such as avocados, mango, papaya and guava, are grown commercially. Ferns and orchids are grown commercially, also sugar cane. The glasslands provide grazing for livestock. The eight-foot-deep muck of the Everglades has been compared with that of the Nile Valley. Three plantings a year are harvested. Growing season is 320 to 365 days.

Opportunities in North Carolina, South Carolina and Georgia

These are states of comparatively small farms, the average being sixty to seventy acres. The variations in types of soil, topography and climatic conditions give rise to considerable variation in the types of farming in different parts of the region.

The agricultural pattern in the past has been centered mainly around cash crops, especially cotton and tobacco. But the agricultural picture of this section of the South is undergoing considerable readjustment. The trend is toward greater mechanization and the use of labor-saving farm equipment. Additional sources of income from a diversity of crops and livestock is being added to the traditional "one cash crop" system of the old South.

The upper coastal plains of Georgia and South Carolina

offer some of the best farm land opportunities to be found in the United States. In these sections land is cheap where the old farm patterns of growing single crops have been abandoned and the new agricultural crop patterns have not yet been fully developed. People are coming into South Carolina and Georgia by the hundreds from many other states. In South Carolina they are buying land the natives used to think worn out for $40 an acre and converting it into good pasture. In Georgia, farm land is advertised for sale at prices ranging from $20 to $80 per acre.

Authorities say that beef production can be multiplied four times without encroaching on other kinds of agriculture. It takes two acres of southern range to support one animal against as much as fifty acres in the West. Some dairy farmers are grossing $40,000 a year with herds of 240 cows and calves on 350 acres of pasture.

The finest opportunities in farming in the Southern states for the next several years are in the production of beef cattle and feed crops, with soybeans as a good cash crop. Other types of agriculture also seem promising—but these are unusually promising.

Poultry farming also offers good opportunities. By way of illustration, we need only consider the number of eggs imported to the larger Southern cities. In Atlanta, for example, during 1950, a total of 655,871 cases of eggs were shipped into the city. Of these only 76,688 cases or 12 per cent came from Southern farms.

There are many farm communities throughout the entire region where persons with modest retirement incomes can establish a semirural home on a small farm and achieve the independent security of producing part of the family's food requirements. Subsistence and part-time farming is increasing and is centered mainly around cities and towns where part-time employment can be found in local industries.

North and South Carolina and Georgia have the soils, the rainfall and the long summers and mild winters under which agriculture thrives best. Since the Civil War there generally has been a shortage of local capital in most of the South. Newcomers, either retired persons seeking new enterprises or farmers migrating from other states, who have adequate capital to buy land and modern laborsaving equipment, can cash in on their investments and efforts.

The topography exerts a very important influence on farming. There are four distinct regions from the mountains to the seashore. The mountain region covers the western portion of the area. Many mountain valleys are at elevations up to two thousand feet, and peaks rise to as high as six thousand feet. The Piedmont Plateau forms the central region and is characterized by rolling hills with a general elevation of five hundred to nine hundred feet. The Sandhills region has elevations from four hundred to six hundred and fifty feet. And the coastal plains runs from sea level to elevations of three hundred feet. The growing season is shortest in the mountains where it is about 190 days. The growing season becomes longer as one goes eastward and southward toward the coast where it is from 240 to 300 days.

The Mountain Region. Agricultural production is devoted to general farming, beef cattle, apples, poultry and dairying. The farms are small, with many classified as subsistence farms.

The Piedmont Region. The main agricultural products are cotton, peaches, apples, poultry, dairying, beef cattle, hay, seed production, soybeans, with some truck farming in local areas. There are good opportunities for beef cattle raising on pastures.

The Sandhills Region. The major crops are cotton, tobacco, soybeans, peanuts, hay, peaches, poultry, turkeys and some truck crops in local areas.

The Coastal Plains Region. The most extensively grown products are cotton, tobacco, corn, sweet potatoes, beef cattle, dairying, poultry and turkeys, hogs and truck crops. Good opportunities for greenhouse and nursery crops.

Opportunities in the Gulf States

Alabama. Alabama's chief cash crop for many years was cotton. The state is now the center of one of the greatest land opportunities in the United States for grassland farming and the production of livestock. The Black Belt section offers one of the best land investment opportunities in the nation today, according to a survey made by one of the country's leading land appraisal organizations.

The state ships annually over four million pounds of honey, and about two hundred thousand packages of bees. This is more than that shipped by any other state. Alabama also leads the nation in tree farmers and its timber resources are enormous. There are also good opportunities for poultry production.

BALDWIN COUNTY is the largest county in Alabama. It is considerably larger than the state of Rhode Island. Baldwin County has a mild climate, a growing season of three hundred or more days and sixty-two inches of rainfall annually. Farmers in the area raise two crops a year. Modern farming methods have brought unbelievable yields in the many agricultural products raised in the county. An example is 149 bushels of hybrid corn per acre. Among the twenty-five agricultural crops are Irish potatoes, soybeans, sweet potatoes, pecan and tung nuts, corn and numerous truck crops. Year-round grazing makes beef cattle and dairying popular. Hogs and poultry are profitable operations. Almost any kind of flower is grown by the acre. As to farm real estate, cut-over, or raw, land starts at $35 an acre. Developed, good soil acreage runs up to $200 an acre.

Mississippi. This region offers similar opportunities to

those of its neighbor states of Alabama and Louisiana. It is an important area for early and late fresh vegetable production. Pecans are widely grown.

Louisiana is the nation's leading producer of sugar, one of the leading rice growers, the leading cultivator of yams. The state produces large crops of timber and forestry products, cotton, soybeans, strawberries, corn, citrus fruit, lilies and other flowers. Excellent opportunities exist in this area for growing early and late market vegetables. As in the rest of the South, cattle raising and grassland farming is rapidly expanding. The rich soils, temperate climate, abundant rainfall and long growing season combine to make the area ideal for agricultural production on a year-round basis. Chicken and turkey production offer good opportunities, since the poultry output is below the consumption of the area.

Texas. The state of Texas is broken down into eighteen major farming areas and many subareas. The coastal prairie area is mainly devoted to cattle ranching, cotton and corn production, with dairying and vegetables in limited production around the larger cities. The Lower Rio Grande Valley area, with its long growing season and irrigation, has a wide range of crops including cotton, corn, grain, onions, watermelons and winter vegetables. Citrus fruits are grown in some subareas. The Panhandle area is in wheat production.

Cotton ranks first in value of Texas crops with corn the leading grain crop. Grazing land for beef cattle comprises about 73 per cent of the area of the state. Some of the best grazing lands are in the Trans-Pecos and the Edwards Plateau. Sheep raising is an important enterprise on many farms. Poultry and eggs are produced in every county, but the greatest concentration is in Fayette and Gonzales counties.

Opportunities in Arizona and New Mexico

Best locations for farming are more or less limited in Arizona to the Gila Valley, Salt River Valley, Casa Grande Valley and the Yuma Valley. And in New Mexico, the best locations are the Rio Grande Valley, San Juan Valley, Messila Valley, Mimbres Valley and Pecos Valley.

Maricopa County in Arizona ranks fifth among the fifty leading agricultural counties of the nation. This is one of the most intensely irrigated areas in Arizona. It has a diversified agricultural crop production covering early vegetables, strawberries, tomatoes, corn, pasture crops, dairying and beef cattle, melons, dates, citrus fruits and honey. Pinal County ranks twenty-seventh among the nation's leading counties.

Arizona and New Mexico are arid states. The cultivation of crops requires irrigation and this normally calls for a large capital investment. The valley country north of the valleys mentioned above is cold in winter and hot in summer. Water is the limiting factor throughout the Southwest, because there is more good land available than there is water to irrigate it. Much of the livestock graze on public range lands under permits. Range and ranching communities are small and far apart. Where there is irrigation, however, and agricultural production is more intense, communities are larger and more compact.

Some goats in Central Arizona and in Southern New Mexico are raised for their mohair. Opportunities for part-time farming are rather limited. Poultry does offer an opportunity for those who would like to supplement their income. Many retired people living in the Southwest have gone into the raising of chickens and other poultry. The production of poultry meat is below the consumption demands in both Arizona and New Mexico. Look into opportunities for hydroponics (soilless gardening).

A Few Case Histories of Farming in Retirement

Nine years prior to retiring, at the age of fifty-seven, a former executive of one of America's leading corporations purchased ten acres of land near Lakeland, Florida. He had nine acres cleared and planted in grapefruit trees. One acre was set aside for his home, lawn, flower and vegetable garden. Upon his retirement from business, he moved to his Florida home. Once there, he set himself up in the mail-order fruit business and developed it into a profitable enterprise that he operated until four years ago. The job of managing the grapefruit grove and selling the fruit he turned over to a cooperative association. This man, now eighty-eight years old, has lived a happy and profitable retirement life. During many of these years, he grossed over $11,000 a year from his Florida activities. His advice to those contemplating retirement is: "Have a plan, a goal, a vision to live by."

Here is the experience of a West Virginian who was formerly in the grocery business. At the age of sixty, he decided to retire. He bought an abandoned farm of 186 acres and started to farm it as a hobby. Without any previous experience as a farmer, he learned to farm by observation, by reading good farm papers, by asking advice of other farmers. His friends laughed when he bought the farm and said they were afraid he was too old. With no experience they thought he would fail as a farmer. By his personal determination and love of the land, he has made more progress than many farmers in the county within the last four years. His fields were originally overgrown with briars and weeds and sage grass. He cut and burned the briars, grubbed the thickets with a bulldozer, plowed under the weeds. Next he applied lime and commercial fertilizer, and sowed mixed grass seeds. His progress in four years is almost beyond belief. The fields are now beautiful pastures that carry fifty-five head of fine beef cattle, along with horses, goats and other livestock. He practices strip farming and grows alfalfa, Ladino clover and other kinds of grass mixtures. A new barn has been erected to store fifty tons of hay. He has a purebred Hereford sire to head his fine herd of cattle. This man who began farming at the age of sixty, without any previous experience, is an inspiration to anyone about to retire or already retired. The secret of happy retirement is to transfer your main interests to a new field, to change your occupation and do some of the things you have dreamed of when alone with your thoughts.

Check This List Before You Decide

The College of Agriculture, University of California, advises prospective purchasers of a farm to answer the following questions frankly to evaluate their preferences and desires.

1. Why do I wish to engage in farming? Is my object primarily investment, a home or a home and business? Do I assume none, some or all the manual tasks and management responsibilities?

2. Do I really want to live in the country? What proof have I?

3. Where do I hope to locate? What are my preferences regarding climate? Regarding distance from stores, doctors, schools, places of entertainment?

4. What sort of dwelling am I seeking? Must I have such conveniences as electricity, piped water, furnace?

5. What sort of neighbors do I like?

6. What do I desire to produce?

7. How big a farm should I buy?

8. What annual income do I require to take care of personal needs?

9. How much money can I command to make initial payments, to buy equipment and to provide necessary seeds, fertilizer, water, taxes, feeds and other operating expenditures?

10. Am I willing to invest my savings, and possibly pledge my future earnings, for the maintenance of a farm?

11. What knowledge of farming do I possess that I can utilize to good advantage? Have I an inquisitive mind that will cause me to delve further into agricultural lore?

12. Have I the required experience and training?

13. Have I the ability to select, direct and supervise hired help?

14. Have I the physical strength for farming?

15. Have I the courage?

16. What are my chances to resell or lease in case of future dissatisfaction? In other words, is this property really marketable?

What to Do to Prepare for Farming in Retirement

Once you have definitely decided that you would like to engage in farming when you retire, here's what you should do next.

Your First Step. Begin to acquaint yourself with some of the down-to-earth problems of work and living associated with your choice of farm activity. Begin a long-range self-education program. The earlier you begin to shape your program along specific lines, the easier it will be to progress rapidly when you actually take up farming.

You should, of course, continue about the everyday business of earning a living as you have been doing. This program of acquiring information on your retirement farm specialty is your after-work hobby activity. You are merely laying the foundation of a program that will save you time and money later on.

If you have had no previous farm experience, begin by systematically reading some of the good farm papers. There are a number of monthly and weekly publications that cover farming in general from a nationwide viewpoint. Other farm magazines confine themselves to the agricultural activities of a particular state. Still others are devoted to a specialized branch of farming.

Perhaps the easiest way to acquaint yourself with the various publications on the market is to ask your local librarian to let you look at the bound volumes of back issues of the various farm publications on file at your local library. Pick out one or more publications that appeal to you and subscribe to them. The features, news stories and advertisements will give you a good background on the latest developments as they occur, experiences of successful farmers, how-to-do-it counsel, market prices, new farm equipment—and much information on various aspects of farm living.

Your Second Step. Begin to study and accumulate a library and reference file of clippings of pertinent information on your farming specialty.

The United States Department of Agriculture spends millions of dollars each year in research and development on a great many phases of agriculture. Briefly, these activities cover studies on the growing, harvesting and marketing of better farm products, advice and guidance on improved methods and how to use them, the successful solution of farm management problems, farm home and living.

Publications are prepared in the form of leaflets, pamphlets, bulletins and books by various bureaus of the Department of Agriculture. Many present information in a detailed, step-by-step manner. They are extremely helpful to farmers and prospective farmers. A number of these publications are distributed free. For a complete listing of both free and for sale publications write to Division of Publications, United States Department of Agriculture, Washington 25, D.C. Ask for a copy of *List of Available Publications,* Miscellaneous Publication No. 60. Publications that are for sale should be ordered from the Superintendent of Documents, United States Government Printing Office, Washington 25, D.C. See listing at the end of this chapter for a few of the many publications for sale.

Personal counseling by specialists in the various bureaus is available on many problems which confront farmers. Direct your correspondence to Office of Information, United States Department of Agriculture, Washington 25, D.C. You can even borrow 16 mm. sound motion picture films. For listing and where to borrow films write to Motion Picture

Service, Office of Information, United States Department of Agriculture, Washington 25, D.C.

Many of the state agricultural departments and agricultural colleges also publish bulletins on various farming activities more specifically related to areas of their states. When you decide on the state where you want to retire, write to these departments and colleges for information pertaining to problems that confront you. Some agricultural colleges offer correspondence courses on various phases of farming.

Your Third Step. Perhaps you're thinking by now that you will get a lot of book learning but no practical experience from this self-education program. The more information you have, the easier it will be to acquire the necessary practical knowledge. But how about some practical experience?

At this stage of your program, it would be a good idea to get to know a farmer who is specializing in the type of farming you have chosen. You will see how some of the knowledge you have gathered is actually used in practical farming. Perhaps you can arrange to work part-time for him, say on week ends or during your vacations. In this way you can get some practical experience along with your book learning. If you can't find such a farmer in your locality, get in touch with the county agent. He will be glad to arrange for you to meet a progressive farmer whom you can call on.

Attend state and county fairs and talk with attendants at the various exhibits. You will pick up a lot of practical information.

Your Fourth Step. Use some of your vacation time to visit the region you plan to retire to. Talk with the county agent and local farmers, and visit the nearest experimental station. Maybe you can spend vacations at a farm-vacation-resort in the region.

You will find that this practical method of learning about farming in your spare time is great fun as a hobby. You will be surprised at how well-prepared you will become to make the transition from your regular business or work-a-day world to retirement on a farm. The greatest fun of all will come from developing your own methods suited to your own particular farm.

Plan also your home and living arrangements for your new way of life on the farm. Include in your planning a program of recreation and participation in the community life. Your financial program should be arranged so that you can take over your new farm free or nearly free of mortgage debt. You should have money to buy the equipment, fertilizer, seeds and livestock, and to cover the other operating expenses required to run the farm. In addition, you should have some surplus cash to provide for emergencies.

Bibliography

Names and addresses of various magazines devoted to farming. Covering farming in general:

The Progressive Farmer, 821 North 19th St., Birmingham, Ala.
Country Gentleman, Independence Square, Philadelphia, Pa.
Capper's Farmer, Capper Publications, Inc., Topeka, Kansas.
Farm Journal, 230 Washington Square, Philadelphia, Pa.
The Farmer, 553 Tenth St., St. Paul, Minn.
Farmers Market Bulletin, 360 N. Michigan Ave., Chicago, Ill.
Successful Farming, 1716 Locust St., Des Moines, Iowa.

Covering farming in various states:

Alabama Farm Bulletin, 201 Clayton St., Montgomery, Ala.
Arizona Farmer, 842 N. Central Ave., Phoenix, Ariz.
California Farmer, 83 Stevenson St., San Francisco, Calif.
Florida Agriculture, Aloma Ave., Winter Park, Florida.
Mississippi Farm Bureau News, 221 N. President St., Jackson, Miss.
New Mexico Agriculture, Farm Bureau Bldg., Las Cruces, N.M.
Carolina Cooperator (North Carolina), 125 E. Davis St., Raleigh, N.C.
South Carolina Farmer, 215 W. Church St., Anderson, S.C.

Texas Ranch and Farm, 400 W. Seventh St., Forth Worth, Texas

Covering various farm products:

American Bee Journal, Hamilton, Ill.
Gleanings in Bee Culture, Medina, Ohio.
Sheep Breeder, 801 Elm Street, Columbus, Mo.
The Sheepman Magazine, 234 N. Upper St., Lexington, Ky.
The Cattleman, 410 E. Weatherford St., Fort Worth, Texas.
Breeder's Gazette, Spencer, Indiana.
National Livestock Producer, 139 N. Clark St., Chicago, Ill.
Hog Breeder, 314 Jefferson Bldg., Peoria, Ill.
American Fruit Grower, 106 Euclid Ave., Willoughby, Ohio.
Citrus Leaves, 810 S. Spring St., Los Angeles, Calif.
The Citrus Magazine, Box 2349, Tampa, Florida.
Market Growers Journal, 11 S. Forge St., Akron, Ohio
Vee-Gee Messenger, Preston, Md.
American Poultry Journal, 180 N. Wabash Ave., Chicago, Ill.
Everybody's Poultry Magazine, Exchange Place, Hanover, Pa.
The Poultryman, Vineland, N.J.
Turkey World, Mount Morris, Ill.
American Nurseryman, 343 S. Dearborn St., Chicago, Ill.
Horticulture, 300 Massachusetts Ave., Boston, Mass.
Flower Grower, 99 N. Broadway, Albany, N.Y.

For additional farm magazines see copy of *Standard Rate and Data;* your library should have a copy in their files.

U.S. Department of Agriculture Publications. Write to: Superintendent of Documents, U.S. Government Printing Office, Washington 25, D.C.
Beef Calf, Its Growth and Development, Cat. No. A1.9:1135. 10 cents.
Beef Production on the Farm, Cat. No. A1.9:1592. 5 cents.
Feeding Cattle for Beef, Cat. No. A1.9:1549. 10 cents.
Handbook for Better Feeding of Livestock, Cat. No. A1.5/2:12. 10 cents.
Livestock for Small Farms, Cat. No. A1.9:1753. 10 cents.
Swine Production, Cat. No. A1.9:1437. 5 cents.
How to Manage Grasslands, Cat. No. A1.10/a:257. 5 cents.
Grasslands in the South, Cat. No. A1.10/a:2061. 5 cents.
Grass, Yearbook of Agriculture, Cat. No. A1.10:948. $2.00.

Farm Sheep Raising for Beginners, Cat. No. A1.9:840. 10 cents.
Range Sheep Production, Cat. No. A1.9:1710. 10 cents.
Farm Poultry Raising, Cat. No. A1.9:1524. 10 cents.
Marketing Poultry, Cat. No. A1.9:1377. 15 cents.
Marketing Eggs, Cat. No. Al.9:1378.15 cents.
Turkey Raising, Cat. No. A1.9:1409. 20 cents.
Duck Raising, Cat. No. A1.9:697. 10 cents.
Harvesting, Handling Citrus Fruits, Cat. No. A1.60:13. 40 cents.
Growing Fruit for Home Use, Cat. No. A1.9:1001. 15 cents.
Breeding Better Vegetables for the South, Cat. No. A.38:578. 10
   cents.
Farm Garden, Cat. No. A1.9:1673. 20 cents.
Mushroom Growing in United States, Cat. No. A1.9:1875. 15
   cents.
Soybeans in American Farming, Cat. No. A1.36:966. 20 cents.
Blueberry Growing, Cat. No. A1.9:1951. 15 cents.
Preparing Strawberries for Market, Cat. No. A1.9:1950. 10 cents.
Fur Farming Possibilities, Cat. No. A1.35:267. 10 cents.
Gardenia Culture, Cat. No. A1. 35:199. 5 cents.
Planning the Farmstead, Cat. No. A1.9:1132. 10 cents.
Planning the Farm for Profit, Cat. No. A1.9:1965. 10 cents.
Getting Started in Farming, Cat. No. A1.9:1961. 15 cents.
Some Questions and Answers on Where and How to Get a Farm,
   Cat. No. A1.35:299. 5 cents.
Part-time Farming, Cat. No. A1.64:14. 5 cents.
Farm Fishponds for Food, Cat. No. A1.9:1983. 10 cents.

CHAPTER VIII

Good Climate Is Part of Good Retirement Living

Location Is Important

Climatologists and physicians are in general agreement that, for persons past sixty years of age, a mild, warm year-round climate is best. The Southern states, as well as Southern California, with their distinctly mild winters, plentiful supply of sunshine, absence of snowfall, warm, moist summers, and generally settled weather, afford good climate for retirement living.

Robert De Courcy Ward, of Harvard, one of America's outstanding climatologists, in his book *Climates of the United States*, says that the great seasonal ranges of temperature between severe, cold winters, in the northern sections of the United States, followed by hot summers, causes a strain on health. The suddenness and frequency of these meteorological conditions, Ward found, are especially harmful to elderly people who don't adapt themselves easily to wide extremes of weather.

In the cold and stormy regions of the United States, people live on a high plane of both physical and mental energy. As we get past fifty years of age, the body does not respond easily to weather changes and may break down under the strain of trying to make adjustments. In the warm sunny climates, the drive of the body to make adjustments is considerably less. Existence is at a more relaxed pace and consequently persons are less susceptible to diseases of exhaustion.

Dr. Clarence A. Mills, M.D., Ph.D., Professor of Experimental Medicine, University of Cincinnati, in *Climate Makes the Man,* gives this advice:

> There are several large classes of northerners who would benefit from seasonal or permanent southward migration. The largest of these includes the millions of elderly people whose tissue fires have pretty well burned out or become chocked with clinkers of degenerative disease. With their arteriosclerosis, diabetes, chronic nephritis, heart troubles, and a host of other chronic ailments, they are no longer fit for the physical struggle it takes to survive the stormy cold of northern winters.

This is good advice for folks living in the North, past middle age, who find the weather increasingly burdensome. It is especially true for any person who suffers from the illnesses mentioned. He can add years to his life by getting away from the too-invigorating cold climate. The farther people of retirement age move into the Southern warmth, the better it will be for them.

It is a common experience to have more colds, more nose and throat irritations and other respiratory diseases as soon as the cold weather sets in and we must rely on artificial heat. The dry, parched air of Northern homes, offices and factories, and the atmospheric pollution of industrial areas, are largely responsible for the high rate of respiratory diseases.

Studies indicate that deaths due to heart failure are many times more frequent in the Northern regions during winter than during the summer months.

It is in the winter months that the greatest differences in temperatures occur between different regions of the United States. Midwinter mean temperatures as low as ten degrees occur over the Northern interiors as compared with fifty-five-degree mean temperatures in Florida, the Gulf Coast and Southern California. In midsummer the distribution of average temperatures is more nearly uniform between the Northern and Southern states. A migration in summer from the South to the North in search of cooler weather does not offer near the advantages of a trip to the South in winter in search of warmer weather.

The mean annual range of temperatures between the heat of midsummer and the cold of midwinter in the North is as much as sixty degrees. In the South and in Southern California, the range between the hottest and coldest parts of the year is only twenty-five to thirty degrees. Some localities, like San Francisco, have a difference of only ten degrees between mean summer and mean winter temperatures.

Below the Snowfall Line

Generally speaking little or no snow falls and lies on the ground in winter south of an irregular line stretching from Cape Hatteras in North Carolina on the Atlantic Coast, through the southeastern section of South Carolina, Georgia and the Gulf States, across southern Texas, across southern New Mexico and southern Arizona (except at mountain altitudes) and over the lowlands of central California to the coast of California (except in the mountains). During exceptional cold spells an occasional light snow may fall in parts of these regions. But when it does fall it is such a rarity that it causes considerable excitement and little discomfort. The world's stormiest region is around the Great Lakes and southern Canada. As we go south from this region, storminess diminishes. Florida has a moderate degree of stormy weather. Southern California, southern Arizona and southern New Mexico are the least stormy parts of the United States.

What Makes a Good Climate?

You often hear people say that a certain place has a "perfect" climate. But climatologists tell us that a perfect climate as such does not exist. Every climate has its own advantages and some disagreeable features at certain seasons. A Southern climate, with its mild winters, abundant sunshine and opportunities for outdoor living the year round, may be hot and moist in summer. The invigorating climate of the North is too cold and stormy for elderly people in winter. Coastal climates may be too damp and foggy for many persons afflicted with respiratory diseases. The high altitudes and chilly climates of mountain regions are too strenuous for those suffering from arthritis, heart trouble and high blood pressure.

Some regions of the United States occasionally subjected to climatic accidents like hurricanes, earthquakes, tornadoes and floods, receive a great deal of publicity when these accidents occur. The inhabitants of the area may go through life without experiencing another such disaster. Inhabitants usually receive ample warning of approaching hurricanes or floods. If they follow prescribed procedures little or no harm comes to them from these experiences.

The best climate for the majority of older men and women is one that encourages them to spend a great deal of their time outdoors in the sunshine and in the open air, with frequent but moderate weather changes, temperatures rarely above eighty degrees during the daytime and fifty-five degrees at night, relative humidity around 55 per cent and variety in the amount of cloudiness. Such a climate is neither too hot or too cold. A variety of moderate changes of weather hardens people and conditions them to resist disease. Some change in weather is desirable to avoid monotony.

Don't undertake the impossible task of trying to find the one perfect climate spot in the United States. Select one out of four or five possible locations, any one of which is suited to your physical and mental condition of health and your personal preference. Live in the selected location for a year on a temporary basis before making it your permanent retirement residence.

From a retirement point of view, the ideal way to live is to reside in the South or in Southern California from November through May. Then migrate to New England, the Great Lakes peninsula or to the mountains of North or South Carolina from June through September or October. Migrants should leave the North or mountain altitudes before the winter storms set in. Because this way of living would require the support of two household units, it is beyond the financial reach of the average retired person.

The next best thing for retired people to do is to take up permanent residence in one of the better all-year-round climate regions that provide an easy, more relaxed existence. This calls for getting away from the rigorous climatic conditions of cold, snow, ice and blizzards of winter.

Control Hot Summer Weather by Air Conditioning

Probably the greatest disadvantage of the climate of the Southern regions is the heat and humidity of the summer months. Yet the trade winds and on-shore sea breezes, especially in the coastal regions, make the Southern seaboard more desirable in the summer months than the hot interior of the Northern regions.

A number of people who can afford it move back and forth each year, between the warm winters of the South and the cooler regions of the Northeast. Fortunately, for those persons who cannot afford to make these seasonal migrations, there is another way to enjoy cool weather. That is by air conditioning.

Even though a man may work or spend considerable time outdoors during the hot summer months, he can be refreshed by a good night's sleep in a cool house. The heat of the day is not nearly so depressing when a comfortable night's sleep is possible.

If the climate is too humid, air conditioning removes the surplus moisture from the air but leaves enough moisture to insure a healthful humidity. Through air conditioning, people living in the South can control the temperature and humidity in homes, offices, stores and other private or public buildings.

Other advantages of air conditioning in the Southern regions are the stepping-up of the human-energy level and the building up of resistance to infectious disease, by night-time cooling during the summer months.

Air conditioning is no longer a luxury item only for the wealthy. Room air-conditioning units, placed in a window, can be purchased for about $230. Console or floor units are more expensive, costing $600 and more, depending upon the horsepower rating of the unit. Air-conditioning manufacturers are experimenting with complete weather-controlled home units. The latest units, run on gas or oil, provide solid comfort the year round by keeping the inside of the house at an even and comfortable temperature no matter what the weather is outside. The total heating-cooling costs for the year on some of these units recently installed in the New Orleans area is about $110 a year.

Additional Ways to Keep Cool

Here are a few things you can do in order to keep cool during the summer's heat: A light-colored roof will deflect the rays of the sun . . . insulation under the roof and in the side walls keeps out heat . . . an attic fan will remove heat . . . attic vents let in fresh air . . . light-colored outside walls reflect heat, dark colors absorb heat . . . cool colors on inside walls and in decoration materials make you feel cool . . . wide overhanging roof and awnings provide shade and keep direct rays of sun from reaching the side walls . . . cross- or through-ventilation carries away the heat . . . vent fan over the stove removes heat . . . fluorescent lighting is cooler . . . portable fans circulate the air . . . trees and a vine-covered trellis on the west side of the house lessen the severity of the heat.

Another way to beat the heat is to wear white or light-colored and loose-fitting clothing. Dark clothes in summer absorb heat and act like a blanket-warmer around the body. Don't stay too long in the direct sun in the middle of the day. Eat light but balanced meals.

Climate and Health

While there are certain areas of the United States where average persons suffering or convalescing from certain illnesses feel better and more comfortable, there are no peculiar properties in natural climates which act specifically to prevent disease. Some local areas, however, do have dusts, pollens, smoke and acids that pollute the atmosphere and cause discomfort to persons susceptible to them.

Temperature, winds, variability in weather changes, humidity and barometric pressure are the factors that make a climate good or bad. Every time there is a sudden or severe change in the factors that go into making good or bad weather, the body has to make adjustments to meet these changes. Normally healthy younger folks make the adjustments fairly easily. For people in ill health, weather changes make drastic demands on the body. They also have a depressive or an optimistic effect on the mental state of the ill person.

See Your Doctor

Everyone suffering from illness should get good medical advice before moving to a new climatic region. Physicians advise that good food and water, pure air, rest and proper exercise, outdoor life, a congenial occupation and freedom from worry is as important as a change in climatic conditions.

People who diagnose their own illnesses and treat themselves run great risks of unnecessary suffering and possible permanent harm. The same is true with reference to choosing a climate for health purposes. *Don't make a drastic change of climate, because of illness, without the guidance of your doctor and possibly one or more specialists.*

Beneficial Regions for Sufferers of Ailments

Although not every good region of the United States is known, most doctors and climatologists recognize, under certain conditions, the following regions as beneficial for persons suffering from specific ailments. Your doctor should be consulted regarding your individual case.

For heart trouble, high blood pressure, hardening of the arteries, diabetes, nephritis, anemia, digestive disorders, and hypertensiveness, the following regions are recommended: southern Florida, southwestern Texas in the vicinity of Brownsville and McAllen, Southern California.

For asthma, sinus, bronchitis, arthritis, rheumatic infections, hay fever, nervous disorders, the following regions are good: southern Arizona in the vicinity of Tucson, Phoenix, Prescott; New Mexico in the vicinity of Santa Fe, Albuquerque, Dening, Truth or Consequences; Southern California in the vicinity of Palm Springs, Banning, Indio, Redlands, Riverside; southwestern Texas in the vicinity of El Paso.

For kidney diseases, liver troubles, dyspepsia, chronic diarrhea, constipation, nervous and general debilities, there is the "Ozone Belt" area of Louisiana in the vicinity of Abita Springs.

For tuberculosis, the dry and cool mountain area of the Southwest, at altitudes high enough to escape summer heat, has long been a popular area for persons afflicted with tuberculosis. Today, however, good sanatorium care near the patient's home usually gives him the best chance of recovery.

If you move to another state, you may not be able to get state tuberculosis hospital care unless you are a legal resident of the state. In some states a person becomes a legal resident only after three years of residence.

Pneumonia, tuberculosis and lung cancer, medical research has found, are more common in the crowded, smoky, industrial cities, especially in the low-lying districts. Retired persons should avoid taking up permanent residence in localities having a smoky atmosphere.

Dr. Clarence A. Mills makes the observation in his book, *Climate Makes the Man,* that cancer in the population, except cancer of the skin, occurs much less frequently in the warm climate of the Gulf of Mexico than it does in the colder regions up north. Science has not yet found the answer to why cancer is more frequent in one climate than another.

For hay fever, have your doctor diagnose the pollens and dusts to which you are allergic. Check with the United States Department of Agriculture, Washington, D.C., to learn in which regions of the country the plants with pollens that affect you have their natural growth and which regions are generally free of such plants. Generally speaking, the Southwest desert regions are beneficial to sufferers of hay fever, because pollen-bearing plants do not grow in these regions.

A change of climate often has helped people who suffer from certain ailments, but it has also failed. For this reason those who seek relief by change of residence should try the new location for several months before making a permanent decision to relocate.

Bibliography

Climate Makes the Man by C. A. Mills (Harper, N.Y.)
Man, Weather, Sun by William F. Peterson (Thomas, Springfield, Ill.)

The Climates of the United States by Robert De Courcy Ward (Ginn, Boston)
Climatology by Thomas A. Blair (Prentice-Hall, N.Y.)

U.S. Government Publication:
Climate and Man, Yearbook of Agriculture (out of stock). See copy in public library.

CHAPTER IX

Where to Live in Retirement

To Move Away or Stay Put?

Should you continue to live in the old neighborhood or move to a new location after you retire? The answer to this critical question is one you will have to reach yourself after weighing all the facts for and against each proposition.

In the old neighborhood you enjoy a certain sense of security. Your personal friends most likely live nearby. Maybe your children or relatives live in the same community. Your church and the local stores fit comfortably into an established pattern of living. Your home through the years has acquired affectionate associations.

But neighborhoods change character. Local newspapers carry obituary notices of close friends who cannot be replaced. Many people find the old neighborhood a difficult place when living in retirement. Their financial income is so reduced that former social and living standards cannot be continued. Neighbors leave for work each workday morning. Children now married have homes of their own. The old home seems too big, too expensive, to run for two people. Children have their own personal life patterns to live and parents are no longer included, except for a Sunday dinner now and then, or an occasional appeal to baby sit. These disturbing factors often bring on a feeling of loneliness, frustration and insecurity.

Moving to a different area brings a freshness into the lives of many retired people. In many regions of the country there are colonies of older folks, all with the same aspirations and desires. Here retired persons find substitutes for old neighborhoods, for old friends who have moved away or passed away, for former family relationships.

In community-sponsored recreation and handicraft centers, in social clubs and church groups, they meet and make new friends, and avoid the sense of frustration and loneliness. Many times these new companionships made in later life, at new retirement locations, are more satisfying than earlier friendships formed with people associated with regular workday life. With fast transportation by airplane, modern streamlined trains, and with the telephone always handy, the old home town does not seem as distant as it did originally. A vacation visit from or to family and friends is something to be appreciated on all sides. Somehow the new location substitutes values and virtues that more than replace those of the old neighborhood. Life again offers a challenge full of new and interesting things to accomplish. Eighty per cent of the frustration of older people is brought on by reliving the past. Residence in a new environment often changes interests, changes the outlook on life. It gives you an opportunity to pick a climate which is suitable for all-year outdoor living and a community where your retirement income will provide a comfortable standard of living.

California Still the Popular Choice

The question was put to a large cross section of the American public on their choice of a state if they had to move away from their present location. California was the first choice by a wide margin. This was particularly true of those who responded from the Midwest, as well as those from the Rocky Mountain area. California, except for its mountain areas, is south of the normal snowfall.

Go South, Old Man

Horace Greeley's famous words, "Go West, young man," electrified the country nearly one hundred years ago. The West proved to be the open door of opportunity and enriched many thousands who migrated there. To retired persons seeking happiness and economical living, the best advice today is, "Go South."

Climatic conditions play an important part in the health and happiness of older persons. The regions of the country south of the snowfall line offer a gentle, sunny climate that is rejuvenating for older people. South of the snowfall line is a land of opportunities to live better on less money. Here you will enjoy savings in food bills, cost of shelter and clothing, fuel and doctor bills. You will find many opportunities to operate a profitable small business enterprise or to engage in subsistence farming.

Costs Less to Live in the South

One of America's leading research organizations made public the results of a nationwide survey on the question: "What is the smallest amount of money a family of four needs to get along on in this community?" Here is the average, or what statisticians call the median, by the size of the community:

$$100,000 \text{ and over} \ldots \ldots \ldots \ldots \$60 \text{ per week}$$
$$10,000 \text{ to } 100,000 \ldots \ldots \ldots \ldots \$60 \text{ per week}$$
$$\text{Under } 10,000 \ldots \ldots \ldots \ldots \ldots \$50 \text{ per week}$$

There was considerable difference by geographical sections. In the South where farming is the chief occupation, the average person says $40 a week is sufficient. In the industrial East where living costs are high, the amount needed is $60 a week. Here are the median averages by geographical areas:

South $40
East and West Central.....................$50
Far West...............................$60
New England and Middle Atlantic..........$60

Estimated Budget for Elderly Couple Is Less in the South

During October 1950, the United States Department of Labor made a study in thirty-four cities of the requirements of a modest budget for elderly couples living in large cities. The budget family consisted of a husband and wife approximately sixty-five years old, who maintain their own two- or three-room rented dwelling and who are able to get about and take care of themselves. The husband is retired or has only occasional employment. The family does not own an automobile. Such a family is typical of many of those now receiving retirement benefits and many potentially eligible for, or actually receiving, old-age assistance.

The elderly couple's budget was designed to represent a level of living which provides the goods and services necessary to maintain health and allow normal participation in community life, in accordance with current American standards. Social and conventional as well as psychological needs are taken into account. The level of living is not luxurious but is adequate to provide for more than the basic essentials of consumption.

Here are the estimated annual dollar costs and relative costs of the total budget, housing and other goods and services for October, 1950, for selected cities:

Budget for an Elderly Couple
Estimated Cost, October 1950

City and State	Total Budget	Housing	Dollar Costs Other Goods and Services
Milwaukee, Wis.	$1,908	$705	$1,203
Boston, Mass.	1,880	640	1,240

City and State	Total Budget	Housing	Dollar Costs Other Goods and Services
Los Angeles, Calif.	$1,866	$605	$1,261
Portland, Oreg.	1,866	630	1,236
Washington, D.C.	1,863	671	1,192
Houston, Texas	1,855	670	1,185
Seattle, Wash.	1,852	583	1,269
San Francisco, Calif.	1,833	567	1,266
Chicago, Ill.	1,818	578	1,240
Detroit, Mich.	1,818	573	1,245
Cleveland, Ohio	1,805	590	1,215
Jacksonville, Fla.	1,795	621	1,174
Philadelphia, Pa.	1,783	587	1,196
New York, N. Y.	1,782	543	1,239
Baltimore, Md.	1,779	603	1,176
Norfolk, Va.	1,774	612	1,162
Pittsburgh, Pa.	1,767	554	1,213
Minneapolis, Minn.	1,765	577	1,188
Atlanta, Ga.	1,748	582	1,166
Denver, Colo.	1,746	577	1,169
Indianapolis, Ind.	1,746	569	1,177
Manchester, N. H.	1,737	550	1,187
Portland, Maine	1,733	548	1,185
Memphis, Tenn.	1,726	563	1,163
Richmond, Va.	1,712	581	1,131
St. Louis, Mo.	1,711	527	1,184
Buffalo, N. Y.	1,698	534	1,164
Kansas City, Mo.	1,687	507	1,180
Savannah, Ga.	1,658	532	1,126
Cincinnati, Ohio	1,650	485	1,165
Mobile, Ala.	1,620	475	1,145
Scranton, Pa.	1,614	463	1,151
New Orleans, La.	1,602	436	1,166

Source: U.S. Department of Labor, *Monthly Labor Review*, September, 1951.

Three out of five of the lowest budget cities are in the South. In 1950, it cost $306 less for an elderly couple to live in New Orleans than to live in Milwaukee. The cost of living has increased since the Department of Labor made this study. The relative differences in the dollar cost of the elderly couple's budget, in the various cities mentioned in the study, probably holds the same relationships today.

One more observation worth noting is that the cost of "housing" covered average rentals in cities, and dollar cost of "other goods" included the purchase of food at retail prices. It is brought out elsewhere in this book that average rentals are lower in noncity areas. The cash outlay for the couple's market basket could also be cut substantially by their producing home-grown vegetables and some poultry.

The South Is Marching Forward

The economy of the Southeast and the Southwest has been one of the most dynamic in the United States. Growth is reflected in the South's expanded share of the United States total income and in the increase in resident population during the past twenty years.

Industry and business, favored by availability of resources awaiting development, by favorable climatic conditions, by low comparative costs, by attractive market opportunities, has expanded faster than the national average.

The resident population of the Southeast grew 25 per cent between 1929 and 1950—a rate faster than that of the entire United States. This region has the highest rate of births and an unusually low rate of deaths. The Southwest, too, has had an accelerated increase in population—27 per cent compared with the national average of 24 per cent.

The expanding character of the South is typified by the construction boom, the trend toward greater industrialization, and the increasing trend toward the importance of the service industries as a source of earnings for residents. Another indication of the South's general economic growth is the expansion of government activities in this region. This is evidenced by the location of many military establishments and other government agencies in the region during the war and the postwar period.

The agrarian South is being rebuilt upon a new structure consistent with the needs of today's changing economy. This provides unusual opportunities for those who bring capital with them to invest in the development of the South's physical and cultural resources. Yes, opportunities are legion for the development of small business and farm enterprises, many of them one-man operated.

Best Way to Live

If you are in reasonably good health, are able to take care of yourself and have the assured minimum income for retirement living—the best way to live is probably in a household of your own. This may be owned outright or rented.

The chances of a mutually satisfactory arrangement in living with a son or daughter are slim. The average American household today provides little accommodation for the privacy and personal living arrangements needed for the heads of a family, growing children and grandparents all living under the same roof. "Keep your own independent household as long as possible," is the advice of many who have tried living the other way. You will probably never be as happy any place as in your own home. As much as you enjoy visits to your children's homes, you probably would find it difficult to make the adjustments necessary to live with them for the rest of your life. You may find it difficult to resist the impulse to boss your children, in-laws and grandchildren. Or, even worse, you may find that they want to boss you. And what about having your own friends visit you? The type of arrangement that usually works out best calls for a separate wing built onto the home of the children. In this little home of their own, the older folks can maintain personal and private living quarters independent of their children's living quarters. A similar solution that has worked out well is the building of a separate, small guest-type of house on the children's property.

Other types of living arrangements to consider are a small apartment, a hotel or a boarding house. If you suffer from chronic illness, perhaps a nursing home would be best for you. Recently there has been discussion about housing developments designed for the special needs of retired persons, at rents they can afford. Few communities have done very much to provide special facilities in housing that older people require. The answers to all these questions should be thought out in your pre-retirement planning.

How to Protect Yourself on Housing

Owning a comfortable house or small farm, fully paid for at the time of retirement, in a small town or village is one of the best ways to provide for security in old age. With your home paid for, you reduce the cost of shelter and the strain on your pocketbook. Otherwise, you will have to make substantial monthly cash payments from your retirement income for rent or to cover the cost of a mortgage. The cost of shelter is the second largest cash expenditure in the family budget.

If you locate in an area where there is a housing shortage, real estate prices will be high. Prices will also be high in the thickly populated resort towns especially during the tourist season. Housing and household operation expenses are much lower in small towns and villages and on a farm than they are in urban areas.

Make your retirement plans several years ahead of the time you actually retire. This gives you an opportunity to buy a home if you are forty or fifty years old and fully pay for it during your high-income earning period before you reach sixty-five. If you decide to relocate in a better retirement area or if your home is too large, you can sell the home and use the cash to buy a small, comfortable home better suited to your needs. Going into debt and becoming obligated to make mortgage payments to buy a retirement home is risky. It is harder to get a mortgage, too, when your income earning capacity is reduced as it is when you retire.

Here are a number of "don'ts" if you plan to build a home:

Don't plan to spend more than twice the average yearly income of your family for a house and lot.

Don't buy a lot without obtaining a clear title.

Don't buy a lot that is subject to damage by floods and other elements of a destructive nature.

Don't buy a lot not served by electricity and not close to transportation lines, schools, churches and shopping centers.

Don't buy a lot just because of its size. The upkeep may become too burdensome for you as you get older.

Don't buy plans which do not conform to building codes, fire restrictions and sanitary laws covering the proposed site.

Don't locate the house too close to side lot lines, or far back from the street. The rear of the lot can be developed for gardening and an outdoor living room.

Don't place the garage at the back of the lot when a location nearer the street will save the cost of extra driveway and maintenance.

Don't make the garage so small that it will not provide adequate space for garden tools and possibly a workshop.

Don't build a house, the exterior design of which is not in character with the neighborhood. You will have trouble finding a buyer if you ever want to sell it.

Dwellings Cost Less in the South

Generally speaking, dwellings cost less to build in the Southern states where the winters are fair and warm. There is less need for expensive house heating systems as you go south. This results in considerable savings in fuel bills—as much as $200 to $250 a year over house heating costs in Northern regions. There is less trouble, too, from the thawing and heaving associated with frozen ground. As a consequence, houses are built without basements, resulting in a saving in the cost of excavation. Since roofs do not have to support heavy snow loads, roof construction can be simplified with resultant lower costs. A closed garage is often an unnecessary expense. In most cases a carport is all that is needed. Land costs, too, are generally lower than in the more densely populated Northern sections of the country. It costs little more to buy the extra land for a private garden, service yard and recreation or patio area.

Planning Your Retirement Home

A place to live in after retirement means more than just a roof over one's head. As you grow older, you probably will spend more time at home. To the retiree, home is a symbol of security and independence. The fact that 68.2 per cent of the heads of families over sixty-five own their homes, while the percentage for the general population is only 53, is evidence of the importance of home ownership to senior citizens of the nation.

There were, in 1951, more than 10,500,000 men and women over sixty-five living in nonfarm areas of the United States, of whom about 7,500,000 were living in their own homes. The remaining three million were living with relatives or friends, in hotels, boarding houses and institutions. Many of the older house owners are couples who own homes built for big families but who refuse to move into smaller quarters after their children are grown and raising families of their own.

The United States Housing and Home Finance Agency reports that too many of the houses in which the oldsters live are rickety, "36 per cent fall below an acceptable standard." A survey conducted in Cincinnati reveals that the majority of retired teachers live apart from relatives and pay about sixty-five dollars a month rent. These retirees do not want to live with other people, not even members of their own families. Many other old people of Cincinnati live in slum tenements. They prefer these to rooming houses, rest homes and institutions. As with the retired teachers, living with relatives and friends is shunned.

The cost of housing was the most important factor in the cost of the elderly couple's budget in the 1950 Survey of the United States Department of Labor. The average yearly rent for a two or three room dwelling, plus the cost of electricity, water and heating fuel ranged from $705 a year in Milwaukee to $436 in New Orleans.

A national survey of the United States Saving and Loan League points out that only about 5 per cent of the mortgage loans handled by savings and loan associations is borrowed by persons sixty years of age and older. And only 2 to 3 per cent of home loans are made to borrowers aged sixty-five and over. This ratio holds true in all states except in California and Florida. Mortgage lenders in these states do a larger percentage of their business in the sixty-and-up brackets.

The 1952 report of the New York State Joint Legislative Committee on Problem of the Aging says: "Our elderly live in houses or apartments constructed for younger people. They ramble around in big homes built for a period when they were raising a family. Or in crowded apartments booby-trapped by slippery floors, sliding rugs, dangerous equipment, death-trap bathtubs, poorly lighted rooms, or steps and stairways that take a toll of the heart. They live squeezed in with their married children with no place of their own to entertain friends, in apartments likely to encourage conflict. You find them in the seedy rooming houses, in the slums, in the deteriorating neighborhoods, over a store, in the back flats, in a cubbyhole in a rooming house."

New York's State Housing Commissioner, Herman T. Stichman, announced on November 26, 1951, "In all state-aided public housing projects in the future it will be required that approximately five per cent of the dwelling units be set aside for the aging and that upon application from the local authorities, this may be increased as the need is shown." This New York State set-aside order is the first of its kind in the history of public housing in the United States.

Apartments for the aged in New York State public projects are: "Type 'A' (tentatively designated for aging couples), double bedroom, separate full-sized living room and combination dining room with kitchen facilities and separate bathroom; Type 'B' (tentatively designated for couples 70 years old and single persons 65 years old doing light housekeeping) combination living and sleeping room, with separate combination dining and kitchen space, with a window and a separate bathroom."

Additional features in the New York State set-aside order designated to serve the special needs of the elderly include:

A. Bathrooms will have nonslip floors.

B. Square bathtubs with seats and hand grips in the walls to facilitate getting in and out of tubs.

C. In some cases, showers with seats and hand grips for aged couples who feel insecure getting into and out of bathtubs.

D. Thresholds eliminated to lessen the danger of tripping.

E. Electric instead of gas stoves to prevent asphyxiation from smothering of the gas flame by the boiling over of liquids.

F. To simplify housekeeping, shelves and cabinets will be placed at low, easy-to-reach levels and windows will have mechanical operators for easy and safe opening and closing of casements.

G. Apartments to face the sunny side and more heat to be provided in these apartments than in those of younger people.

H. Special recreation and visiting rooms for the elderly.

Housing for the retired and the aged is also slated in Boston to provide noninstitutional dwellings for older persons who prefer to live normal lives on their own. The pilot structure, it is said, will contain one hundred dwelling units of one or two rooms each. Plans include rooms for social activities, lectures, concerts and other entertainment for the tenants and their friends; workshops for the study and pursuit of hobbies, either to produce new skills or to carry on part-time activities also are planned. A physical recreation area for light exercise and a cafeteria are being considered. In addition, an infirmary for the care of routine illness and a group of stores carrying groceries, drugs, stationery and similar items add to the conveniences to be enjoyed under one roof. The Commonwealth Housing Foundation has retained an architect to work out the design details of the project.

The Florida State Improvement Commission, Citizens Committee on Retirement in Florida, is actively promoting the Sponsored Neighborhood Village idea among large corporations, labor unions, fraternal organizations and others interested in sponsoring a planned community. A group of businessmen in Florida is engaged in planning such a development which will be open to any retired person. Four plans of financing a home in the village have been proposed. Two of the plans provide for the purchase of the home, in which case the occupant would have a cash equity in it and would be responsible for repairs and upkeep. Two other plans provide for a lifetime lease for the retired couple, in which case the occupants would have no cash equity and the sponsor of the village would be responsible for maintenance.

The Sponsored Neighborhood Village, if constructed, would be located in the suburbs of a Florida city. One-eighth to one-fifth of the inhabitants of the community would live in apartment houses, while the rest would live in separate one-story dwelling units. About half of the homes would have two bedrooms, while the remainder would have one bedroom. More than two-thirds of the Village citizens would take part in a planned program of recreation. Slightly over 70 per cent of the senior citizens who answered a questionnaire on the Sponsored Neighborhood Village proposal indicated that they would prefer living in a community made up largely of retired people, and 80 per cent felt they would like to leave their present location and make their home in Florida.

Another nationwide survey conducted in 1952, by Investors Diversified Services, Inc., of Minneapolis, Minnesota, focuses the spotlight on what those about to retire want in a home. Most of the retiring couples who answered the questionnaire—82 per cent—expressed a desire for a one-floor residence; 36 per cent said they would like a large lot with garden space; 24 per cent wanted an acre or more. Fifty-seven per cent indicated they prefer a two-bedroom house. Only 21 per cent voted in favor of a one-bedroom dwelling. More than two-thirds of the couples answering now own their homes; another 32 per cent rent. About 17 per cent said they would like to settle in Florida; another 10 per cent favored California. But more than one-third stated they wanted to stay in their present communities. While 55 per cent said they expected to work to supplement their retirement incomes, more than half indicated they expected to retire with upwards of $200 per month. Thirty-nine per cent preferred not to work in retirement. Of those who replied, 17 per cent were professional men and women, 10 per cent office workers, 7 per cent self-employed business people, 6 per cent salesmen, 4 per cent factory workers and 4 per cent other workers.

Safety, Health and Recreation Features to Include

If you plan on building a new home for retirement living, or buying or renting one, here are a few checklist guides to follow:

House: One story with no steps, steep thresholds or stairs. Ground-level entrances. Nonskid floors. Wide doors. Good view from windows. Adequate electrical outlets. Good heating system. Good ventilation. Good lighting. Good insulation. As good fireproofing as possible. Building materials well suited to climatic conditions.

Bedroom: Close to bathroom. Good light for reading. Plenty of storage space.

Bathroom: Safe step-in type bathtub with grab bars in the wall. Ample size medicine chest.

Kitchen: Laborsaving and stepsaving type. Electric range. Electric water heater. Good ventilation. Easy-to-reach shelves and cabinets. Adequate storage space. Dining corner.

Living Room: Picture window. Raised fireplace.

Cellar: Dry. Well lighted. Stair handrail.

Heating System: Automatic oil burner. Electric heating (if power rates are low).

Garage: Near to street. Easy lift-up doors. Wind and rainproof passageway to house.

Workroom or Hobby Shop: Good heating and ventilation. Good lighting. Nonskid floor. Ample storage space.

Patio or Outdoor Recreation Area: Private for sunbathing. Outdoor fireplace.

Cesspool: Large. In good working order.

General Information: Deal with a reliable and experienced real estate agent. Don't sign or pay anything without checking with a lawyer. Don't be in a hurry to close the deal. Don't plunge into mortgage debt over your head. Remember this purchase of a house is likely to be the most important investment of your retirement life. If you plan on building a house, consult an architect for advice on design and materials. If you plan on buying, experienced local appraisers and builders can help you select a retirement house in the community where you plan to settle.

You will not find it easy to locate homes already built and on the market that include all the special facilities listed above. However, with a few remodeling alterations and modern equipment, you can often make over a house already built into a more livable and easier-to-maintain house for your needs in retirement living.

As a result of the housing shortage created by World War II, there grew up a tremendous demand on the part of young couples and middle-aged families. Architects and builders are concentrating their efforts on satisfying the demands of this great boom in housing. The home ideas of today's architects and home builders feature the ranch-type and split-level styles adapted for the living requirements of house-hungry younger families.

As the demand diminishes for the popular type of house being built today, builders may turn their attention to the great untapped market for retirement housing. Until private enterprise recognizes that there is a large demand for homes with special facilities for the retiree and the elderly, the burden of furnishing retirement housing appears to be on government agencies, large public groups, such as labor unions, fraternal organizations and the like.

Here and there, a few forward-looking architects and builders are showing evidence of recognizing the housing problem facing retired couples and are coming to the front with practical suggestions. No overall national pattern, however, is yet in sight. The huge planning and development job is still ahead. It may be some time before we see any mass planning and development for the kind of retirement housing our senior citizens want and need.

Planning your future home for the later years can be one of your most exciting and rewarding hobbies. You will get into the study of finances and budgets, search through home-planning magazines and articles for new and fresh ideas, have lively and stimulating conversation sessions with friends, and then discuss with architects and builders the practical applications and cost of your ideas for your model retirement home.

Save Money by Doing Your Own Repairs

You can save a substantial part of house maintenance costs if you do your own outside and inside house painting. Learn to make plumbing, electrical and carpentry repairs yourself. Buy a good home handyman's guide and study its how-to-do-it instructions. Also write to Superintendent of Documents, United States Government Printing Office, Washington 25, D.C., for a copy of selected lists of publications on household service and on home economics. The more fix-it-yourself jobs you are able to do, the less you will pay out of your cash income for labor to keep your home efficient and comfortable, and to make valuable additions and improvements. In addition to the financial gains you enjoy by doing the work yourself, you also gain the satisfaction of a job well done, and of preserving and adding to the value of your property.

You Can Save Money on a Build-It-Yourself House

If you are handy with tools, can read blueprints and follow how-to-do-it instructions, you can save almost half the cost of building a small home. More than 40 per cent of the cost of building a house goes for wages and to contractors as overhead and profit. Build your own home yourself and save the cash outlay for outside labor.

Building industry experts estimate that more than one hundred thousand families have built their own homes since World War II, doing all the work or most of it themselves. A couple of retired men handy with saw and hammer could pool their time and efforts on owner-built homes for themselves. Even if they let contracts for part of the work, they could save considerable money. To build a house, even a small one, from start to finish is a big job. But this is one way to beat the high cost of housing and to save hard-earned dollars. It is also a profitable and practical way to use leisure time.

There are a number of small-home plans on the market. You buy a complete set of blueprints and specifications and a lumber list. If you plan to do the building yourself, turn the mill and lumber list over to a lumberyard. Some yards will cut the lumber to size before delivering it. You can also buy ready-cut homes direct from the factory. All the lumber and basic materials are accurately cut to fit, marked and numbered, ready to be assembled. This eliminates hand measuring and cutting. You save as much as 30 per cent on labor and 18 per cent on waste. One factory offers 110 designs of houses to choose from.

However, be sure to check local building codes, fire restrictions and sanitary laws before you start to build. Some work, like plumbing and electrical work, is covered by strict local codes. You may have to employ a licensed plumber and electrician to do this part of the job. If you plan to obtain a loan backed by the Federal Housing Administration or other lending institution, to build a stock-plan house, check with the local office to discover whether the stock plan and specifications are acceptable. FHA offices, both state and regional, differ in their requirements, depending on local climatic and other conditions.

A concrete block, five-room house is being built in many locations by amateur builders, complete with plumbing, electrical wiring and heating system for less than $3,650. Another popular plan on the market features a modern-design ranch house. It's a year-round house, eighty-one feet long and twenty feet wide, fully insulated, finished outside and inside with durable plywood, requiring no plastering. A heating and ventilating system and electric wiring are included in the plan. You build the basic house, which includes living room, dining area, two bedrooms, kitchen, bath, utility room and carport, for about $5,000.

A Good Home Is a Good Hedge Against Inflation and Insecurity

Houses and farms are bought by many as a hedge against inflation. A dollar used to purchase bonds may be worth only

50 cents when the bonds mature. Houses and land, though, tend to keep pace with economic conditions. Their value may fluctuate but they will still be there when they are needed. As long as it is paid for or the mortgage payments are kept up, no one can take your house or land away from you. A good house, a well-bought farm, will care for you in your old age, and do the job all over again for your children. If you own it outright by the time you retire, it's one of the best safeguards for security you can have.

A number of retired couples in Florida have small apartments built over their two-car garages. They move into these apartments during the winter season and rent their houses to tourists. From four months rent they get the income needed to pay the taxes plus enough to live on comfortably all year.

The executive of an oil company who prefers alpine sports bought fifty-five acres on a Vermont hillside. His retirement home is being constructed bit by bit during his summer vacations. When it is eventually finished, the entire upper floor will be rented to ski lodgers. With additional ski lodges he is planning and some farming in season, he expects to have fun as well as make money when he retires.

Nine Reasons Why It's Smart to Live in a Rural Town or Village

1. Cash expenditures for family living are lower. In the city, land values and dwellings are higher, taxes are higher, the conveniences of community water supply and sewage disposal costs money. These add up to higher monthly rents and higher costs of home ownership. The cost of rental for the average nonfarm rural dwelling unit is about one-half the cost of the average urban dwelling unit.

2. The average expenditures for household furnishings and equipment tend to be somewhat lower in villages than in cities. It is not surprising then to find that the proportion

of husbands and wives sixty years old and older is greater in villages than in cities. It costs them less to live in villages and towns than in cities. Village families are less style-conscious with respect to home decorations than city families and are less likely to replace furnishings in order to keep up with fashions, or to keep up with the Joneses.

3. Because of the informality of rural living, you don't have to dress as expensively as you would in the city. Informal living calls for informal clothing. Consequently, cash outlays for clothing, the fourth largest expenditure in the cost of living, is less for rural families.

4. The job of bringing electric power lines and telephone service to America's rural communities is virtually complete. You can locate where you can enjoy these advantages.

5. You can do much of your shopping by mail. The mail-order houses, because of their method of group selling, almost without exception offer merchandise to the purchaser at a saving. Some of the mail-order houses offer a larger selection of merchandise than many large retail stores.

6. The development of the automobile and the building of good roads has done much to promote both suburban and rural living. The desire to live in the country was always present as shown by the fact that even in the old days, well-to-do families had summer homes to which they would go to escape the conditions of city dwelling. But in the winter the country summer home was uninhabitable because of the difficulties of communication and transportation. Today the automobile has solved the difficulties of transportation and the telephone those of communication.

7. Many good rural retirement spots are located adjacent to national and state parks, lakes, dams, rivers, fertile valleys, seashore or mountain regions. They provide virgin territory for recreation and vacation projects of retired persons. They offer opportunities to establish income-producing tourist cot-

tages, motels, guest houses, tearooms, gift shops, boats and fishing equipment for hire, summer camps and other enterprises catering to the tourist and vacationist.

You don't have to isolate yourself deep in the backwoods country to enjoy the economy and informality of rural living. You can locate on good roads with accessibility to large towns, or in a lovely rural village, with scenic or historic attractions. Generally speaking, many good retirement spots for happy living can be found within a half-hour drive from a town boundary line.

8. Another advantage of rural or country living is that it is comparatively easy to supplement your income by raising and selling a specialty crop on a few acres.

9. Rural living will give you a workable set of values which will help you to achieve thrifty and comfortable living, while maintaining a level at which you can live with dignity.

Trailer Homes for Mobile Living

The United States Department of Commerce estimates that there are more than a half-million trailer coaches in use in the United States today. A large number of converts to trailer living are retired people—doctors, lawyers, farmers, three ex-governors and people from all walks of life. Most of them find trailer living the most economical way of spending winters in Florida, California, Arizona and other sections of the United States from coast to coast. For many retired couples with limited incomes the trailer coach way of life with its easy mobility, simple way of living is a happy solution. Over one hundred thousand house trailers visit Florida during the winter season. Over seventy thousand house trailers are registered in California. Retired couples have found, in the trailer coach, an economical way to enjoy the pleasures of travel.

Some modern house trailers are forty-five feet in length, have five rooms, including two bedrooms, shower and tub bath, oil heater, cooking stove, electric refrigerator, plenty of closet space and room for television or radio.

Practically all leading vacation areas now provide attractively landscaped plots or trailer parks for the use of trailers. Some of these parks offer additional facilities, such as laundries, food stores, private baths, recreational areas and moving picture theaters. Some of them can accommodate as many as two thousand trailers. Charges are usually about $20 a month including all facilities. De luxe parks charge as much as $40 a month.

Trailer living has come a long way. No longer is it a gypsy way of life. For many a trailer is a permanent home for living a normal, happy and economical life. The price of a new, modern trailer coach runs from $2,500 to $5,000, depending on size and the number of conveniences. Classified advertisements in newspapers often offer bargain values in used trailers.

A Compact Home Afloat

You can live a life afloat, enjoy a "dash of salt" and the leisurely pleasure of cruising without chartering a liner or owning a palatial yacht. You can do this in the same comfort as those who live ashore in house trailers.

You can spend many interesting days around yacht yards and basins looking for a bargain buy in a thirty- to forty-foot pleasure cruiser, or for a commercial fishing craft that has outlived its usefulness for deep-sea runs but is still good for use in protected waters.

I know of a man who lived this way for many years in Florida. He earned enough income from writing and doing publicity jobs ashore, not only to support himself but also to pay for his son's college education.

Here are a few of the many advantages of living on a boat. You can cruise up to Maine in the summer and down to Florida in the winter. You can pick interesting spots along the coast for short stays or choose a location for a permanent home afloat. Berth space can be found in protected harbors, at private or public docks offering electricity, drinking water, telephone, ice, gas, showers, laundromat and recreation rooms. A boat can be used as an economical home afloat while you are engaged in pleasure-seeking activities, or as temporary living quarters while looking for a permanent house or apartment ashore.

Bibliography

How to Retire to Florida by George and Jane Dusenbury (Harper, N.Y.)

How to Retire to California by Aubrey Drury (Harper, N.Y.)

Where to Retire and How by Fessenden S. Blanchard (Dodd, Mead, N.Y.)

Where to Retire on a Small Income by Norman D. Ford (Harian, N.Y.)

You and Your Aging Parents by Edith M. Stern (Wyn, N.Y.)

CHAPTER X

Selecting a Location for Retirement Living

Since personal preferences vary so widely, it is impossible to list every location that offers good prospects for retirement living. However, the localities described in the pages that follow are those most frequently recommended in my research of important retirement areas. The omission of any specific location does not necessarily mean that the particular city or village has little to offer for a happy, healthful and enjoyable retirement. The localities included, however, have proved their value as retirement sites, and deserve your serious consideration.

The principal points to consider in selecting a place for retirement are: *Climate,* which has much to do with physical comfort and good, healthful living. *Avocation, hobby and work opportunities* as they fit into your retirement plans and desires for keeping busy. *Facilities for intellectual and cultural outlets* covering libraries, museums, lectures, concerts, art, adult education classes, etc. *Recreation facilities,* such as golf, fishing, yachting, shuffleboard and other forms of amusement, depending upon whether you want an active or quiet community life. *Social and religious groups* providing opportunities to meet friendly people and to make new companionships according to backgrounds and interests. *Scenery, altitude and topography* with reference to the view and the charm of the place and facilities. *Financial requirements.* In many desirable locations the cost of a home, taxes and other living expenses may be too great a strain on your retirement income. The problem is to find the best locations within the means of your budget. In some instances, the answer will be to settle in a new suburban development or in a neighborhood village which is part of a larger community offering the advantages you are looking for. *Personal preferences* which may be influenced by any number of considerations, such as nearness to relatives or friends, availability of medical care, the tempo of living, preference for urban or rural living, opportunities to engage in a small business enterprise and other special and personal reasons.

Each of these considerations carries a different degree of importance for each individual. Decide for yourself which ones are most important for you, which ones will assure the rich life you are looking forward to in retirement.

Keep in mind, however, that there are many things about a place that cannot be measured statistically. These have to be discovered by personal experience while actually living in the community. If you plan to move to a new locality, it is wise to live there on a temporary basis for a while. Try it out through all seasons of the year before taking up permanent residence.

The selection of a retirement location is tied up with many factors, some emotional, some financial, others purely personal. No specific geographical location in itself can guarantee a happy retirement. An early start in planning where to live in retirement will avert errors in judgment, save a good deal of money and make adjustments to retirement easier. Somewhere in the United States, there are retirement localities seemingly made to order for your needs and desires. The earlier you start searching for them, the better your chances of finding them.

CHAPTER XI

California

Southern California, Coastal Areas

Climatologists classify the climate of Southern California as Mediterranean in type—one of the best four-season climates in the world. The summers are tempered by sea breezes with almost no rain for two to six months; winters are mild with light to moderate rain coming in periods of a few days' duration separated by many days of brilliant sunshine.

Because of the proximity of the Pacific Ocean, freezing temperatures are extremely rare. Average temperatures along the coastal plain range from forty-eight degrees to sixty degrees during the winter months with a daily range of about twenty degrees. In the summer months the temperatures vary from seventy-two to seventy-eight degrees during the daytime to around sixty degrees at night with a daily range of about fifteen degrees.

Southern California has about forty-five days of rain, amounting to ten to twenty inches, as an annual average. There are normally twelve rainy days in spring and nineteen in winter. Relative humidity at noon in winter averages 45 to 56 per cent and during the summer months 52 to 60 per cent. This region has 179 clear days and 77 cloudy days annually. During daylight hours in winter, the sun shines 68 to 71 per cent of the time, and in summer 70 to 80 per cent.

In the interior valleys, winter temperatures are sometimes below freezing at night and summer temperatures rise to ninety-five degrees. Low humidity, however, moderates the effect of high temperatures. The nights are usually cool and comfortable. The desert areas of the southern part of the state, near Nevada and Arizona, are hot and dry—among the most arid places on the North American continent.

The coastal areas and nearby foothill districts are subject to night and early morning fogs which are more frequent in summer than in winter. The fog increases as latitude and altitude increase.

San Diego. Pop. 322,000. Alt. Sea level to 19 ft. County Seat of San Diego County. The oldest Spanish settlement in California is 125 miles south of Los Angeles and about 15 miles from the Mexican border. The city and county enjoy a dry subtropical climate, considered by many experts as one of the world's finest climates. Because it is one of the great military bases of the nation, San Diego is geared, to a large degree, to international developments as they affect the armed forces.

The city is built around beautiful, fourteen-hundred-acre Balboa Park which contains a large zoo, museum, art galleries and many diversified recreational facilities, exposition buildings and outdoor organ recitals. Back of the city is the Coastal Range affording snow sports in season, as well as camping and hunting. San Diego is well equipped to satisfy every cultural desire. Art galleries, floral gardens, symphonies-under-the-stars, theaters, starlight operas, social clubs, churches, missions—all are here in numbers and quality. Every form of diversion from deep-sea fishing and boating to golf, surfing and shuffleboard is available in the area. San Diego Public Library has thirty-two branch libraries.

San Diego's aircraft plants are the leading industrial activity. Other manufacturing includes patio furniture, machine tools, dairy equipment, building materials, etc. Landscaped, three-bedroom homes, with fruit trees, are advertised at $13,500; two-bedroom bungalows at $9,000 to $12,000.

A large retired population lives in the surrounding communities, especially retired Navy personnel. Here there are opportunities to establish a small business or to engage in subsistence farming.

La Jolla, a suburb of San Diego, is one of the most delightful retirement communities in the United States. It is located on a picturesque rocky headland, fronted by many pleasant sandy coves, with beautiful and comfortable homes and impressive estates around the beaches and on the hill slopes. This charming community was originally settled by artists, writers and theater-folk. Many of them have permanent homes there. Everybody, including celebrities, dresses informally. They lounge along the winding streets and frequent the Community Playhouse.

The shopping center has charming shops with unique names, such as The Little Pink House, The Green Dragon, etc. The Art Center offers art and craft classes open to everyone of all ages. At the Scripps Institution of Oceanography there is an aquarium and marine museum where you can study ocean life. For golf there is the La Jolla Country Club and championship tennis is played at the Tennis Club.

You will find many retired business executives and Army and Navy officers living in this distinctive and cultural community, which is blessed with one of the most delightful climates in the United States. Ranch-type homes with three bedrooms are listed from $25,000 to $42,500. You will need about $300 a month to participate in, and enjoy, the community standard of living.

Coronado. Pop. 18,000. Alt. 25 ft. San Diego County. A fashionable community of beautiful homes, resort hotels, modern apartments, fine restaurants, shady avenues, parks, beaches and a famous yacht harbor, located across the bay from San Diego. Recreation facilities include yachting, deep-sea fishing, golf, tennis, lawn bowling, swimming in ocean or bay, in a climate where every month is an out-of-doors month. Rather on the expensive side for retirement living.

Escondido. Pop. 7,500. Alt. 700–900 ft. San Diego County. A number of retired and semiretired families have chosen Escondido because of its excellent year-round climate and happy, healthful, informal way of living. Many families live on a small acreage and grow avocados, citrus fruits, poultry and turkeys. Escondido (meaning Hidden Valley) has beautiful rolling hills, canyons, highlands and lowlands, and affords ideal locations for diversified types of farming and retirement homes. It possesses practically everything for healthful and comfortable living.

You will find the usual number of clubs, social and service groups here; twenty-five churches, representing every important denomination; an excellent school system; opportunities for many forms of out-of-doors recreation; a philharmonic society; painting and art groups and devotees of the drama; a well-stocked library and a well-equipped hospital. Escondido is the southern gateway to the famous Palomar Mountain Observatory and its two hundred-inch telescope. Very close to the area are the Warner Hot Springs and Rincon Springs. The town is situated beyond and above the coastal fogs, lying fifteen miles inland from the Pacific Ocean. The chamber of commerce reports that opportunities for establishing small businesses exist in the community. Real estate offerings: two acres with two-bedroom house $7,200. Family orchard, four and a half acres with six-room house $11,000.

Oceanside. Pop. 13,000. Alt. 50 ft. San Diego County. Located on the coast, thirty-eight miles north of San Diego, this community at the mouth of the San Luis Rey Valley offers good prospects for retirement. The four-mile beach is considered one of the cleanest and safest in California. A municipal fishing pier, picnic facilities, open-air theater, fishing, swimming and playground equipment add to the attractiveness of this fine resort town. The Mission San Luis Rey and the estate of the Rosicrucian Fellowship are located here, which indicates that the area offers advantages for retirement living. One of the largest United States Marine Corps bases adjoins Oceanside.

Laguna Beach. Pop. 12,000. Alt. 17 ft. Orange County. This attractive village is the home of a number of distinguished playwrights, musicians, actors, ceramists, photographers and artists. At the art gallery you will find painters and sculptors mingling with guests at monthly teas. Here, too, you will find schools of painting, photography, ballet, sculpture and ceramics. The artists' studios have uniquely-shaped roofs and bright-colored shutters. Many of them are built on the hillside. If you like to live in an atmosphere of art, lectures and concerts, where living is easy and informal, you'll enjoy Laguna Beach. The Festival of Arts and Pageant of the Masters, presented each summer, is a famous and popular attraction. Recreationwise, you can enjoy surf fishing and bathing, motorboating and sailing, golf and tennis, lawn bowling, beautiful trails for riding or hiking. Laguna's churches represent almost every denomination. All the principal service clubs and fraternal organizations are represented. The Orange Coast Junior College and Santa Ana College provide academic and college sports atmosphere.

It is strategically located fifty miles south of Los Angeles and eighty miles from the Mexican border, in the center of Southern California's famous climate belt. Laguna is a town of artistic homes and gardens noted for individuality and hospitality. It is very popular as a retirement community. Attractive homes start at $12,000. Tax rate is $5.18 per $100 assessed value.

Santa Ana. Pop. 45,500. Alt. 135 ft. County Seat of Orange

County. This growing city, located thirty-three miles south of Los Angelos and ten miles inland from the Pacific Ocean, has been for years a delightful place to live in retirement. Its 132 clubs and service organizations, thirty-two churches, Community Players, Municipal Bowl, Bowers Memorial Art Museum and parks offer an active community life. Nearby beaches and mountains provide additional recreational facilities.

Santa Ana is the center of a rich orange-, walnut- and avocado-growing and packing empire. It has a surprising number of industrial plants that manufacture everything from ornamental lamps to hydraulic presses and farm machinery. The surrounding area is dotted with ranch homes, poultry and turkey farms, groves of all kinds and large estates of retired business executives. Two-bedroom homes are for sale at $8,000; three-bedroom homes from $7,000 to $18,000. Groves and ranches, five acres, sell from $13,000 to $25,000. Furnished apartments rent from $30 to $75 a month.

Orange County, extending forty miles along the coast and twenty-five miles inland, a combination of flatland, rolling hills and mountains, offers a great variety of choice locations for those seeking varied living, pleasure, farming or business opportunities.

Pasadena. Pop. 104,500. Alt. 700 to 1,200 ft. Metropolitan Los Angeles Area. Located ten miles northeast of the city of Los Angeles, at the foothills of the Sierra Madre Mountains in the San Gabriel Valley, it is a city of above-the-average homes, gardens and estates. It is best known as the site of the annual Tournament of Roses and Rose Bowl football games. The California Institute of Technology, Huntington Library and Art Gallery, Pasadena Community Playhouse and the College of Theatre Arts provide plenty of opportunities for lectures, plays, concerts and other cultural activities. Brookside Park's five hundred-acre recreational preserve and fifteen other parks afford a variety of outdoor recreational activities.

Most houses for sale in this location are advertised at from $20,000 to $50,000 and more. This includes homes in San Marino which is a rapidly growing suburb of Pasadena. Many millionaires have large estates here, and thousands of moderately wealthy families also live in retirement throughout the Pasadean area. You'll need a monthly income of $400 or more for reasonable retirement living. People with more moderate financial incomes will find delightful quiet living in locations like Sierra Madre and Altadena in the mountain foothills surrounding Pasadena.

Long Beach. Pop. 224,000. Alt. 35 ft. A celebrated seaside resort and year-round playground, about twenty miles southwest of Los Angeles. For many years this has been a haven for retired folks. It was here that Dr. Francis Townsend organized his famous old-age pension movement. Many people now consider Long Beach too commercialized with too much tourist activity for peaceful retirement living. However, thousands of retired families have settled here.

An eight-mile smooth and wide ocean beach plus stillwater beaches provide for swimming, aquatic sports and fishing. In its one thousand acres of parks and playgrounds are numerous recreation facilities for retired folks—everything from shuffleboard and horseshoe pitching to flycasting and picnics. Lectures, plays, concerts and community programs are held throughout the year at the Municipal Auditorium. Homes in the residential areas range from modest bungalows to pretentious estates. Long Beach ranks among the four top cities of its size in the United States from the standpoint of health. Many retired people who live here are from the Central and Midwestern states. The Wayside Art Colony sponsors exhibitions, schools and activities of artists and craftsmen in several forms of art ranging from painting to woodworking.

City-owned oil wells have brought in huge revenues for the city government which has resulted in lower tax rates for residents. A municipal golf course is located at Recreation Park and in addition there are two private courses. There are one hundred churches representing twenty-six denominations. The library system includes the main library, seven branch libraries and four subbranches. Bixby Park is a picnic park noted as the site of state society picnics. More than six hundred industries are located in Long Beach and it is the home port of the United States Navy Battle Fleet. Five well-equipped hospitals provide modern facilities.

Santa Monica. Pop. 72,000. Alt. Sea level to 400 ft. Located sixteen miles from Los Angeles in an area of scenic beauty "where the mountains meet the sea," Santa Monica is in the ideal year-round climate zone where frosts, thunderstorms and strong winds are virtually unknown. A great many of the Hollywood movie stars have their residences here. This is a city of attractive homes and estates with beautiful gardens. Residential districts extend from the ocean front up into the foothills of the Santa Monica Mountains. Santa Monica with its palm-lined streets is the kind of city Eastern people dream about.

The University of California (UCLA) and Loyola University provide college-town atmosphere, as well as excellent facilities for social and cultural life. The Junior College Technical School offers classes for adults. Things to do in Santa Monica include visits to Municipal Pier and to the Ocean Park Amusement Pier, fishing, swimming, paddleboard, yachting, bathing along three miles of beaches; tennis playing in city parks, bowling on the green, playing shuffleboard; golfing and riding nearby and attending the open-air theater. The city has fifty churches, the usual social and service clubs, and an excellent public library and art gallery. It is an easy place in which to make friends and is a popular retirement location for people from the Midwest states.

The average ocean water temperature in summer months is sixty degrees and in winter months, fifty-five degrees. The average air temperature in July is seventy-nine degrees and in January, sixty-one degrees. Rainfall averages only about twelve inches a year. City tax rate is $1.99.

Oxnard. Pop. 26,000. Alt. 45 ft. Ventura County. The climate is about ten degrees cooler than that of Los Angeles in summer and winter. Maximum temperature for January is sixty-seven degrees; for July, seventy-four degrees. Minimum average for January is forty-one degrees and for July, fifty-three degrees. There are high fogs in the spring and fall seasons. Thunderstorms are a rarity; lightning occurs very seldom; the area is practically frostless. Oxnard is located sixty-three miles northeast from Los Angeles and thirty-eight miles from Santa Barbara, four miles from the Pacific Ocean, in the center of a rich agricultural empire of lemons and truck crops.

Everything in recreation and relaxation is within minutes of the community—deep-sea and surf fishing; sun bathing and swimming; hunting and fishing in mountain-stream country. Riding, hiking, golf and other outdoor recreation are easily accessible. Adult evening classes furnish added diversion, as do the many musical, dramatic, art and cultural groups which are active throughout the county. Practically every denomination is represented in Oxnard's sixteen churches.

A great share of Oxnard's growth and present activity is due to military and defense activities. These have created a temporary housing shortage which is being relieved by new home construction. A new five-room house sells for about $7,500 and a six-room house for around $9,000. Land values are high, ranging from $1,500 to $3,000 per acre. One-bedroom, unfurnished apartments rent for $50 to $85 per month. City tax rate is $1.82 per $100 assessed valuation. County tax rate is $2.28. This is not a resort town. Outside of vacationers, the people locating in this community have clear-cut reasons such as business, agriculture, industry or retirement.

Mindful of the importance of water supply, Oxnard has taken a lead in the development and preservation of adequate future water supplies by planning river-source dams, open and underground reservoirs. Average annual rainfall is eleven inches.

Ojai. Pop. 2,519. Alt. 900 ft. Ventura County. Here is an unusual, cheerful and active community, whose cultural and recreational facilities, blended with leisurely living, have attracted many people looking for a place to settle in retirement. Lying in a sunny and fertile valley in the mountains of the Los Padres National Forest, Ojai Valley is called the "Valley of Enchantment." The Ojai community enjoys smog-free air, warm summer days and cool summer nights. July temperatures reach a maximum of ninety-two degrees, with night temperatures around fifty-three degrees. The dry climate has helped many who suffer from asthma and hay fever. Arts and crafts flourish in the community aided by classes and exhibitions of the many outstanding artists and craftsmen who reside in Ojai Valley. Late in May, a week-long festival presents outstanding artists of the music and concert world. Many attractive resorts and hot springs are located in the valley. Fishing may be enjoyed in the mountain streams and hunting in the hills. Golf, tennis, riding, picnics and shuffleboard are a few of the outdoor activities to be enjoyed the year round. Orchid raising, started as a hobby by one resident, has grown so that he now has an eighty-acre Orchid Town. Other retired persons raise flowers, ornamental shrubs or citrus fruits.

Three-bedroom homes sell for $8,000 to $9,000 in the village. Better homes on hillside locations cost as much as $25,000. Because it has no industrial area and is off the beaten path, Ojai has been able to retain its spirit of peace and tranquility.

Santa Barbara. Pop. 53,000. Alt. Sea level to 850 ft. County Seat of Santa Barbara County. For gracious living and an atmosphere of natural beauty in oak-covered hills, mountain background and expanse of seashore, Santa Barbara is a favorite retirement location for business men, professional people and ex-military personnel. It's a bright, clean city of flowers, red tile roofs, white stucco walls, with a reputation for ease and leisure. Many internationally famous writers, painters, sculptors and musicians reside in this community. Flowers and shrubs grow the year round in home gardens and on the landscaped estates and ranches of the retired wealthy.

Average temperatures during summer are in the high seventies and night temperatures average forty-nine degrees. Winter temperatures average sixty-five degrees maximum to forty degrees minimum. Annual rainfall is eighteen inches. Relative humidity averages 78 per cent.

Santa Barbara stands out for its high level of cultural activities. The Civic Recreation Center is the headquarters for dance groups, plays, orchestra and singing groups, as well as card and chess games. Instruction in arts, crafts and trades is provided by the city school and university extension systems. Santa Barbara College, of the University of California, is planning to spend $21,500,000 on a 408-acre site on Goleta Mesa. Goleta is ten miles from Santa Barbara and at the present time there is little in the way of private housing accommodations within reasonable distance of the Goleta campus. This presents a good opportunity for investment in new homes and college service businesses, as the future will see this section built up as a thriving college community area. Santa Barbara has a museum of art and a museum of natural history.

From a social and recreational viewpoint, Santa Barbara has much to offer retired people with its social and service clubs and groups covering all manner of special interests. The Retired Business and Professional Men's Club (similar to the Old Guard) has over 150 members. Archery, baseball, tennis, golf, lawn bowling, swimming, yachting, hiking, picnics, riding, rifle and skeet shooting and fishing are a few of the recreational facilities available. Outstanding concerts, plays, recitals and road shows are presented at the Lobero Theatre. Santa Barbara Mission is said to be the most photographed of all the missions.

Farming activities in the vicinity include citrus, walnut and avocado groves, vegetable growing, cattle and horse raising, dairying and flower growing. Typical real estate values recently advertised include a cozy one-bedroom cottage with garden for $9,200; ranch-style, two-bedroom home at $11,950, larger homes with "view" locations from $15,000 to $26,500; a three-bedroom, frame home, with ten-acre walnut grove and pasture land at $18,000. Apartment rentals range from $75 up per month. Real and personal property taxes in city $1.20; county tax in city $4.46 per $100. City assessments are based on 60 per cent and county on 50 per cent of market value of property.

Santa Barbara is so well thought of as a retirement location that you will find families from all sections of the country living in retirement there.

Southern California, Interior Areas

The climate of Southern California varies with the distance from the coast and the topography of the locality. In general, the climate is warmer and dryer in Riverside County than in the coastal counties. Low average relative humidities, absence of smog and infrequent fog, predominantly clear skies and warm temperatures, are considered beneficial to persons afflicted with asthma, bronchial diseases, neuritis and sinus. During the summer months the maximum daytime temperatures are usually below ninety-five degrees and the relative humidity averages 45 per cent. The effect of the low humidity is that, though the thermometer is high, people feel comfortable. Summer nights are cool, with temperatures in the fifties. In the winter months temperatures range between thirty-six degrees minimum to sixty degrees maximum, with relative humidity around 50 per cent. There are about 233 clear days and wind averages seven miles per hour. This is a land of contrasts—rich valleys filled with orange, lemon, cherry, walnut and date palm trees, lakes cupped in wooded hills, famous desert resorts and hot springs. Those seeking quiet living in a dry climate for health reasons, within accessible distances from a great metropolitan center like Los Angeles, will do well to consider retirement locations in Riverside County.

Riverside. Pop. 46,000. Alt. 800 to 1,200 ft. County Seat of Riverside County. One of the outstanding inland cities of Southern California on the Santa Ana River. The birthplace of California's navel-orange industry, Riverside is famous for its Mission Inn, a unique hotel with a collection of art objects and pioneer relics. The city has sixty-five churches. Nearby is Mt. Rubidoux, site of the original Easter sunrise service. Several homes were listed from $8,000 to $12,000. Ranches and groves, on five acres, were being offered at $15,000 and up. This community ranks high as a retirement location.

Banning. Pop. 7,000. Located on the slopes of Mt. San Gorgonia, this town is in the midst of citrus fruit and almond groves.

Corona. Pop. 10,200. Alt. 600 ft. A charming garden city laid out in a circle among lemon groves. Living costs are reasonable and there are many attractions in the area to interest retired families.

Beaumont. Pop. 3,100. Located in the San Gorgonio Pass, which is the principal pass connecting the coastal plain and Imperial Valley, it is the center of cherry, peach, apple and apricot orchards and the home of the Cherry Festival.

Palm Springs. Pop. 7,500. Alt. 425 ft. A fashionable desert, winter and social resort, resting on the shelf of Mt. San Jacinto, it is located 105 miles east of Los Angeles, and is famous for its sulphur springs and mud baths. The desert soil is fertile; flowers and palm trees bloom profusely. This oasis in the desert is a playground for Hollywood movie stars, artists and rich Americans from October through May. A number of persons who have benefited from a health standpoint from the climate have stayed and opened modest wayside inns and other resort-type businesses. While Palm Springs is a wealthy resort community, it is not snobbish. The atmosphere is that of a friendly village. Some of the finest shops in California are located on tree- and flower-bordered streets of this fascinating little desert city.

Central California, Coastal Region

This region comprises the counties of San Luis Obispo, Monterey, Santa Cruz, San Mateo, Marin, Contra Costra, Alameda and Santa Clara. These counties have a marine type of climate. Mild temperatures prevail the year round and result in the absence of clearly defined seasons although periods of gradual transition are apparent. The region is characterized by low temperatures near the coast and high pressures during the summer, while the interior is characterized by higher temperatures and low pressure. Saturated air passing over the colder water surfaces is cooled until the moisture condenses into fog. Strong westerly winds carry the fog inland. The entire coastal area is subject to fogs which occur most frequently during the evening and early morning in the summer months. The fog is usually "burnt out" by midmorning. These fogs cause a large number of partly clouded days and reduce sunshine to 60 percent of daylight hours. Average annual temperatures are seventy degrees maximum and forty-seven degrees minimum along the coast. Inland they reach into the eighty-degree range. Average rainfall varies from fourteen inches in the valleys to twenty-five inches in the foothills, with most of the rainfall occurring from November to March. During most days clear, sunshiny afternoons prevail. There is no snowfall.

San Luis Obispo. Pop. 14,162. Alt. 215 ft. County Seat of San Luis Obispo County. This is an old mission community, located halfway between Los Angeles and San Francisco, in an area where everything is raised, from wheat and cattle to citrus fruits. Average January temperature is fifty-two degrees and average July temperature is sixty-four degrees, which allows the community 320 growing days per year. This accounts for its marvelous vegetable crops and flower seed industries. The California State Polytechnic College provides an academic and sports background.

One good testimonial for the city and its surrounding community is that a great many ex-servicemen have made this their home, as have quite a large number of retired persons. Deep-sea fishing, clamming and small-game hunting are all close at hand. For quiet and inexpensive living in town or on a small farm, it is worth while looking into a number of fine locations in San Luis Obispo County. A good general rule to follow when looking for retirement locations is to investigate the site where the old missions were established. The original reasons for selecting these sites are still good, practical ones for selecting a retirement location.

The Monterey Peninsula Area, called the world's most spectacular meeting place of land and sea, has long been famous for its natural beauties, renowned pines, invigorating climate, and as a place to live in retirement. More than seventy-five years before the Pilgrims set forth to establish a colony in New England, Rodriguez Cabrillo sailed up the West Coast and sighted this great wooded promontory. Since then many of those who have come to the Peninsula as visitors have fallen in love with it and settled there in retirement. Artists, writers, musicians, intellectuals, business and professional men and ex-military officers from all parts of the United States have chosen this part of California for their retirement. Robert Louis Stevenson made his home there. A seventeen-mile drive, one of the most beautiful scenic roadways in the country, follows the rugged coast. Five golf courses, several of championship caliber, make the Monterey Peninsula the golf capital of the world. The Peninsula has come to mean a way of life and to be a haven for those more interested in living than in merely making a living. They live in Carmel, Monterey, Pacific Grove and in several unincorporated areas. The location of these communities, only a few miles apart, affords easy participation in the assets of each community.

Carmel. Pop. 4,351. Alt. 20 ft. An informal, individualistic community, situated on Carmel Bay on the southwest side of the Peninsula. No concessions, hotels or other commercial activities are permitted to operate at the beach or its immediate area. It has grown from a village of artists and writers to a famous art and literary center of California, while still maintaining the flavor of a village. There are no sidewalks or street lights in the residential area and no house numbers. Villagers go to the post office to get their mail. The Carmel Bach Festival is ranked as one of the major music festivals in the country. Fine arts are fostered by the Art Association, whose members work in ceramics, metal, leather, plastics, wood and other materials. Carmel is said to have one of the most lovely beaches in California. It also has good schools, a library and an art gallery.

Carmel Valley is becoming so popular that farm, orchard and pasture land is rapidly giving way to residential lots. New two-bedroom ranch-type homes are advertised from $10,000 up. There are just about as many people living outside the village limits as in the village, so that the Carmel area has a population of around ten thousand.

Monterey. Pop. 16,200. Alt. 20 ft. This community is rich in tradition and history. It was old California's first capital. Monterey Bay is popular for its deep-sea fishing, shore fishing, fishing from rocks, wharf or boat. The First Theatre in California, established over one hundred years ago, still holds to a regular schedule of productions each week end the year round. Small ranch-type homes are selling at prices ranging from $10,000 to $15,000. While living is extremely pleasant in Monterey, the community does not have quite the same atmosphere as the art colony of Carmel which is only three miles away.

Pacific Grove. Pop. 9,623. Alt. 20 ft. This is another quiet peninsula community for relaxing and refreshing retirement living. The town maintains as a park its own rugged waterfront coastline, municipal swimming pool, sheltered cove beach with marine gardens, boating, picnic and barbecue facilities. It operates a municipal golf links, playground, tennis and roque courts, in addition to its museum and exceptional library. Scientists and students from all over the world come to the Hopkins Marine Station at Pacific Grove.

Los Gatos. Pop. 4,907. Alt. 600 ft. Santa Clara County. If you would like to retire to a delightful, small community at the foothills of the mountains, yet not too far away from the ocean, and within easy distance of a large shopping center, take a look at Los Gatos. It is called the "Gem City of the Foothills." The community is located in sheltered hills at the mouth of a forest canyon, with lovely views and picturesque trails. According to one great English medical authority, Los Gatos has one of the world's most equable climates, like that of Assouan, Egypt. Average summer temperatures are eighty-four degrees maximum to fifty-two degrees minimum, and in the winter months the thermometer stays fairly steady at from fifty-six degrees maximum to forty degrees minimum. This community is recommended often to sufferers of asthma and bronchial troubles as a place where they may find relief. You will find many interesting and friendly people in Los Gatos. New two-bedroom and three-bedroom homes, on 75 x 125 foot lots, were advertised at $9,450 to $10,000.

There is an organized dramatic club, as well as several other social clubs, a public library, active adult education groups. For recreation there is hiking, riding, fishing, hunting, and golf. Santa Cruz on the Pacific Ocean is about twenty miles away. Many residents commute daily to San Jose. Four miles northwest is the community of Saratoga which looks down on orchards as far as the eye can see. In this home and resort center is located Congress Springs, also Villa Montalvo, a haven for artists and writers.

Los Altos. Pop. 12,000. Alt. 200 ft. Santa Clara County. A retirement garden spot within an hour's rail commuting of San Francisco, Los Altos is a ten-minutes' ride by car to Palo Alto, fifteen minutes from Santa Clara, with its well-known college, twenty minutes from San Jose, an hour from the beaches at Santa Cruz. This charming community is one of the choice retirement locations of the entire country. No wonder the late Walter B. Pitkin, the authority on retirement, made his home there. There are no cramped, crowded residential sections. Every home has its garden, its trees; many have orchards and shady groves. Among its oak-studded hills, in cozy cottages and on estates, retired families enjoy gracious living in the California tradition.

Socially, Los Altos is democratic and modern. Much of the

community life centers around the Country Club with its attractive clubhouse, golf course, tennis courts and swimming pool. For college atmosphere and adult educational programs, within half-an-hour's drive you can reach Stanford University, the University of Santa Clara, San Jose State College and San Jose Bible College. Recreation facilities, libraries, museums, social clubs and organizations in nearby communities cover almost everything you can think of.

The climate is ideal with summer temperatures averaging seventy-four degrees maximum and minimum forty-eight degrees, while the average winter maximum is sixty-two degrees and the minimum forty degrees. Rainfall from September to March averages twelve inches, and for the rest of the year about two inches.

Palo Alto. Pop. 25,475. Alt. 20 to 90 ft. Santa Clara County. A community where retired men and women of the arts, sciences, professions, business, including ex-President Herbert Hoover, have chosen to live to enjoy the advantages of a university community and a mild, sunny and dry climate. A distinguished Palo Alto citizen, Kathleen Norris, describes the community as an exquisite, tree-shaded city of beautiful, spacious homes, of gardens and tennis courts, of matchless climate, good neighbors and honest standards.

Stanford University, adjoining Palo Alto, is one of the world's great centers of higher education, cultural and college athletic activities. The Community Center has diversified indoor and outdoor recreational activities for everyone. Adults and children have their own theaters, libraries and swimming pools. The public school system offers adult evening classes in practical and cultural subjects. Adults enjoy civic theater programs, folk dancing, song fests, lectures and concerts. Museums include the Hoover Tower and Library, Stanford Museum, Stanford Art Gallery and the Children's Junior Museum. There are nine parks, three libraries and thirty-two churches.

Average summer maximum temperature is seventy-four degrees, average minimum fifty-two degrees, and for the winter months the average maximum is sixty-two degrees, with forty-five degrees the average minimum. The relative humidity daytime average is 52 to 62 per cent. Average rainfall for the year fifteen inches. New two-bedroom homes were advertised from $10,000 up. For about $20,000 you can buy an attractive modern ranch-type home. Tax rate for the city is $1.302, for the county $4.69 per $100, of assessed valuation.

Palo Alto Yacht Harbor is located three miles from the center of the city on the shore of San Francisco Bay. Many residents commute daily to San Francisco which is only thirty-one miles away. Other residential communities within a six-mile radius are San Carlos, Redwood City, Woodside, Atherton, Melo Park, Los Altos and Mountain View.

Berkeley. Pop. 113,805. Alt. Sea level to 300 ft. Alameda County. On the eastern shore of San Francisco Bay, facing the Golden Gate, is the charming and cultural city of Berkeley. It is situated on a gently-sloping wide plain that stretches upward to a range of tree-clad hills and wooded canyons. While Berkeley is the home of the world-famous University of California, it is more than a college town. It is a suburban city of comfortable homes from which thousands of people commute daily to work in San Francisco. Berkeley is also a thriving business and industrial center. The topography of the land affords a wide choice of residential sites with picturesque views, suiting the means and tastes of various groups. A tunnel through the Berkeley Hills provides quick and easy access to a fertile valley where many retired families have settled.

The beautifully landscaped University of California is the center of numerous musical, dramatic, educational and sports activities. Open-air musical and dramatic performances are given in the Greek Theatre which seats over seven thousand persons. The California Memorial Stadium, seating capacity seventy-eight thousand, is the center of college sports activities. The University offers various correspondence courses and class instruction covering a wide range of subjects of interest to adults.

Other interesting sidelights for Berkeley residents are the Pacific School of Religion, the ten-thousand-acre East Bay Regional Park, the Berkeley Aquatic Park, the Berkeley Yacht Harbor, the Tennis Club, the University Art Museum and Gallery and the Botanical Gardens. Golf is played at Tilden Park the year round. Berkeley residents can also enjoy the advantages of its neighboring city, Oakland, or drive across the bridge to San Francisco. The Berkeley area is a superior retirement location.

Marin County Area. Across the Golden Gate Bridge from San Francisco is the broad triangular peninsula of Marin County. This is a region of garden communities, forests of redwoods and eucalyptus trees, rolling hill ranges, beaches, bays and lagoons, dominated by Mt. Tamalpais. The seacoast and bayshore provide swimming, yachting and motor boating. In the waters of San Francisco Bay bass fishing is famous, and salmon and steelheads are caught. The lakes and streams afford trout fishing. Hunters bring down deer in the fall months; in winter months they shoot ducks. Golf and tennis are played at all seasons of the year. Hiking and horseback riding are popular.

Residents of Marin County enjoy a rich community life amid delightful surroundings. The typical residence stands within a large lot or estate. It would be hard to find a home without a garden. Roses bloom from June to June. Service clubs, women's organizations and other civic groups contribute to the fullness of community life. Fifty churches are established here. A wide variety of events, from fiestas to rodeos, mark the year-round activities. New residential districts are being developed in many localities. Dairy farms and poultry ranches, stock ranges, truck farming and orchards are inviting many rural residents. It is only about half-an-hour's drive to downtown San Francisco. The leading residential areas are:

Sausalito. Pop. 4,828. This area has many delightful homes on wooded hills overlooking the bay.

Mill Valley. Pop. 7,331. This charming community at the base of Mt. Tamalpais, with a good climate for retirement living, is surrounded on three sides by wooded hills. Attractive homes are advertised from $10,000 upwards.

San Rafael. Pop. 13,848. County Seat of Marin County. This popular retirement area is largely populated by commuters to San Francisco. Many attractive homes are priced at $12,000 to $15,000. It is headquarters of Marin Yacht Club, also Municipal Yacht Harbor.

Santa Rosa. Pop. 17,902. Alt. 153 ft. County Seat of Sonoma County. Situated fifty-two miles north of San Francisco, twenty-five miles from the Pacific Ocean, its climate is moderate, winter and summer, with an average temperature of fifty-seven degrees and average rainfall of thirty inches. Trade breezes from the Pacific Ocean prevent hot spells and insure cool summer evenings. More than 90 per cent of the city's residents own their own homes. Pride of ownership is exemplified in well-kept lawns and flower gardens that bloom the year round. The rich soil and gentle climate so delighted Luther Burbank that he chose this place for his experiments in plant breeding. There are eight parks, a city symphony orchestra, churches of all denominations. The famous recreational area of the Russian River and the Redwood Empire is fifteen miles away. Petaluma, one of the foremost poultry districts of the world, is sixteen miles south of Santa Rosa. The slogan of Santa Rosa is: "The city designed for living." If you would like to retire to gardening and relaxation, like so many have already done, take a look at Santa Rosa.

Paradise. Pop. 7,000. Alt. 1,200 to 2,500 ft. Butte County. On the western slope of the Sierra Nevada Mountains, above the floor of the great Sacramento Valley, is a unique settlement appropriately named Paradise. Because the area departs so definitely from the conventional community arrangement, it is difficult to describe just what Paradise is. It isn't a city, though its population is over seven thousand. It isn't a village because it has a business district and civic services geared to its population figures. It isn't a farming colony, yet the growing of garden and orchard crops represents a major source of income. It isn't a health resort but its climate has attracted many who recognize Paradise as an ideal place for healthful retirement. It is a community of homes and gardens; a few are large and impressive but, for the most part, they are modest, attractive cottages on small intensely cultivated plots. Here you will find olives and almonds growing among pine trees.

A number of retired families who have settled there are raising poultry and eleven small experimental farms have proven successful raising chinchillas. One retired citizen writes: "Right at our doors grow the justly famous Paradise apples, grapes, cherries, almonds, the sweetest walnuts and most luscious raspberries I ever ate; and in the streams close by swim fine young trout just waiting to be caught."

There are more than thirty social, fraternal and service organizations and clubs in Paradise, sixteen churches representing leading denominations. A nonprofit, nondenominational sanitarium has recently been opened. Nutritional and physical therapy of the type originated by the Battle Creek, Michigan, Sanitarium is a featured program of the institution. If you are looking for one of the smaller communities featuring rural living, this may be it.

CHAPTER XII

Florida

In survey after survey among people contemplating retirement and in polls taken throughout the nation as to where Americans would most like to live, Florida rates at or near the top in popularity. Only California competes with Florida for first choice, as a retirement spot.

Each year new records are being chalked up in the number of families moving to Florida to take up permanent residence, as well as in the number of tourists who visit the state. United States Census figures show that the population of Florida is growing three times faster than the national average. If the state maintains its present rate of increase in the number of permanent residents, the population of Florida could easily double during the next twenty years.

If you take a look at a map of the United States, you will see that Florida lies farther south than any state of the Union. The northern boundary of Florida is one hundred miles south of San Diego, California. The sweeping curve of the Atlantic Coast pushes Florida directly south of eastern Ohio, while Florida's northwestern boundary lies directly south of Chicago. Miami is the closest of any American city to the geographic center of the population of the Western Hemisphere. Within eight hours, by air, Miami can be reached from the entire East and Midwest, eastern Canada, Central America, the Caribbean, Colombia and Venezuela.

Climate is one of Florida's great assets. While the greater part of the nation is freezing and the North and East are blanketed in snow, the January average temperature in southern Florida is sixty-eight degrees and for north Florida, fifty-four degrees. Winters in Florida are nearly fifty degrees warmer than in the northern states. Florida has from five to six hours of sunshine per day in winter, while the northern part of the United States has less than three hours per day. During the summer months the highest temperatures are no higher than those of New York or Chicago. July average temperature for the whole state of Florida is eighty-one and eight-tenths degrees. Florida's hot days are relieved by afternoon semitropical rains of short duration that cool the atmosphere so that evenings are almost always cool. In addition, prevailing breezes from the ocean speed evaporation of perspiration and keep the body cool. Sunstrokes and heat prostration in Florida are unknown.

Florida offers other advantages for the retired person. A modern two-bedroom house costs about 30 to 40 per cent less to build than the same type of house would cost in the Northern states. Comfortable, simple, small homes can be built on the outskirts of cities and towns or in rural sections for as little as six thousand dollars.

There is no Florida State Income Tax. Personal and property taxes are low. Farm homesteads up to 160 acres, and city dwellings on lots of half an acre or smaller, are allowed "Homestead Exemption" up to $5,000. Since assessed valuations seldom represent more than 50 to 75 per cent of the actual cost, you can own a costly house and have little tax to pay. City, county and other taxes are moderate.

It is not fair to judge Florida from the publicity of show girls and the "sports" who crowd Miami, the horse-race followers who flock to Hialeah, the millionaires hibernating in Palm Beach. These people congregate along the Gold Coast, a narrow coastal strip stretching 75 miles from Palm Beach to Miami. Florida is more than 450 miles wide at its northern boundary, 150 miles wide across the middle of the Peninsula. From north to south it extends more than 500 miles. In this vast territory there are many excellent communities for retirement. The majority of permanent residents in Florida are quiet, ordinary, middle-class Americans.

What about hurricanes? The chances of hurricane-force winds reaching the Florida coast in any given year are, for Miami, about one in seven; for Daytona Beach, one in thirty; for St. Petersburg, one in twenty; for Jacksonville, one in fifty. The United States Weather Bureau at Miami says: "Damage totals have been declining over the past 25 years, due to 'Hurricane Building Codes' and other concerted efforts to protect property. Protective measures consist primarily in building 'hurricane proof' homes according to the codes, and staying in them during the storm." If a building is properly constructed, with the proper type of roof, and is securely anchored to the proper kind of foundation, it will not sustain serious damage in a hurricane of major intensity. It is apparent that Florida folks have no fear of hurricanes. If one does come along, the Weather Bureau gives from three to four days' warning, folks stay away from the waterfront and settle down in their homes until the storm passes by. The months of greatest hurricane frequency are September and October.

The rapid growth of Florida's tourist business, now becoming a year round activity, increase in agricultural activities, industrial development and business expansion, comfortable climate the year round, wide choice of inexpensive recreational opportunities, low cost of living, friendliness of residents to retired persons—all add up to new and expanding opportunities for retired people.

East Coast Section

Coral Gables. Pop. 19,837. Alt. 10 ft. Dade County. The city of Coral Gables is not a tourist resort. It is a refined and preplanned community of comfortable homes set in park-

like surroundings. People make Coral Gables their permanent home and live in houses mostly of Mediterranean-type
design, though zoning permits French and Dutch Colonial
architectural designs in certain sections, and in other subdivisions, adaptations of West Indian, African and Chinese
add a foreign note. There are no saloons, no bars and practically no facilities for tourists. The name Coral Gables is
well known as a "hundred million dollar" real estate development of George E. Merrick at the end of World War I.
Through the years, the high standards of building and land-
scaping conceived by Merrick and his original city planners
have been adhered to. Though Coral Gables is at the back
door of Miami, it is not "tourist" as is Miami and Miami
Beach.

Coral Gables is a university city, the home of the University of Miami, the cultural center of south Florida. The
campus contains the Bing Theatre production center of the
Drama Department, Lowe Art Gallery, Playing Field for
college sports events. Coral Gables has its own one-hundred-
piece symphony orchestra and active little theater group,
music and garden clubs, concerts, and over fifty social and
service organizations. The Coral Gables Library and Community House, Art Center and Country Club all contribute
to good living. You can fish in Coral Gables' canals or move
over to Miami Beach where some of the world's finest fishing
is available. Salvadore Park maintains tennis courts, shuffleboard, horseshoe, croquet and other adult recreation facilities. Golf can be played at Coral Gables Country Club,
Riviera Golf Course and Miami-Biltmore Country Club.
Since Coral Gables is adjacent to Miami, local residents have
the opportunity to participate in the cultural and social life
of Miami and Coconut Grove, and to take advantage of the
entertainment, recreational shopping, beach, parks and
sports facilities of Miami and Miami Beach. One great ad-

vantage is that one can always withdraw from the tourist stream to the relaxing tranquillity of life at Coral Gables.

From a climatic standpoint, the area occupies on the Atlantic Coast a position similar to that of Los Angeles on the Pacific Coast. Coral Gables, however, has no smog, no fog. During the winter months Coral Gables is about twelve degrees warmer than Los Angeles. The average January temperature for Coral Gables is sixty-eight degrees and for Los Angeles fifty-six degrees. The summer average temperature for Coral Gables is eighty-one degrees, for Los Angeles seventy degrees. The Los Angeles climate is much drier. Average annual rainfall for Los Angeles is fifteen inches and for Coral Gables fifty-five inches. It rains only 39 days a year in Los Angeles compared with 134 days in Coral Gables. Sunshine during daylight hours in Coral Gables is 66 per cent, in Los Angeles 70 per cent. Coral Gables is approximately six hundred miles nearer to the equator than Los Angeles. Year-round house rentals start at about $110 per month. The average price of a new modern, custom-built, two-bedroom home ranges from $14,500 to $17,000 and a three-bedroom, two-bath home from $17,000 up.

Fort Lauderdale. Pop. 36,328. Alt. 10 ft. County Seat of Broward County. This is a city of waterways, rivers, bays, canals and inlets, with the Atlantic Ocean at its front door. There are about two hundred miles of ocean, river and canal waterfronts within the city limits, bordered by tropical gardens, palms, lawns and lovely homes. Many wealthy residents with homes on the waterfront keep their yachts and pleasure craft tied up to private docks in their front yards. Other yachtsmen tie up their craft at Bahia-Mar Yacht Basin where they find every provision for pleasant living. Fort Lauderdale has long been famous as a yachtsman's and fisherman's paradise. Both inshore and deep-sea fishing rank with the best in Florida. The city is in the heart of the Gold

Coast, twenty-five miles north of Miami. The Gulf Stream is only two miles offshore. New River, which flows through the center of the city, is connected by a canal with Lake Okeechobee. Hugh Taylor Birch State Park and Pan-American State Park are within a few miles of the city.

There are three local golf courses, a large shuffleboard club, a community center with day and evening adult programs for canasta, bridge, dancing, arts and crafts. Surfbathing and sun bathing can be enjoyed the year round on a five-mile ocean beach. Fort Lauderdale's library has twenty-five thousand volumes. There are thirty-one churches representing sixteen religious denominations. For those who desire excitement and activities, there is always something going on like regattas, beauty contests, concerts, festivals, fishing tournaments, forums. And Miami is only a half-hour drive from the city.

Fort Lauderdale is popular as a retirement location with New Englanders, New Yorkers and Middle Westerners. The standard of living is rather high and requires an income of at least $100 a week to enjoy living in this community.

As to climate, January temperatures average seventy-six degrees maximum to sixty degrees minimum, and for July, ninty degrees maximum to seventy-three degrees minimum, with the usual onshore sea breezes to temper the hot weather. Suitable retirement homes are priced from $10,000 to $20,000 according to type of construction and location. If you want a waterfront home with a private dock be prepared to pay up to $40,000 to $50,000 for this luxury.

Hollywood. Pop. 14,351. Broward County. This is a modern city located seven miles south of Fort Lauderdale. It is an attractive resort community with a six-mile ocean beach and wide palm-bordered streets and many attractive homes. Seven parks provide facilities for shuffleboard, tennis and other recreation. There are two eighteen-hole golf courses.

Hollywood has an annual fishing tournament and the Kennel Club holds dog races. The Baltimore Orioles have their spring training camp here. In Hollywood you can enjoy quiet living in the shadow of Greater Miami which is only fifteen miles to the south.

Daytona Beach. Pop. 30,187. Alt. 7 ft. Volusia County. Permanent residents of this summer-winter resort community are about equally divided between those who have come to establish a retirement residence and those who earn their living catering to the needs and tastes of summer and winter tourists. Parks with palms and flowers, residential streets shaded by large moss-hung oaks, magnolias and palms give the community a restful beauty.

You may live in Daytona Beach as luxuriously as anywhere in Florida. Many wealthy persons have estates here and you can pay $60,000 for an oceanfront home. You may also live in the Daytona Beach area as simply and as economically as you choose. A cozy cottage with two-bedrooms, on a 55 x 132 foot plot, was offered at $6,650. Several modern masonry two- and three-bedroom homes, with red tile roofs, were selling for $11,500. The majority of permanent residents are middle-class Americans who enjoy informal living in the Florida manner.

Daytona Beach attracts over thirty thousand visitors in the winter and almost as many in the summer. Tourists come from the Northeastern states in winter and from south Florida, Georgia, Tennessee and the Midwest to enjoy cool breezes during the summer. January average maximum temperatures are seventy degrees with minimum temperature of fifty degrees. In July average maximum temperatures are eighty-nine degrees, with seventy-one degrees the average minimum. Afternoon showers and pronounced sea breezes during the summer months keep temperatures from soaring to uncomfortable levels. Average annual rainfall is forty-eight inches. Ocean water mean temperatures in January are 60.3 degrees and in July 78.9 degrees.

There is a mile-long promenade adjoining the famous beach. The beach itself is five hundred feet wide at low tide and twenty-three miles long providing all-year swimming, sunbathing, motoring on the beach and sand sailing in sailboats equipped with wheels. Other daily diversions include shuffleboard, lawn bowling, golf, skeet shooting. Fishing facilities include deep-sea fishing from chartered boats, surf casting and fishing from bridges which span the Halifax River. Thousands of motor yachts and commercial craft pass through the heart of the city. A bathing-beauty contest, golf tournaments, Fourth of July Frolics and a $10,000 fishing tournament are annual events. Dozens of women's clubs, fraternal organizations and social groups are represented. There are outdoor and indoor community concerts. This is a retirement location where you can take your choice of an active community life or live in quiet seclusion with neighbors and friends.

Ormond Beach, eight miles north of Daytona, where the late John D. Rockefeller had his winter home for many years, is a popular cottage and resort colony. The once Rockefeller winter home is now a private girl's school. The golf course where he gave out new dimes is one of the best courses in Florida. Tomaka State Park is nearby.

Central Section

Lakeland. Pop. 30,851. Alt, 227 ft. Polk County. A city of well-kept homes amid rolling hills in almost the exact center of Florida. Lakeland is located on one of the highest elevations in the state and is built around twelve lakes which are within its corporate limits. Temperature in January is seventy-two degrees maximum to fifty-one degrees minimum, and for July ninety-one degrees maximum to seventy-two degrees minimum. Sunshine during daylight hours is 62 per cent. Annual average rainfall is fifty inches.

The United Brotherhood of Carpenters and Joiners of America have a national multimillion dollar home on the shores of Lake Gibson on the outskirts of town. The home is a small community center and includes such facilities as a hospital, theater, laundry, eighteen-hole golf course, etc. Lakeland's million-dollar Civic Center on the shores of Lake Mirror is the focal point for recreational activities, including lawn bowling, shuffleboard courts, tennis, dances, card parties and teas. Florida Southern College, the only college with an orange grove for a campus, has exceptionally fine schools of music, art and dramatics. It is architecturally famous for its college buildings designed by Frank Lloyd Wright. Lakeland has a little theater group, Civic Music Concert Association and two eighteen-hole golf courses. Munn Park has facilities for horseshoe pitching, card and checker playing, while Municipal Park has barbeque pits, picnic tables and a swimming pool. The Detroit Tigers have winter training quarters here. The Orange Cup World Championship Motorboat Regatta on Lake Hollingsworth is held in March.

There is a heavy concentration of orange groves in the Lakeland area and the Florida Citrus Commission has its headquarters here. Fishing is good in the many nearby lakes.

Winter Park. Pop. 8,250. Alt. 100 ft. Orange County. This charming community, known as "The City of Homes," is also famous as "the town that became a university." As one of its well-known author-residents writes: "When you become part of the Winter Park community, you automatically become a student of Rollins College whether you register in the college or are just a citizen entitled to vote in the next election. The churches, clubs, halls have all become allied departments of Rollins College. Famous men and women are delivering lectures and presiding over discussions in them every day and every evening." The climate, location, natural attractiveness, together with the fine citizens who are attracted to Winter Park, combine to make it a foremost spot for retirement.

From November to May the days are usually dry and sunny. The average temperature for this period is sixty-five degrees. The nights are cool with the winter climate similar to the sunny fall weather of the North. The temperatures from May to October average seventy-five degrees, with cooling showers and lake breezes to moderate the highs of summer heat. It is an outdoor climate the entire year where elderly people add years to their life's span. Winter Park has become the Florida home of a large number of authors, painters, musicians, educators, clergymen and nonprofessional people whose tastes and interests tend to music, art, drama and lectures.

Winter Park is located in the citrus and lake section of central Florida. It has sixteen lakes within the city limits. Homes are attractive and individual, representing Mediterranean, Spanish, Colonial, Cape Cod and other styles. Comfortable two- and three-bedroom homes range from $9,000 to $25,000. Lower-priced homes, not shacks, are available in the rural sections adjacent to the city. And, of course, large estate homes are available for those who desire to live on a more sumptuous scale. Many suitable building sites are still available.

The life of the community centers around Rollins College. The Rollins Adult Education Program includes varied series of lectures covering a wide range of material. A unique *Animated Magazine,* published each February, presents leaders in literature and world affairs who appear in person to read their contributions. The Town Hall Series also presents a varied program by noted lecturers, musicians and entertainers. Dramatic productions by both professional and collegiate casts are presented at the Annie Russell Theatre and at the Fred Stone Laboratory Theatre. The Civic Music Association presents a series of concerts at the Orlando Auditorium. A Bach Festival is held in March. The University Club of six hundred members has over one hundred listed in "Who's Who in America." The Shuffleboard Club, with over four hundred members, holds weekly social meetings, tournaments and occasional picnics. Winter Park's Women's Club has a membership of over five hundred. The Public Library at Rollins College, Beal-Maltbie Shell Museum, Kraft Azalea Gardens, Mead Botanical Gardens, are features of interest. Golf, boating, bathing, fishing, hunting, intercollegiate athletic contests, shuffleboard, croquet and card games offer additional recreation and entertainment for residents and visitors.

Orlando. Pop. 52,367. Located six miles south of Winter Park is the largest inland city in Florida. It is a popular residential and resort center that has attracted an enthusiastic retired colony. There are thirty lakes within the city limits, more lakes than in any other city in Florida. Orchestras, the Central Florida Exposition, concerts, a little theater group and the cultural facilities of nearby Rollins College offer a well-rounded program of retirement activities. Pleasant country retirement five-room homes at the edge of town were offered for $5,500. Homes at the lakeside on 150 x 200 feet plots could be bought for $15,500 to $35,000. The Washington Senators have a spring training camp there. Orlando Country Club has an eighteen-hole golf course, and there is a Yacht Club on Lake Conway.

Gainesville. Pop. 26,861. Alt. 185 ft. County Seat of Alachua County. You may retire from your business, work or profession but you need not retire from life, from cultural, recreational and sports activities if you locate in this college town in central Florida. You will find a bonus in the University of Florida located at Gainesville. The University offers courses in many fields for people of retirement age. Your experience in life meets all the admission requirements to enroll for a course in two hundred fields of knowledge through ten colleges and four schools of the University. Retired persons who plan on settling down on a small or large farm can benefit from courses offered by the College of Agriculture. Noted lecturers, authors and musicians regularly make appearances at activities sponsored by the various University groups. Other active cultural groups are the Civic Music Association, Fine Arts Association, Little Theatre, Philharmonic Society and Twentieth Century Club, as well as the Florida State Museum and numerous civic and social organizations and clubs.

Gainesville has a full-time recreational program. There is an eighteen-hole golf course at the Country Club, skeet shooting at the Gun Club. Close by Gainesville are many fine fishing lakes famous for their bass. An abundance of quail, turkey, duck, rabbit, deer and bear await sportsmen.

The hill country of this area enjoys low humidity, a factor appreciated by sufferers of bronchial ailments. Maximum average temperature in January is sixty-eight degrees, the minimum, forty-six degrees—somewhat cooler in winter than points further south. In July maximum temperatures reach ninety degrees and drop to seventy-one degrees in the evenings. Average annual rainfall is forty-nine inches. The United States Veteran's Administration selected Gainesville as the site for one of its regional hospitals. Agricultural products of the area include cattle raising, poultry, truck farming, citrus orchards and the commercial growing of flowers and bulbs. Several trailer parks are located in Gainesville; many occupants are year-round residents. Two-bedroom homes were priced at $7,900 to $15,000 and three-bedroom homes from $13,500 to $22,400. A 102-acre farm with six-room house, ten miles from Gainesville, was selling for $11,000.

West Coast Section

Naples. Pop. 1,500. Alt. 10 ft. Collier County. The Tamiami Trail from Miami through the Everglades reaches to Naples, a pleasant resort community, the most southerly town on the west coast. Naples has for years been known for its fishing and its hospitality toward fishermen. A one thousand-foot fishing pier extends into the Gulf. In addition to pier and surf fishing, there are many boats available for charter, manned by experienced guides. A few miles south of Naples are the Ten Thousand Islands, a fisherman's paradise, which stretch southward for fifty miles along the coast of the Everglades National Park.

Naples is growing very rapidly and a number of retired folk have settled here. There are indications that it will develop into a community populated by the upper-income group. While there are a few houses selling for about $9,000, it takes from $12,000 to $15,000 and up to buy one of the better houses available. Two recent subdivision developments are at Crayton Cove with its smart shops and docking facilities for cruisers, and at Port Royal with its $30,000 to $50,000 houses. Architecturally, many of the mansions in the Naples area resemble those of Palm Beach.

A series of concerts with top talent are presented at the high school auditorium. Swamp Buggy Day is a colorful event featuring races with swamp buggies. Besides fishing and golf, other recreation facilities include surf bathing, hunting, shelling, boating, skeet shooting and shuffleboard.

Average temperature for January is seventy-five degrees maximum to fifty-five degrees minimum, and for July ninety degrees maximum to seventy-three degrees minimum. Average annual rainfall is fifty-four inches. The cost of living is lower than at Miami, slightly lower than at Sarasota, but higher than at St. Petersburg.

Fort Meyers. Pop. 13,195, Alt. 15 ft. County Seat of Lee County. Known as the "City of Palms" because its streets are shaded with over sixty varieties of palm trees, Fort Meyers is a desirable retirement spot for year-round outdoor living. The city is located on the Caloosahatchee River, about fifteen miles from the Gulf of Mexico, and has a climate that is classified as subtropical. Thomas A. Edison selected Fort Meyers, in 1886, for his winter home. Edison was responsible for the planting of the great variety of tropical palms, shrubs and flowers which give the city a tropical character. Henry Ford also bought an estate alongside his lifelong friend Edison. Many resort islands with fine beaches are in the Fort Meyers area, including Boca Grande, La Costa, Captiva, Sanibel, Pine and Fort Meyers Beach. These are nationally famed as shell-hunting grounds. The rivers and inlets of the surrounding territory provide excellent fishing for silver king tarpon, trout, red fish and snook.

The Municipal Auditorium seats six hundred. Evans Park provides facilities for shuffleboard, roque and tennis, and a swimming pool and chess pavilion. The city has beautiful churches, good schools, eighteen-hole golf course and an art school. During the winter season a series of concerts and lectures add to the cultural life of the community. While the chief source of income is from the tourist trade, there are a great many gladioli farms and citrus orchards. Living costs are said to be lower than on Florida's east coast and very comfortable living can be enjoyed for about $175 to $200 a month. Temperatures range from an average of sixty-five degrees in winter to eighty-two degrees in summer. Prevailing winds from the Gulf cool off the summer evenings. Chances of a hurricane in this area are about one in twelve.

Fort Meyers has a good yacht basin and is the terminus of the Cross State Canal, a 120-mile canal connecting Fort Meyers on the Gulf of Mexico with Stuart on the Atlantic Ocean. Ten-acre farm homesites, fronting a paved road leading to the coast, six miles from the city, served by electricity and bus service, were advertised in early 1953 for $2,500. Other real estate prices are about the same as for Sarasota.

Venice. Pop. 2,000. Alt. 10 ft. Sarasota County. If you would like to be part of a pleasant community that is on its way up as a resort and retirement spot, take a look at Venice. About thirty years ago, Dr. Fred H. Albee, a famous orthopedic surgeon of New York, conceived the idea of building a city around a modern hospital in the center of the mild west coast climate belt. Dr. Albee selected Venice as the ideal spot and engaged a famous town planner to lay out the ideal town. The Brotherhood of Locomotive Engineers acquired vast holdings of land and started to build Venice according to the original plans, but abandoned the project during the great depression of the 1930's. In recent years, Venice has been rediscovered as a resort and retirement location and the community is regaining its place on the popularity map. Its population has increased 100 per cent since 1950. Venice is located directly on the Gulf between Sarasota and Fort Meyers with a seven-mile beach in the town's front yard. The nationally known Kentucky Military Institute maintains winter headquarters in Venice. The Florida Medical Center, founded by Dr. Albee, is staffed with physicians and surgeons from leading hospitals. There is not yet much in the way of formal entertainment or organized excitement. Fishing and swimming are excellent. There is a Country Club with a nine-hole golf course, a woman's club, little theater group and a city park with shuffleboard courts.

Homes can be purchased from $6,000 up depending upon location and type of construction. For $10,000 to $15,000 you can buy a modern home in a good location. Many retired teachers, army officers and business people have settled here. Artists, writers and others interested in creative arts and crafts have also been attracted to Venice. Situated in the practically frost-free belt, the surrounding countryside is ideal for truck farming, cattle raising and subtropical fruit growing. There are good opportunities to establish small businesses and services catering to the needs of tourists. A retired couple can live comfortably here on an income of $2,400 a year.

Sarasota. Pop. 18,896. Alt. 5 ft. County Seat of Sarasota County. Sportsmen, artists, writers and professional people as well, as seekers after health and good retirement locations, all find what they are looking for in this friendly community.

Sarasota has miles of sandy beaches along Sarasota Bay and outlying keys or islands that extend twenty miles north and south fronting the Bay. On these keys are beautifully planned residential subdivisions. Siesta Key, Long Boat Key and St. Armands Key are as good retirement spots as you will find anywhere in the United States of America.

Sarasota also claims the honor of being the art center of Florida. The Ringling Art Museum, now state owned, is said to rank second to the Metropolitan Museum of Art in New York City in size and value of its contents. The Art Association, Summer Festival of Arts, several art schools, daily classes in shellcraft—all provide stimulus for those who follow some form of art as a hobby. The Players, an accomplished little theater group, Palm Tree Playhouse, Community Concerts Association, Choral Society, Music Club, Symphony Orchestra, all present full programs. Near the Museum is the Jungle Gardens which features exotic plants and bird life. Mayakka River State Park, one of the most tropical woodlands in the state, is sixteen miles east of the city. Four fishing tournaments are held during the year. Sarasota has excellent facilities for yachts, sailing craft and motor boats. The Recreation Center has facilities for bowling on the green, shuffleboard, card parties, tennis and indoor games. The famous public Lido Beach Casino has shuffleboard courts, a swimming pool and a golf course. There are two additional eighteen-hole golf courses in the city. The Boston Red Sox hold spring training here and play exhibition games. Ringling Circus makes its winter home in Sarasota.

As to climate, the winter is mild with daily temperatures around seventy-two degrees maximum and fifty-three degrees minimum. Daily average summer temperatures are ninety degrees maximum to seventy-two degrees minimum with cool breezes at night. Homes on the keys and around the bay water front run from $10,700 to $40,000 depending upon type of construction and location. New two-bedroom homes in recent subdivisions can be bought for $13,000. Older homes in good condition further inland cost about $7,000 and up for a two-bedroom home. A thirty-two-acre ranch was offered at $14,500. For a ten-acre orange grove just outside the city limits the price was $20,000. Several income-producing properties were listed ranging from duplex homes at $10,000 to apartment buildings for $90,000. There are several trailer parks on the outskirts of the city with rental space at $15 to $40 a month. In Sarasota County, agriculture is an important industry. Cattle, celery, dairy products, vegetables, citrus fruits, honey, litchi nuts and trees are the main products.

St. Petersburg. Pop. 96,738. Alt. 20 ft. Pinellas County. Many thousands of retired men and women have taken up residence in St. Petersburg to regain their health, to lengthen their lives and to enjoy the companionship of people of their own age who seek the same kind of healthful living and recreation. The Retirement Research Division, Florida State Improvement Commission, recently made a survey among retired persons living in St. Petersburg. More than eight out of ten of the retired persons are from other states of the nation. Over 42 per cent of the residents interviewed formerly lived in New England, New York, Pennsylvania, New Jersey, West Virginia, Delaware and Maryland. Over 27 per cent came from the Middle-Western states. Retired men and women reported an average income of $158 per month per family or individual. Half of them had monthly incomes of less than $120 a month. Most of the persons interviewed had retired voluntarily. Cards, gardening, fishing and shuffleboard were the most popular recreational activities. Over 75 per cent preferred to own their own homes rather than rent. Nearly 62 per cent had not visited a doctor during the preceding six months and 82 per cent had not summoned a doctor.

Asked why they had decided to spend their later years in St. Petersburg, most people mentioned the climate, its healthfulness and the recommendation of relatives and friends. In answer to another question, "What do you think is best about St. Petersburg?" the climate and the friendliness of its people were mentioned most often. Most retired people were enthusiastic about the community and found little to criticize. More than any other city, St. Petersburg has gone out of its way to attract and entertain elderly people. Thousands of green benches line the downtown sidewalks and city parks. Ramps are provided for wheel chairs at the curbs of major street intersections. St. Petersburg's Shuffleboard Club (world's largest) with over seven thousand members is another famous institution.

Climate is a great asset especially for older folks. The average mean temperature for the year is seventy-two degrees. For the winter months it is seventy degrees maximum and fifty-two degrees minimum and for the summer months between eighty-nine degrees maximum and seventy-three degrees minimum. The sun shines, on an average, 360 days a year, with 6½ hours of sunshine per day during winter months. Annual rainfall is forty-nine inches, only one-sixth of which occurs during the winter months. Relative humidity averages 80 per cent at night, drops to about 50 per cent in midafternoon.

Mirror Lake in the downtown section is a recreational center offering all manner of outdoor activities from shuffleboard (over two hundred courts) to card playing, checkers, chess, horseshoe pitching and similar forms of recreation. The Municipal Pier extending a half-mile into Old Tampa Bay is a popular spot for fishermen and a favorite social center. Treasure Island and Pass-a-Grille Beach have their own residential beach communities. St. Petersburg has over four hundred social, cultural and hobby clubs and organizations where one may meet others with similar interests. The New York Yankees and the St. Louis Cardinals maintain spring training camps in St. Petersburg. There are four eighteen-hole golf courses within the city limits, excellent fishing facilities, fine boating, yachting, swimming and sun bathing.

Among the large number of homes advertised for sale were small economy homes built on "your own lot" for $6,380; new two-bedroom, masonry homes from $7,650 to $15,000; distinctive three-bedroom, tile roof, landscaped in new developments from $13,000 to $16,000; Gulf-beach and bay-front homes from $10,000 to $35,000.

Clearwater. Pop. 15,581. Alt. 75 ft. County Seat of Pinellas County. Situated on the coast between the Gulf of Mexico and Old Tampa Bay with the highest coastal elevation of any city in the state, it is practically surrounded by salt water which assures a temperate climate throughout the year. Average temperature for the winter is from sixty to eighty degrees and for the summer seventy to ninety degrees, with temperate breezes drifting back and forth across the city. Clearwater enjoys more hours of sunshine than any other city in the eastern United States. Relative humidity averages 54 per cent during the daytime. There are practically two springs, two distinct seasons of new vegetation growth—February to March and June to July. A committee of the American Medical Association is said to have selected this area as the healthiest spot in the entire United States.

Clearwater is a popular vacation resort both winter and summer. It has excellent facilities for year-round bathing, boating, fishing, tennis, golf, lawn bowling and shuffleboard. The Tourist Center provides opportunities for newcomers to meet and get acquainted. There are one hundred clubs and organizations offering participation in music, art, dramatics and social and recreational activities. The Gulf Coast Art Center at Belleair maintains programs of exhibitions, lectures and instruction in painting, silk screening, woodworking and ceramics. The Clearwater Art Group also sponsors exhibitions and lectures. A series of musical programs is presented by the Community Concert Association. Since Clearwater is surrounded by the residential communities of Belleair, Dunedin and Safety Harbor, the facilities of these communities are easily accessible. St. Petersburg is only twenty-one miles away. There are four golf courses in the area, all eighteen-hole, open all year. Clearwater is the spring training camp for the Philadelphia Phillies. Safety Harbor has mineral springs offering therapeutic values. Clearwater Beach, one of the best bathing beaches on the West Coast, has a fishing pier and a yacht club.

Attractive homes range in price from $10,000 up to ultramodern three-bedroom homes in the $35,000 class. Small two-bedroom homes outside the city are listed at $7,000. In the Belleair Estates, a community which is restricted, home sites range from $1,000 to $30,000 and plans for construction of homes must be approved. Other homes in the town of Belleair are priced at $15,000 and up.

Retirement Community Developments

Several retirement communities are being promoted in various sections of Florida, usually in the outskirts of well-established and growing cities and towns. They provide for low-cost living for persons with modest incomes, pensions and annuities.

The sponsors of these properties assemble large-acre tracts which they subdivide usually into quarter-acre home site lots. The lots provide room for a small home, vegetable garden and a dozen or more fruit trees. Lots are priced from around $500 to under $1,000, depending on their location and size. In some developments lots are also available for business sites.

The developers usually have standardized plans for homes containing one- two- or three-bedrooms, bath with shower, kitchen–living room combination, a breezeway and carport. Developers will build these homes for as little as $4,290 up to $8,950, depending upon the size, design and location of the home.

Recreational and social activities center around the community club house and the facilities of the nearby towns, beaches or lakes.

Here are a few of the outstanding retirement communities:

LEISURE CITY, fifteen miles southwest of Miami. Eventually will contain nearly six thousand homes.

PLANTATION ESTATES, on Lake Monroe in central Florida.

FLORIDANA BEACH, a suburb of Melbourne.

TYRONE GARDENS, in St. Petersburg.

PARADISE PARK, TROPIC ACRES, HARMONY HEIGHTS and SUNLAND

GARDENS, near Fort Pierce—Over two thousand retired families will live in these four communities.

DELRAY GARDEN ESTATES, in Delray Beach.

ROYAL PALM ESTATES, adjacent to West Palm Beach.

FLORIDA TROPICAL HOME SITES and LITTLE FARMS, near Venice.

ELLINOR GARDENS, at Ormond Beach. When fully completed will provide living accommodations for more than two thousand persons.

FLORASOTA GARDENS, at Sarasota. Offers furnished apartment and cottage units.

PALM BEACH SHORES, near Palm Beach. Located on an island.

FLORIDA ACRES and DRUID HEIGHTS, at Clearwater.

The postal clerks maintain a Postal Colony Company, at Clermont, that operates a large acreage of citrus groves for retired members. The Colony does not own or rent houses or sell home sites.

Penny Farms is a model community for retired clergymen and their families, and for retired YMCA workers. A resident buys a residential annuity costing $3,500 which entitles him or her to a home as long as he or she lives. At death, the apartment-home reverts to the Christian Herald Association, operators of the project, and is available to a newcomer.

The Brotherhood of Railway Engineers sponsors a retirement colony for members in Venice.

The United Brotherhood of Carpenters and Joiners of America operates a national home for retired members at Lakeland.

At St. Cloud there is a retirement community of war veterans.

The Sponsored Neighborhood Village

The state of Florida has a special interest in helping retired people to live happily within its borders. Mr. Walter E. Keys, Director of the Florida State Improvement Commission, advocates the establishment of sponsored Neighborhood Villages. In brief, the plan proposes that "large employers, labor unions and other interests sponsor communities in Florida built to meet the needs of retired people. The houses or apartments would be of good quality, and the monthly rental would be low. This would be accomplished through long-term financing at low interest rates without speculative profit. Each village would have a manager to direct recreational and social programs and to take care of maintenance—but every resident would be independent, free to come and go as he wished.

"A Neighborhood Village would be made up of perhaps 500 or more living units. Nearby would be a town or city where most shopping needs could be satisfied. Radiating outward from a community center, the houses, apartments, and dormitories would be situated on lots of varying size —some with space for garden plots, all with ample well-developed lawns and flower plots. Recreation, adult education, social and religious interests, and crafts or other hobbies would be carried on, permitting all residents to enjoy a full and satisfying life.

"The Neighborhood Village Plan has been suggested by the Florida State Improvement Commission in the hope that it will give threefold benefits: to retirees and their families, who will get quality low-cost housing and an excellent climate; to unions and employers through its labor-relations and public-relations value; and to the state of Florida, since it may head off a potential social problem."

CHAPTER XIII

Georgia, South Carolina and North Carolina

Nature has favored this area with a moderate climate. It is not quite so warm as Florida, not so cold in winter as New England, and does not have the wide range of annual climatic extremes of the Northern and Central states.

Along the coastal plain section, the mean temperature in January averages sixty degrees maximum to thirty-eight degrees minimum. Oranges and grapefruit grow in the sheltered seacoast regions as far north as Cape Hatteras. Cold waves are of short duration and practically no snow falls. There is no record of zero temperatures in any coastal county and hard freezes are rare.

In the interior sections, winters are cool enough to be invigorating. Snow almost never falls before Christmas and many winters have none at all. When snow does fall it disappears quickly. A series of frostless zones, called the "thermal belt," are found in the Carolinas where the winter climate is milder than that of the surrounding mountain areas, with the temperature on the slopes from one to fourteen degrees warmer than at the top of the mountains or the valleys at the bottom. These favored locations are popular as both summer and winter resort areas.

Summers in the coastal counties are tempered by ocean breezes. July mean temperatures average around eighty degrees. In the interior, summer temperatures generally are about ten degrees warmer than in the coastal plains, but at rises of altitude of one thousand feet the temperature usually is five degrees lower. That's why the nights are cool in the mountains during July and August.

Georgia, South Carolina and North Carolina offer an abundance of small, congenial communities where retired couples can find good friends and may live in pleasant surroundings without high costs. Those who wish to do a little farming, or to raise poultry or turkeys, can find many opportunities to do so. Average land prices are not high. In some localities there are opportunities for part-time or full-time work in the many new industries locating throughout this part of the South.

In selecting a site for retirement, you can choose between beautiful mountain areas and moss-draped, low-country near and along the seacoast. Modest incomes are frequently sufficient for economical living, particularly in rural areas not fully developed and in areas that are past their population peaks. There are many places where life can be taken as quietly or as vigorously as anyone could wish—and in which retirement life can be budgeted to almost any income.

Georgia

Albany. Pop. 31,155. Alt. 215 ft. County Seat of Dougherty County. Albany is located on the banks of the Flint River, which is one of Georgia's largest streams, in the southern coastal plain section of the state. The climate is characterized by short, mild winters and long warm summers. Only about three-fourths of an inch of snow falls during the year. The normal temperature for the winter season is sixty-two degrees maximum, forty-two degrees minimum. Some winters are so mild that very little heat is needed in the house. Mean summer temperatures reach ninety degrees during the day and drop to the low seventies at night. Heat is not oppressive, owing to the relatively low humidity which averages 50 to 63 per cent. Sunstrokes and heat prostrations are unknown. Rainfall averages forty-nine inches for the year.

The Civic Music Association brings nationally known artists to Albany each season. Several plays are presented by the little theater group. Albany's Male Chorus is outstanding. A civic drama association, philharmonic orchestra and several stage shows provide for cultural activities. As to recreational facilities, Radium Springs, one of the South's best resorts, located four miles south of Albany, affords swimming, golfing and fishing. Chehaw State Park, a game preserve and picnic ground, provides all kinds of recreational opportunities including swimming, boating, fishing, horseback riding and several miles of trails and bridlepaths. There is a nine-hole golf course in Albany and an eighteen-hole course at Radium Springs. Albany is the site of the spring training camp for St. Louis Cardinals B, C and D teams. The library has over twenty thousand volumes. Seventeen churches for whites represent the leading denominations.

Columbus. Pop. 79,611. Alt. 248 ft. County Seat of Muscogee County. This is one of the few cities whose site was deliberately selected and laid out in advance. It is located on the banks of the Chattahoochee River, on the fall line between the Piedmont Plateau and the coastal plain, in a region famed for its scenic beauty. Retired persons will like its tree-lined streets, green lawns and home gardens. Attractive well-planned residential neighborhoods and numerous home developments are in evidence throughout the metropolitan area.

During the winter months, temperatures range between sixty degrees maximum and thirty-nine degrees minimum. Snow rarely falls. Moderate winters reduce the cost of heating and winter clothing costs. Average summer temperatures reach ninety degrees and fall to sixty-eight degrees at night. Relative humidity at noon is around 59 per cent rising to 71 per cent at night. Total annual rainfall is fifty-three inches.

The University of Georgia maintains an off-campus center in Columbus offering a variety of courses. Over four thousand persons are enrolled in adult education courses in the public school system. A full-time recreational department plans year-round recreational programs. A little theater group and numerous clubs and organizations foster special interests such as literature, drama, art and music. Columbus has an excellent library, seventeen parks and playgrounds, two golf courses, an auditorium and a stadium for college and high school football games. Golden Park is the home of the Columbus Cardinals. Pine Mountain State Park, one of Georgia's state parks, is twenty-five miles away. There is good fishing and hunting in the neighborhood area and nearby forests and streams. Warm Springs, the famous health resort, is little more than an hour's drive away. Fort Benning and Lawson Air Fields are located three miles south of the city. Columbus offers good opportunities to retired United States military service personnel who can take advantage of the facilities of the commissary, post exchange and officers' clubs of Fort Benning and Lawson Air Base. For nonmilitary people, too, who prefer retirement in an inland community, Columbus is well worth serious consideration.

Atlanta. Pop. 331,314. Alt. 1,050 ft. County Seat of Fulton County. The capital of Georgia is a city that's always going places, yet never in a hurry. Atlanta is a city where folks take time to live. It is a Georgia city, a Southern city and a Yankee city that attracts people from every section of the country. The metropolitan area of Atlanta embraces the cities of Decatur, East Point, College Park, Hapeville and Avondale Estates, as well as the counties of Fulton, De Kalb and Cobb. During the winter months temperatures are fifty-five degrees maximum to thirty-five degrees minimum. The Blue Ridge Mountains act as a partial barrier against cold waves sweeping in from the north. Snow falls so rarely and remains on the ground so short a time that snow is of little importance as a climatic factor. Summer temperatures have a daily mean of eighty-seven degrees maximum and sixty-seven degrees minimum. Relative humidity is 55 to 66 per cent. Summers are not hotter than in the Middle West or North. Normal annual rainfall is fifty-one inches.

With three universities and four colleges located in Atlanta, residents enjoy a great many opportunities to participate in the college's educational, cultural and sports activities that are open to the public. North Georgia resorts and trout streams are within easy driving distance. The High Museum School of Art is rated among the better art schools in the nation. The Southeaster Fair, held in October, is a big annual event. The city is one of the music centers of the United States and has its own ninety-piece orchestra. Grand opera, light opera and popular concerts are presented throughout the year. The entire area abounds with points of historical interest. Atlanta's enthusiasm for sports and recreation can be traced to its eighty-eight parks and the city's long range multimillion dollar program of recreation improvements. Golf can be played at twenty-two golf courses the year round. Library facilities are excellent, with a large public library and eighteen branch libraries plus the state and college libraries. There are over three hundred churches for whites. Recreational facilities also include the Fernbank Forest and nearby are Kennesaw Mountain National Park and Chattahoochee National Forest.

There is a substantial supply of new, brick, two- and three-bedroom houses for sale in the Greater Atlanta area at prices ranging from $7,000 to $19,000 and, of course, there is always a supply of more pretentious homes in exclusive residential districts at higher prices. Apartments with one-, two- and three-bedrooms rent at prices ranging from $75 to $150. Decatur, College Park and Avondale Estates are the residential suburban communities with shady streets and attractive homes. Many people live comfortably on small farms within commuting distance of the city.

South Carolina

Beaufort. Pop. 5,081. Alt. 10 ft. County Seat of Beaufort County. Located midway between Savannah and Charleston on the Atlantic seacoast, Beaufort is one of the historic spots on the American continent. It was on these shores beginning 433 years ago that the Spaniards, the French and the English first settled and over which they fought for 100 years. The flags of six nations have floated over this section—a fact worth noting as indicative of its desirability as a place for retirement living.

Beaufort is a small community, pleasant in summer and winter. Average temperature in winter is around sixty degrees maximum to forty degrees minimum while in summer temperatures are ninety degrees maximum to seventy degrees minimum. With a constant southwest breeze blowing, summer climatic conditions are enjoyable. Beaufort is wholly surrounded by salt water and the air has a sea tang. Some of the homes are stately old Southern mansions built by wealthy Sea Island cotton planters. Here you will find magnolia trees, oleander, palmetto palms, camphor trees, as well as olives and oranges. Moss-draped live oaks, flowers and birds are everywhere and the forests are green all winter. Practically every farmhouse has its own home orchard and homes have beautiful lawns and flower gardens.

The Beaufort section has more game preserves than any other section of the United States. Over one thousand yachts on their way to and from Florida pass by each year. There is good fishing everywhere and practically every sort of fish is caught in the area, many of them the year round. A number of people from the North are buying estates or building small, comfortable homes in and around Beaufort, many of them former servicemen once stationed on nearby Parris Island. Hunting Island across from Beaufort is a state park and wildlife sanctuary with long, wide beaches for picnics, swimming and surf fishing. Golf is played at the Lady's Island Country Club. The United States Navy has a large hospital located here. This is destined to become a popular retirement town for those who like an easygoing and quiet spot.

You can obtain a five-room house for $6,000 and up, a six-room house for $7,000 and up. Taxes are low and on the units described they would be about $50 a year. Many retired people are living very comfortably here on an income of $200 a month. Beaufort County, with its sixty-four islands, is one of the finest truck farming sections in the country. It has a growing season of 290 days, producing four crops a year. Undeveloped or partially developed beaches await those who are looking for soothing scenic spots on the ocean for retirement living. Good farm land can be bought at an average of $50 per acre and this often includes a good home and buildings. Good opportunities exist for bulb growing, poultry raising, hog raising and cattle raising.

Charleston. Pop. 70,174. Alt. 25 ft. County Seat of Charleston County. This is a fascinating, quaint Colonial city of narrow streets, homes and churches that date back to the seventeenth century. It is widely known as a shrine of history, as a superb seaport and is famed as an all-year resort. Six miles from the city limits is Sullivan's Island with a fine beach. Three miles further along the coast is a delightful beach community at the Isle of Palms where a number of retired families live the year round. South of the city is Folly Beach.

Located in Charleston are the College of Charleston, the oldest free municipal college in America; The Citadel Military College; and the Medical College of South Carolina. The city has an excellent school system which permits a child to go from primary grades through college tuition free. There are seventy-six churches of all leading denominations and four hospitals for whites. The Magnolia Gardens, Middleton Gardens, Cypress Gardens and Pierates Cruze Gardens are outstanding showplaces. Bulls Island, near Charleston, is a semitropical island noted for its great number and species of birds, both migratory and native. The Footlight Players and the Dock Street Theatre Players present original and Broadway successes. Art classes are conducted by the Carolina Art Association. A series of concerts is given by the Charleston Symphony Orchestra. Residents enjoy excellent salt- and fresh-water fishing and swimming, sailing, good hunting in season, golf and home gardening.

Charleston enjoys sunshine during 65 per cent of daylight hours. Winter temperatures average fifty-eight degrees maximum to forty-three degrees minimum. There is no snow. Summer temperatures average eighty-eight degrees maximum to seventy degrees minimum. The average year-round temperature is sixty-four degrees. Annual average rainfall is forty inches. Rentals for small unfurnished apartments range from $50 to $75 per month; two- and three-bedroom unfurnished houses rent for $75 to $125 per month. Charleston has many lovely suburbs where real estate costs are from $8,500 to $25,000 for two- to four-bedroom houses.

Georgetown. Pop. 6,004. Alt. 9 ft. County Seat of Georgetown County. There are many retired persons living in this area, some on small farms, some on large plantations and others in town. Georgetown is South Carolina's second oldest city. It is not a resort area but a substantial residential community with fine old streets lined with giant oaks and elms and many quaint historic buildings. Climatic conditions are similar to those of Charleston. The mean annual temperature is sixty-four degrees. Pawley's Island, twelve miles from the city, is noted for its quiet uncommercialized residential area, surf fishing, shady beaches and surf bathing. Brookgreen Gardens is an outdoor museum of American sculpture. Belle Isle Gardens is a nationally known beauty spot. The Community Concert Association presents three or four concerts during the year. The Yacht Basin is a favorite stopping place of yachtsmen using the Intracoastal Waterways. This is a restful community for those who enjoy easy living.

Columbia. Pop. 86,949. Alt. 332 ft. County Seat of Richland County. This is the capital of South Carolina and is located in the geographical center of the state in the Sandhills section. The mean annual temperature in January is forty-six degrees. There is an annual snowfall of about two inches. In July, the mean annual temperature is eighty-one degrees.

Columbia is the site of the University of South Carolina, Columbia College for Women, Lutheran Theological Seminary and the Columbia Bible College. The South Carolina Opportunity School offers courses for adult education. There are 171 churches representing practically all denominations.

The city provides thirteen parks. At Sesquicentennial Park, fifteen miles from the city, there are excellent picnic facilities and a lake for swimming. Within the Columbia area are four public golf courses and two country clubs each with an eighteen-hole golf course. Excellent fishing is available in nearby lakes and streams. Hunting is primarily for deer, bob white quail and wild turkey. Collegiate sports are provided through the University. The Town Theatre, Music Festival Association and other literary and art groups provide for cultural outlets. As to real estate, five-room brick veneer houses were advertised at $10,500. Better built, seven-room, two-bathroom houses in the best residential sections were priced at $25,000 and up. General property tax for the city is 44 mills and for the county 52½ mills, figured on 25 per cent of actual value of the property.

Spartanburg. Pop. 36,795. Alt. 875 ft. County Seat of Spartanburg County. This residential community has attractive assets for retirement living. Located in the rolling country of the Piedmont, in close proximity to the thermal belt. The climate is mild and bracing. During the winter months, the mean temperature is fifty-two degrees maximum with a mean low of thirty-five degrees. A chain of mountains to the northwest serves to block the movement of the cold waves from reaching the city. Year after year goes by without any snow observed or at most only a trace. In summer the average daily maximum is eighty-eight degrees with nighttime temperatures in the high sixties. Summer nights are usually cool and pleasant. Annual rainfall is about fifty-four inches. Relative humidity averages 55 per cent around the middle of the day.

The cultural and intellectual atmosphere is heightened by Wofford College, Converse College and the Spartanburg Junior College. Residents enjoy the faculty recitals, chorus, orchestra and glee club concerts, also the Lyceum featuring outstanding lectures and speakers. A little theater group presents several plays each year. Summer stock presents a full program in the nearby mountain playhouse. Symphony orchestra and Civic Music Association presentations afford a balanced series of concerts. Croft State Park, five miles from town, has an excellent swimming pool and picnic grounds. Spartanburg is located close to several resort areas. Other retirement advantages are good fishing in streams and lakes, two golf courses, three hospitals, fourteen churches and three good libraries. Real estate is priced at $7,000 to $15,-000 for five- to six-room homes. Spartanburg County is the Peach Capital of the United States.

North Carolina

Wilmington. Pop. 45,043. Alt. 32 ft. County Seat of New Hanover County. Hundreds of families from every state in the Union looking for cultural and intellectual activities, combined with an agreeable climate and economical cost of living, have selected Wilmington as their location for retirement. These include ex-military personnel, businessmen, educators and professional people. During the short winter season, the average daily maximum temperature is fifty-seven degrees with a minimum of thirty-nine degrees. Very rarely does any snow fall. Several varieties of palm trees grow in the city and many varieties of flowers bloom throughout the winter. For the summer months the average daily maximum temperature is eighty-seven degrees with average minimum of seventy-two degrees. The sun shines during 65 per cent of daylight hours. Annual rainfall averages forty-nine inches. A survey by the North Carolina Department of Labor found that, in December 1951, the average cost of family food for Wilmington was $21.05 per week—the lowest figure for the six cities in the state. The cost of living in Wilmington is estimated to be from 12 to 15 per cent lower than in Northern states.

Wilmington is famous for its formal flower gardens. Greenfield Lake and Park, Orton Plantation and Airline Gardens are ablaze in the spring with blooms of azaleas, roses, camellias, dogwood, wisteria, magnolia trees and other flowers and shrubs. The Azalea Festival, in March, is attended by more than one hundred thousand people. The Community Concert Association brings in foremost concert artists during the fall and winter season. The Thalian Association, oldest little theater group in the country, produces several plays each year. Nationally known speakers are brought in by the Executives Club and other organizations. All the leading religious denominations are represented by seventy-two churches. Health welfare is provided for by five hospitals. All kinds of recreation are available from organized sports to golf, tennis, boating, fishing and hunting. In the immediate vicinity of Wilmington are five popular beach resorts.

The cost of building a home is said to be 25 to 30 per cent lower than in many Northern and Southern states. New, modern five-room homes sell for $8,500 to $10,000 and six-room (two-bedroom) units from $9,500 to $12,000. The city tax is $2 per $100, county tax, $1.10 per $100, based on 60 per cent of assessed valuation. Both taxes are assessed within city limits.

Additional coastal towns where life moves at a slow tempo and living is inexpensive are New Bern (pop. 15,812), Edenton (pop. 4,468), Elizabeth City (pop. 12,685) and Southport (pop. 1,744).

The Outer Banks (estimated population 3,500). The country's first national seashore recreational area is being developed on the famous Outer Banks. This area consists of a chain of islands along North Carolina's coast and is the most extensive tract of undeveloped seashore remaining on the Atlantic Coast. Here you can find year-round ocean and inland fishing that is without equal. These islands have no local government or taxes, no incorporated towns, mayors, policemen or jails. Living can be as primitive and easygoing as you would like and as inexpensive. A moderate income is sufficient for economical living, particularly if relative isolation is desired. Oranges and grapefruit can be grown here because of the mild winters. The growing season is forty-two weeks of the year. Houses are for sale at $4,000 and up. There is nothing else like the Outer Banks. More and more people are discovering them every year. Principal communities are Hatteras (pop. 500), Buxton (pop. 500), Manteo (pop. 571), Ocracoke (pop. 500) and Nag's Head, a well-known resort.

Chapel Hill. Pop. 9,177. Alt. 501 ft. Orange County. You will find many well-to-do people, as well as those academically inclined, living happily in retirement in this college town, the site of the University of North Carolina. The cultural, social and sports life of Chapel Hill is dominated by "the University." There are no industries in the town. The atmosphere is informal and friendly and the community is in no way stuffy or reserved. Annual events include statewide Dramatic Festival; Folk Festival; University Day and major college sports. Entertainment is provided by Playmakers Theatre, Forest Theatre, Grass Roots Opera Company, University Memorial Hall, Hill Music Hall, the Morehead Planetarium and the Person Art Gallery. The University library contains four hundred thousand volumes and is open to the public. In this community you can enjoy lectures and forums, concerts and plays, discussions and conferences with faculty members. Chapel Hill offers golf, swimming, fishing and hunting.

Climatically, the winters are temperate with average daily temperature of fifty-two degrees maximum and thirty degrees minimum; summers average maximum temperatures of ninety degrees and average minimum temperatures of sixty-seven degrees. Only a few days in winter are unpleasantly cold, and a few days in summer can be called hot. About nine inches of snow fall during the winter season but snow does not stay on the ground long. Average rainfall is forty-seven inches.

Southern Pines. Pop. 4,272. Alt. 516 ft. Moore County.

Nine retired, top-ranking United States army generals have selected Southern Pines as their community for retirement. This town in the Sandhills section of North Carolina affords quiet and peaceful living. The mild, dry winter climate makes outdoor activity attractive. Except in a military sense the nine generals living here are far from retired. On the contrary, you may find them hoeing, fertilizing and weeding their gardens. They ride horseback, golf, putter about their remodeled farm homes, hunt quail, fish in nearby streams and lakes and are active in local community projects. Ask the nine generals why they selected Southern Pines. They will tell you it was the climate, the green golf courses, the quiet and restful countryside, the friendly people who make up the community.

Maximum average daily temperature in January is fifty-five degrees, minimum is thirty-three degrees; in July daily maximum is ninety degrees, with minimums of sixty degrees. About eight inches of snow usually fall during the winter months. Average relative humidity at noon is 58 per cent. Average rainfall is forty-five inches.

Seven golf courses are easily accessible from Southern Pines, including four magnificent clubs at Pinehurst six miles away. Other activities include horse shows, gymkhanas and participation in the social life at nearby Pinehurst. There are many beautiful estates and retirement farm homes throughout the area. Living is rather expensive, especially if you want to keep up with the Joneses. A fifty-acre tract between Southern Pines and Aberdeen was advertised at $3,000; a new, five-room house for $7,500; and a three-bedroom brick house within walking distance of shopping area at $13,500.

Tyron. Pop. 2,000. Alt. 1,085 ft. Polk County. Located on the southern foothills of the Blue Ridge Mountains in the thermal belt, Tyron affords a fairly even climate the year round. This is a well-established residential community and popular resort area, most attractive in the spring and fall, but maintaining an all-year season. The surrounding countryside is known for its vineyards and fruit orchards. Winter temperatures average maximums of fifty-three degrees with minimums of thirty degrees. About seven inches of snow fall during an average winter. In summer, temperatures average eighty-nine degrees maximum to sixty-five degrees minimum. On the average, fifty-eight inches of rain fall during the year.

The community has a very friendly atmosphere and many families from the East and the Middle West make up a happy retirement colony. The Tyron Country Club provides golf, swimming and tennis, and is the social entertainment center. The Riding and Hunt Club maintains bridle and hunt trails. Other activities include foxhunting, boating, camping, hunting and fishing in nearby mountains, lakes and streams. One can live comfortably in this locality on an income of $4,800 a year and up depending upon the living standard adopted. You can buy a small but comfortable and modern home for about $10,000; more elaborate homes are available at higher prices.

Hendersonville. Pop. 6,103. Alt. 2,200 ft. County Seat of Henderson County. A beautiful community located in a broad plateau region of the Blue Ridge Mountains. This attractive town affords all the modern conveniences of a larger city, only on a smaller scale. It is the center of a prosperous agricultural and industrial activity, and is a vacation resort area. The chief sources of income of Henderson County are tourists, $9 million; industry, $5 million; agriculture, $4.5 million.

Hendersonville has been called the "dancingest town in America," because of its numerous community street dances. Recreational events include dramatic performances, horse shows, golfing, county fairs, fishing, hunting, swimming and shuffleboard tournaments. The Huckleberry Arts and Craft Camp at Lake Kanuga promotes and encourages native handicrafts. Brevard Musical Festival, Apple Harvest Festival and religious conferences and camps are outstanding summer events. This section is also the youth camp center of Eastern America.

The mean maximum temperature during the winter months is forty-nine degrees and mean minimum is twenty-seven degrees. Snowfall averages about nine inches for the winter months. In summer the maximum daily temperature is eighty-three degrees at midday, dropping to sixty-one degrees at night. Retirement on small farms is quite in vogue in the Hendersonville territory. The area has a wide appeal to those retiring, and has already built considerable reputation among people of the Midwest, New York, Florida and the Panama Canal Zone. An eight-room, three-bathroom, century-old residence on a plot 200 × 500 ft. was offered at $13,500. There are good buys in comfortable homes priced at $10,000 and up.

Asheville. Pop. 53,000. Alt. 2,203 ft. County Seat of Buncombe County. Asheville is situated on a plateau between the Blue Ridge and the Great Smoky Mountains in the "Land of the Sky." Here you can retire and take it easy, or engage in as active a life as you choose. Whatever your tastes, you'll find yourself in good company for many retired military personnel, business executives, professional people, educators and plain ordinary folk live in retirement in the countryside of this happy inland community.

From the point of view of climate, the area is far enough south and sufficiently protected by mountain barriers to escape the extreme severity of winter storms and cold. Average daily temperature in the winter months is forty-eight degrees maximum to twenty-nine degrees minimum. Snowfall averages eleven inches for the winter season. In summer, daily maximum temperatures reach eighty-three degrees and drop to sixty-three degrees at night. Asheville is popular with Northerners in January and February and with Southerners in July and August. It has long been a favorite health area for those afflicted with pulmonary and similar ailments as well as nervous disorders.

Asheville offers all kinds of recreational facilities associated with resort areas, plus social activities at numerous clubs and community organizations. The Annual Mountain Dance and Folk Festival is noted for its picturesque revelry. Many religious groups maintain summer assemblies and conferences throughout the area. There are two country clubs with golf courses plus three public courses, lots of scenic beauty, good fishing in numerous lakes and streams, shuffleboard and swimming. The Southern Highland Craft Guild sponsors handicrafts and many outstanding craftsmen maintain workshops and classes in weaving, ceramics and woodcarving.

As to real estate, two- and three-bedroom homes in Beverly Hills, West Asheville and North Section were selling at $8,000 to $16,000; in the Kimberly and Lake Park residential sections, three-bedroom homes were priced at $21,000 to $30,000. Relatively cheaper real estate can be obtained in the Piedmont counties near the Virginia border and in the smaller mountain communities. Quite a number of retired families live comfortably on small farms in the countryside around Asheville.

CHAPTER XIV

The Gulf Coast Country

The Gulf Coast country is an amphitheater-like region that includes the coastal area bordering the Gulf of Mexico from Alabama to Texas. This section of the United States has a personality all its own with little resemblance to the interior of the states.

Few areas of the South have a more varied and colorful history than the Gulf Coast. Seven flags have flown over the territory since the French first established a settlement in 1699 at Biloxi. The influence of the French, Spanish and English is still evident in the Gulf Coast architecture and customs. Early Spanish and Civil War forts, presidential homes, legendary pirate hide-outs and Indian myths give charm and interest to this section of the nation.

Numerous bays, islands and streams along the Gulf Coast shoreline afford the fisherman wonderful opportunities to catch many species of fish as well as crabs, oysters and shrimp.

Everywhere there are wonderful oak trees and Spanish moss, flowers, pine trees, and the special atmosphere that makes this a good place to live and play the year round. The Gulf Coast is a way of living—a gentle, gracious, unhurried way that often seems unreal to visitors from other sections of the country. It has a reputation for good food, warm hospitality, fun and frivolity. Residents and visitors of the area can pursue a variety of outdoor sports and recreation at little expense and without traveling great distances.

Winter weather is normally mild. January, the coldest month, has an average mean temperature of fifty-two degrees. Snow is so rare that it causes considerable excitement. Summers are consistently warm with average mean temperatures around eighty-one degrees. Summer temperatures are usually checked by daily onshore sea breezes and the temperature is brought down to around seventy-two degrees at night. The average annual rainfall is about sixty inches, usually of the shower type. Long periods of rain are rare. While the area is located in the hurricane belt, one hurricane every fifteen years is the general average. Relative humidity averages 62 per cent. The average number of clear days is 120 a year and partly cloudy days, 138. The growing season is 274 days or more.

On the Gulf Coast prices are in general very reasonable. The mild winters permit lower costs in home construction and reduced costs for house heating. Vegetables are easily grown the year round. The abundance of fish, crab, oysters and shrimp reduces Gulf Coast food bills. The year-round outdoor living and the informality help cut down the clothing budget. The purity of the water in many communities and the mild climate promote healthful living. These are but a few of the many advantages that await those who plan a happy life of retirement under the warm Gulf Coast sun.

Alabama

Fairhope. Pop. 3,354. Alt. 125 ft. Baldwin County. On the eastern shore of Mobile Bay, an hour's drive from the city of Mobile, friendly Fairhope offers small-town comfort with big-town advantages. The area is cooled by breezes from the Gulf and the Bay in summer and, in winter, temperatures reach freezing only a few times a year. Here you can swim from sandy beaches with shade trees growing to the water's edge. There are four piers for salt-water fishing, crabbing or just relaxing. Fresh-water fishing is available within the town limits. Good hunting for wild fowl and small game is to be found in the immediate area. Fairhope has a country club, a night-lighted athletic field and tennis courts. There is a yacht club and over thirty clubs and organized groups covering social and civic activities, as well as the arts. The library is well stocked. Classes are held for the study of metalcraft, weaving, art, sculpture and creative writing. The Civic Music Association brings a series of well-known artists to town during the winter season. Golf is available nearby. Shuffleboard courts are maintained by the Tourist Club.

Houses can be bought at $5,000 and up, and small houses and apartments may be rented at $40 and up per month. Fairhope has a single-tax plan under which some of the home and farm property falls. The lots or acreage are obtained under ninety-nine-year leases which are renewable. There is a good opportunity here to establish small rental cottages or courts. Another good-paying opportunity exists in the wholesale flower-blooming-pot-plant business with a big market in Mobile and the surrounding towns. Excellent opportunities also exist for establishing poultry farms. Chickens are now shipped in. Nearby Mobile would also be a good market for eggs and poultry.

The towns of *Daphne* and *Montrose* a few miles southeast of Mobile have become increasingly popular as year-round residential communities for people working in Mobile. Many retired families have located in this area. *Point Clear,* to the south, is a beautiful resort colony of summer homes, vacation cottages and boasts the luxurious Grand Hotel.

Mobile. Pop. 129,000. Alt. 10 ft. County Seat of Mobile County. The city of Mobile is located on the Mobile River at its entrance to Mobile Bay, thirty-one miles from the Gulf of Mexico. Mobile is regarded as the economic capital of sixty counties of the Greater Gulf area. It is a modern sea-coast city where ocean steamers call from the world's great ports. This is a community noted for the friendliness of its citizens. Mean temperature in January is seventy-two degrees maximum to fifty-eight degrees minimum. In July mean temperatures are eighty-eight degrees maximum to seventy-three degrees minimum. Relative humidity at noon averages 60 per cent and 74 per cent at 6:00 P.M. Average wind velocity in winter months is thirteen miles per hour and in summer nine miles per hour. Annual rainfall averages sixty-two inches.

During all seasons of the year, this area provides many types of recreation. Deep-sea and fresh-water fishing are popular. The Alabama Deep Sea Fishing Rodeo is a big attraction during July and August. Wild game is hunted in the deep forest and swamps. Swimming facilities are found in the shores of the Bay and in nearby lakes. Mobile's seventeen-mile Azalea Trail winding past ante-bellum homes attracts thousands of visitors during the late winter and early spring. Mardi Gras is celebrated during February or March.

More than two hundred churches provide services for all leading denominations. The United States Marine Hospital, Providence Hospital, City Hospital and the Mobile Infirmary are located in the city. Some citrus fruit is grown and there are many outdoor nurseries. The growing season is 274 days. The United States Department of Labor study on the cost of living for an elderly couple ranked Mobile as the second least expensive city among the thirty cities studied. This is a place where living is fun and the future is a happy challenge, especially for those in comfortable homes on the outskirts of the city proper.

Mississippi

Ocean Springs. Pop. 3,058. Alt. 10 ft. Jackson County. This was the original site of Biloxi. When Biloxi was moved across the bay, the remaining community was called Ocean Springs, because of the mineral springs in the area. Ocean Springs, in addition to being a health resort and residential community, is also a vacation resort. Its climate and many opportunities for outdoor recreation, fishing, hunting, boating, swimming and similar pastimes bring visitors back year after year. A number of persons from many different states have found the Ocean Springs area a pleasant place in which to enjoy retirement life. Some of the popular activities are golf, square dancing and horseback riding. A few miles east of town is Magnolia State Park, a perfect picnic area with facilities for camping, cooking and swimming, and headquarters during the summer for the Gulf Coast Marine Research Laboratory. Up-to-date churches, a community center, a score of clubs and organizations and the friendliness of the people offer good prospects for unhurried retirement living.

The Memorial Bridge across the bay connects Ocean Springs with Biloxi, the second largest city in Mississippi. Biloxi is the shipping center for shrimp, oysters and fish from the Gulf of Mexico. It is also the site of the Keesler Air Force Base, Electronics Center and a large Veteran's National Soldiers Home and Hospital. Here you can enjoy special pageants, parades and celebrations. At Ocean Springs you can live among beautiful moss-draped oaks and in homes set among camellias, azaleas and other flowers. The land is well suited to truck farming, pecan orchards and the growing of tung trees.

Gulfport. Pop. 22,659. Alt. 10 ft. County Seat of Harrison County. This new modern city with a deep-water port is destined to be one of the most popular winter and summer resort areas of the deep South. The mild climate, together with the cordiality of happy residents, have won for Gulfport the title of the "Hospitality City." The average annual temperature is sixty-eight degrees, ranging from a minimum monthly average of fifty-one degrees in January to a maximum of eighty-two degrees in July.

Golf, tennis, swimming, city parks, sandy beaches, the West Side Community House, the East Side Community House, the Recreational Center and a long pier extending out into the Gulf are a few of the facilities offered by Gulfport. Fourteen miles north of the city is a large recreational area and picnic grounds. The great number of lakes, rivers, bays and bayous within a few minutes' drive from Gulfport, in addition to deep-sea fishing, make this a fisherman's paradise. A little theater group and the Knife and Fork Club are active. Gulfport, according to physicians, "has the making of the finest spa in the U.S.A. Its mild climate and the purity of its water offer relief to sufferers of asthma, chronic bronchitis, insomnia, organic heart disease and kidney ailments. These, of course, are not all cured at Gulfport, but sufferers report relief and comfort that they can obtain nowhere else." Artesian water from deep wells is said to be among the purest drinking water in the United States. Opportunities are numerous to establish various tourist and health enterprises that should prosper with the continued growth of Gulfport.

Mississippi City (pop. 3,400), just a few miles east of Gulfport, is another town to win fame as a resort-retirement area. It is referred to as the "Fruit Basket of the Gulf," because of the pears, grapes, oranges and other fruits marketed there.

Long Beach (pop. 2,703), a quiet and restful community of homes three miles west of Gulfport, has a twenty-seven-mile-long sandy beach.

Pass Christian. Pop. 3,383. Alt. 20 ft. Harrison County. This is a typical year-round Gulf resort town. For many years it has been the headquarters for a "Coast colony" of people from New Orleans. Pass Christian is, year-in and year-out, being rediscovered by tourists traveling the Old Spanish trail. It was first settled as a colony of France over 250 years ago. The Pass, as it is affectionately referred to, has an atmosphere and a culture all its own. Oriental trees, shrubs and flowers thrive to the edge of the sea wall. Physicians have recommended this area for reasons of health for more than a century.

Some of the more magnificent old homes of the South will be found here. Many are famous, such as that of the well-known columnist Dorothy Dix, and the Dixie White House which was occupied by President Wilson. Pass Christian Reef is one of the most prolific oyster reefs in the country. Shrimp, crab and excellent salt-water fishing, as well as surf bathing and other water sports, are all part of life at the Pass.

Louisiana

New Orleans Area and the "Ozone Belt." Across Lake Pontchartrain from New Orleans is St. Tammany Parish called the "Ozone Belt." Many people commute daily to New Orleans from the delightful residential towns of this parish. This section of Louisiana also rates high as a retirement location, because of the healthful climate, quiet tempo of living and the hospitality of the people. Yet residents of these towns, within an hour, have easy access of the recreational, cultural and rich atmosphere of the historic and cosmopolitan city of New Orleans.

The characteristics of the Ozone Belt are pine forests whose towering trees give off a fragrant balm, exuding the evaporation of pine oil, artesian waters of real purity and pleasing taste, medical springs that yield waters acknowledged to have high therapeutic value and the mild climate. The area is similar to the Ozone Belt of the Hartz Mountains in Germany. To such areas, on advice of physicians, go sufferers from diseases of the heart, the lungs and the respiratory system. The death rate in Louisiana's Ozone Belt is 9.3 per 1,000, while the death rate for the United States as a whole is 14.67 per 1,000.

For generations St. Tammany Parish has been famous as a resort for convalescence and recuperation of invalids. This region is now also becoming a popular location for persons seeking a desirable spot for retirement living.

Temperatures during the winter months average sixty-three degrees maximum to forty-seven degrees minimum. During the summer months average temperatures are eighty-nine degrees maximum to seventy-five degrees minimum. No snow falls in this area. Annual rainfall measures sixty inches, distributed fairly evenly throughout the year. Relative humidity around noon is 62 per cent.

Slidell, Covington, Hammond and *Abita Springs* are good retirement locations and are destined to become more popular as they become better known outside the state of Louisiana.

Slidell. Pop. 3,500. Alt. 11 ft. St. Tammany Parish. This is a suburban residential town just thirty-two miles from New Orleans, located near Lake Pontchartrain and Pearl River. Practically everyone owns his own home and rentals are scarce. A frame dwelling costs about $8 per square foot to build. Real estate taxes are low. Because of the mild climate and good water supply, home owners have beautiful flower and vegetable gardens. Many grow a large variety of vegetables for the family table the year round. Fruit trees do very well, especially pear, fig, plum, mandarin and persimmon.

Covington. Pop. 4,000. Alt. 35 ft. Parish Seat of St. Tammany Parish. A beautiful suburban-country town on the banks of the Bogune Falaya, a clear-water and sandy-bottom river. Covington has splendid, friendly homes and residential areas that stretch for miles along paved, shaded streets and rival those of much larger cities. Several floral gardens and trails are regionally famous. Only a few blocks from the center of the town is Fontainebleau State Park, a resort and recreation center for the city of New Orleans, providing swimming, water sports, hiking, picnicking and other forms of outdoor activities. Lake Pontchartrain and numerous smaller lakes and streams are within easy reach of fishermen and boatsmen. Many New Orleans businessmen live here and commute daily to their work.

Covington industries depend chiefly on the pine forests in the area. Where forests have been leveled, truck farms grow a variety of produce. Open land costs $30 to $60 an acre. Homes in town run about $10,000 for a comfortable five-room house. Covington has a library and many social clubs and organizations. Living costs are about average for the South or perhaps a bit lower because of the great variety of truck crops grown around the countryside. "This is a place that attracts artists, writers and those who are sensitive to their surroundings as well as many charming people who have taken up residence in Covington," is the comment of a citizen who has lived in Covington for many years.

Abita Springs. Pop. 700. Alt. 56 ft. St. Tammany Parish. Here, where the sea breezes from the Gulf mingle with the ozone-laden air of the pine woods, Abita Springs affords an ideal place for a summer or winter residence to escape the rigors of a Northern climate. Since the discovery, in 1854, that the springs are highly medicinal, this small town has become a favorite health resort. Abita Springs has been added to the Louisiana State Parks System and plans are under way to make this one of the most attractive spots in the state. In the midst of rolling hills, covered with great pine trees, sweet gum, oak, magnolia and other trees, it makes a beautiful and enchanting spot for rest, recreation and retirement. There are several springs here, all noted for their health-giving qualities in the healing of kidney trouble, liver trouble, dyspepsia, chronic diarrhea, constipation, nervous and general debilities. The climate is mild and free from dampness and is highly recommended by physicians for the relief of respiratory ailments. The climate is said to be the equal and in many respects the superior of many parts of Southern California.

This lovely retirement spot is located about eight miles from the shores of Lake Ponchartrain, is sixty-five miles from New Orleans and is in the center of the Ozone Belt. Undeveloped resources give ample opportunity for enterprise and the profitable investment of capital. It is an ideal site for home seekers who wish to combine health and a profitable occupation. The climate is peculiarly adapted to farm products and fruit culture, especially figs, peaches, grapes, plums and strawberries. The area also offers great opportunities for livestock, poultry raising, flower and plant culture. In and near Abita Springs is good hunting for deer, wild turkey, squirrel and quail. Splendid fishing, camping, boating and swimming are also available.

Morgan City. Pop. 9,759. Alt. 6 ft. St. Mary Parish. About eighty-nine miles southeast from New Orleans surrounded by Lake Palourde, Grand Lake and the Atchafalaya River is the town of Morgan City. A correspondent writes: "Morgan City is probably the easiest place a man could find to sustain life. Anyone with a fair vision and the ability to toddle to the waterfront can, in a short time, catch enough shrimp and fish for an average family's meals. A branch of native willow, secured to a stake on shore, can be lowered into the stream, and in two hours will have harbored a multitude of shrimp, which can be shaken into a net and used for food or as live bait for larger fish, in the same stream. A small plot can be made to produce vegetables in almost every month of the year. Our average temperature for January is fifty-two degrees, and for July, eighty-two degrees. These moderate temperatures are assured by the water that surrounds us, and our proximity to the Gulf of Mexico."

Morgan City offers a year-round recreation program under a trained director. The Concert Association brings in nationally known artists each winter. A fine library, very friendly people, numerous civic and social groups and clubs, a golf course, good hunting, are a few other advantages that make this good retirement territory.

Cost of real estate varies with the location. City building lots sell for $300 to $3,000. The city tax is low, which helps overcome the state tax. A resident writes, "Life in Morgan City is so easy that residents have not had to be aggressive and have left open many unexploited avenues for those who would like to establish and operate a small business enterprise."

Texas

Austin. Pop. 132,449. Alt. 463 to 700 ft. County Seat of Travis County. Austin is the capital of Texas and the seat of the University of Texas. It has a mild and pleasant climate, a university-town atmosphere and nearby lakes and hills, all of which make it a natural location for retirement living. The citizens of the "Friendly City," as Austin is called, include government officials, college professors and students, businessmen and more professional and semiprofessional people than most cities of similar size. The economic life of Austin, in addition to the activities of the state government and the University of Texas, includes several regional offices of the Federal Government, many small manufacturing and processing plants, headquarters for state-wide associations, home offices of several insurance companies. In Austin and the adjacent territory are several springs and wells where water of the highest medical quality flows abundantly.

Living in the shadow of the University of Texas, residents of Austin have the opportunity of attending a wide assortment of concerts, plays, sporting events and other forms of entertainment. The Austin Symphony Orchestra, the Junior Symphony Orchestra and the Mixed Chorus Society present a series of complete programs. The Cultural Entertainment Committee of the University also sponsors several concerts monthly. A number of dramas and plays are sponsored by the Civic Theatre and the Exchange Club. Works of well-known artists are exhibited at the Elisabet Ney Museum. The O. Henry Memorial Museum contains the works of the famous short-story writer and other items of interest. Art classes are available for both children and adults in sketching, painting and ceramics. Adult education classes are offered by the city school system and the University of Texas offers correspondence courses to all Texans who cannot come to the campus. The City Library, State Library and the Library of the University of Texas have a total of over a million volumes. The city has 5 hospitals, 110 churches and a great number of the usual social and civic clubs and groups. Austin Municipal Park affords swimming, boating and fishing. Zilher Park has landscaped areas for picnicking. Pease Park and Woolbridge Park are also popular outdoor recreational areas. There are three golf courses.

The climate lacks the dampness of the coastal area. Winter temperatures seldom reach freezing, the lowest monthly average being forty-nine degrees. The average daily summer temperature is eighty-three degrees with average daily minimums of seventy degrees. Annual rainfall is thirty-four inches. The area enjoys sunshine during 65 per cent of daylight hours. Relative humidity averages 57 per cent.

This combination of a generally mild climate together

with the picturesque, rolling countryside has encouraged many former university students, legislators, military personnel and others who have spent time in Austin to return to make it their permanent home. Within a short drive from Austin are five lakes and six major dams which are becoming famous. They open up unlimited opportunities for resort and vacation developments. Within the next decade hundreds of vacation and recreation enterprises will be established in this virgin area. It is destined to become one of the South's most popular resort regions and the site for year-round homes. Low-cost electricity and irrigation have opened up the lower valleys of this region to provide rich opportunities for better living and a large volume of agricultural products.

San Antonio. Pop. 421,700. Alt. 700 ft. County Seat of Bexar County. Once a Spanish stronghold, San Antonio today is the headquarters of the largest military establishment in the United States. Once the capital of a province in New Spain, it is now the commercial and financial center of south and west Texas. The city's mild climate and sunny skies appeal alike to persons seeking retirement and to an expanding city population seeking happy and healthful living. The average winter temperature is fifty-nine degrees, with temperatures dropping to freezing only a few days each winter. The average summer temperature is seventy-nine degrees with cool Gulf breezes on summer nights. Average humidity in summer months is 52 per cent and in winter months, 56 per cent. Average annual rainfall is twenty-seven inches. The sun shines during 50 per cent of daylight hours in winter and during summer 70 per cent.

The city's fifty-six parks and recreation system of more than two thousand acres includes facilities for golf, tennis, baseball and swimming pools. The Alamo Stadium is the scene of outstanding sporting events. At the Coliseum, livestock shows, rodeos, ice shows and other events are popular.

There are 250 churches covering the leading denominations. San Antonio is a city of culture. Its symphony orchestra is well rated. There is a weeklong opera season, a constant series of concerts, plays and other cultural diversions. There are numerous fine libraries, art galleries and museums. Among San Antonio's colleges are Trinity University, San Antonio College, St. Mary's University and four junior colleges, plus military academies and schools of music and art. There is much of historic interest to see including the Alamo and several early missions. San Antonio is well known as a health resort and medical center. There is every indication of further steady increase in San Antonio's popularity as a retirement location.

Brownsville. Pop. 36,066. Alt. 35 ft. County Seat of Cameron County. The only city in the United States which is a port of entry to Old Mexico by water, highway and air, Brownsville is on the shortest route to Mexico City for 70 per cent of the people of the United States. Matamoros, Mexico, is just opposite Brownsville on the Rio Grande River.

Brownsville celebrates a four-day fiesta called Charro Days, when everyone wears a costume typical of some part of Latin America. Programs are sponsored throughout the year by the Knife and Fork Club and the Rotary Club featuring prominent lecturers on world topics. The Civic Music Association presents outstanding concert artists. There is a wide variety of social groups including the Art League, garden clubs, study clubs and many civic organizations. The area affords fresh-water, salt-water and channel fishing—you can catch fish any time of the year without driving more than thirty miles. Excellent hunting includes game in Mexico. Sailing, boating and bathing are popular in the Ship Channel and at the beaches at Padre Island, Boca Chica or Del Mar on the Gulf twenty-five miles from

Brownsville. The Country Club provides an eighteen-hole golf course. Bullfights, dining and other recreation facilities in Mexico are just across the international toll bridges.

Almost every crop is grown in the Lower Rio Grande Valley. The Brownsville Board of City Development is actively soliciting capable farmers to specialize in small-tract, high-value crops. There are also good opportunities for small business enterprises. Several good opportunities exist for professional, service and retail enterprises. The attitude of the people is to encourage new industries, retail establishments, professions and small farmers. They are not anxious, however, to encourage such innovations as will destroy what they feel to be an admirable way of life. They have officially stated that "Brownsville is one of the last places left in the world where a man can live as he wants to. We aim to keep it that way."

The climate is pleasant throughout the year. Average winter temperatures are sixty-nine degrees maximum to fifty-one degrees minimum. During summer, temperatures average ninety degrees maximum to seventy-four degrees minimum, but cool breezes from the Gulf make living comfortable throughout the day and night. Rainfall averages twenty-seven inches annually. Relative humidity at noon is around 60 per cent. The cost of living is considerably lower than in the North or East and lower than in the larger cities of the South. Tropical winters reduce the cost of fuel for house heating and winters do not require heavy clothing.

The entire Lower Rio Grande Valley, of which Brownsville is the largest community, is rapidly achieving prominence as a good retirement area. There are other fast-growing communities in the Valley.

McAllen (pop. 23,000), "cottages rent from $30 to $60 a month and small homes can be bought for $5,000 to $7,500. Total taxes on a $7,500 house are about $120 a year, which pays for county, state, school and city taxes. Good opportunities for raising poultry exist here."

Harlingen (pop. 23,202) is a modern, progressive and pleasant residential community with many advantages for quiet, enjoyable retirement living.

CHAPTER XV

The Southwest

Arizona and New Mexico are both in mountainous and deep-canyon country. The altitude of the northern tablelands ranges from six thousand to twelve thousand feet; in the central parts of the states, altitudes are about five thousand feet. In general, these altitudes are too stimulating for elderly persons and may even be injurious to those with diminished vital powers.

In the southern section of Arizona, and to some extent in New Mexico, there are a few river valleys with altitudes varying from five hundred to two thousand feet with a mild, dry climate and an abundance of sunshine. These valleys are rapidly becoming well known as health resorts and popular vacation playgrounds. They deserve serious consideration as localities for retirement, particularly by those who prefer the inland, mountain-country type of living. Many will choose this area because of low humidity, dryness, sunshine, mild winter temperature and proximity to natural mineral springs conducive to health building.

As to the cost of living, surveys indicate that about $150 a month is the minimum income on which a family may live comfortably in Arizona and New Mexico.

Winters are mild and sunny during the day and cool at night. The mountains protect the area from a good part of the extreme cold from the north. December to February mean monthly temperatures are fifty to sixty degrees for southern Arizona and forty-five degrees for southern New

Mexico. At night, the temperature in New Mexico often drops below freezing. Snowfall is rare in the valley areas but is heavy at the higher altitudes.

The summers are long and hot, lasting from May to October, with wide variations in temperature between daylight hours and night. Temperatures of one hundred degrees and over occur very frequently during the day in the summer months. These high temperatures drop to sixty to seventy-five degrees at night. Many homes and commercial buildings are equipped with summer air conditioners or evaporative air coolers. Persons who can afford it sometimes move to northern locations and higher elevations or to California to escape the summer heat.

The relative humidity, however, is very low, around 30 per cent at noon. It often falls below 10 per cent during the afternoon. This low humidity tends to mitigate the high summer temperatures and is responsible for the small number of heat prostrations throughout the area. In southern New Mexico relative humidity is slightly higher than in Arizona. There are two main rainy seasons. The first occurs during the winter months from November to March. The second and heavier in July through September when the area is subject to thunderstorms. Generally, there is less than eight inches of annual rainfall in the southern valley areas. Winds are light, averaging only 5.8 miles per hour in southern Arizona but stronger in New Mexico, especially during the spring. The climate is considered beneficial for persons suffering from respiratory diseases and rheumatic illness.

Arizona

Tucson. Pop. 45,454. Alt. 2,400 ft. County Seat of Pima County, Arizona. Located in the heart of a cactus and mesquite-covered desert plateau, Tucson, "The Sunshine City," is surrounded by rugged mountains. Four flags have flown over the city—Spanish, Mexican, Confederate and Union. Winter temperature averages sixty-seven degrees maximum to thirty-seven degrees minimum. Snowfall in Tucson is rare, particularly accumulations exceeding an inch in depth. The summer season is long and hot, beginning in April and ending in October. Maximum temperatures above ninety degrees are the rule with daily minimums in the sixties. Annual rainfall is 10.53 inches. Relative humidity ranges from 30 to 45 per cent. The sun shines during 85 per cent of daylight hours. Mean speed of wind is 7.2 miles per hour.

The unusual setting of Tucson, its sunshine and dry climate are largely responsible for its growth as a resort and health city and for the fact that the number of permanent residents has more than doubled in the last decade. Many business men, professional men, writers, farmers and others who originally went to Tucson for a brief visit have returned to make it their permanent home. In spite of its health resort character, Tucson does not appear to be a city populated by invalids. The really sick people are in hospitals and sanitariums. The other health seekers are those with sinus trouble, asthma, rheumatism, arthritis in stages that benefit from sunshine and dry air.

The University of Arizona, located here, is largely responsible for the varied cultural activities of the community. The university has attracted many people who need a desert climate for health reasons and yet want an intellectual environment. Artists and musicians have gathered there in great numbers. The Tucson Fine Arts Association encourages arts and crafts of all kinds. Nationally known guest artists appear with the Tucson Symphony Orchestra. The Little Theater is active in drama presentations. Well-known speakers are heard on the Sunday Evening Forum program. The community offers a wide range of group activities, with several hundred civic, fraternal, social and special interest groups to choose from. The Tucson Visitors Club entertains three times weekly. Informality is the order of the day and night throughout the community.

For recreation you have a choice of golf, shuffleboard, swimming in municipal pools, picnics, hikes and horseback riding. The Cleveland Indians have a spring training camp there. More than one hundred churches represent all leading denominations. The beautiful San Xavier del Bac Mission is nine miles south of the city. Tucson Mountain Park, full of game, hiking trails and picnic grounds is nearby. The Mt. Lemmon, Sabino Canyon, Santa Cataline Mountains and Saguaro National Monument are just a few of the nearby points of interest. Old Mexico and the border town of Nogales are little more than an hour away by automobile.

No one should come to Tucson seeking employment unless he is prepared to be self-supporting for several months. The area usually has an oversupply of workers in all lines. There is a large colony of retired people living happily in Tucson, the great majority of whom have moderate retirement incomes. About $7,500 is the minimum price asked for a comfortable four-room house. Small homes in the better parts of the city range in price from $8,500 up to $15,000 and more.

Phoenix. Pop. 106,818. Alt. 1,080 ft. County Seat of Maricopa County, Arizona. This is the capital of Arizona. It occupies an area of some ten square miles on the broad plain north of the Salt River. Although reclaimed from a virtual desert, the city has developed surprising landscape beauty. The climate of Phoenix has been compared to that of the Upper Nile Valley of Egypt. In the winter months, daily maximum temperatures are around sixty-five degrees with minimums sometimes dropping below freezing, but afternoons are usually sunny and warm. The summer months frequently bring temperatures over 100 degrees with night temperatures dropping to the low seventies. Relative humidity during daytime averages 30 per cent dropping to 15 per cent in the afternoon. During the past few years, summer air conditioning has brought greater comfort to residents. Thousands of homes are equipped with inexpensive, home-made, excelsior window-box coolers. Artificial summer cooling for homes and office buildings is now the rule for living in Phoenix.

The simplicity of living, the friendliness of the people, the beautiful scenery surrounding the city, the healthful fresh air, the sense of freedom and relaxation, rather than economic advantages, have attracted new residents to Phoenix. The city has much to offer for retirement living and relaxation. There are sixteen city parks, nineteen motion picture theaters, radio and television stations, city symphony orchestra, free lectures at five art galleries and two museums. All the usual civic, service and social clubs and groups are represented and are active. All the major sports activities are available, including golf, tennis, shuffleboard, swimming, fishing and hunting in nearby streams and mountains, rodeos, horse and harness racing and horseback riding. Phoenix is the winter training camp of the New York Giants, and nearby Mesa is the training site of the Chicago Cubs. The Phoenix Technical School offers night classes for adults. Over two hundred churches care for the religious needs of all leading denominations. A great number of the permanent residents visited the city during vacations and later returned to stay.

Phoenix is one of the few rapidly growing cities that does not have a housing shortage. Modern, new, two-bedroom brick homes can be purchased for as little as $7,500 and three-bedroom, two-bathroom homes for $10,000. Unfurnished apartments and homes rent for $65 to $125 per month. While a rapidly growing city like Phoenix offers numerous opportunities to establish new small businesses, anyone thinking of going into such activities should make a personal survey to determine whether the area can support the business contemplated. Part-time employment is difficult to secure. But for those who have assured retirement incomes, Phoenix has much to offer.

Obendler. (Pop. 3,799), *Glendale.* (Pop. 8,179), *Mesa.* (Pop. 16,790), Maricopa County, Arizona. These three communities located within thirty minutes' drive from Phoenix offer the same climatic advantages with opportunities for less expensive living. Each community offers its own recreation and social activities at a quieter tempo and in a more rural atmosphere. Yet each community is within easy reach of the more active city life of Phoenix. These communities are trading centers of a rich agricultural area in the Salt River Valley noted for irrigated truck farms, citrus, date and fig groves. Arizona State College is only six miles from Mesa.

Globe. Pop. 6,419. Alt. 3,500 ft. County Seat of Gila County, Arizona. This is the "City of the Hills" whose main street lies in a canyon and whose pleasant homes overlook the tremendous vista of the Apache Indian Reservation and the Pinal Mountains. It is a former mining town that refused to become a ghost town and continues to grow and prosper as a residential and business center. You can enjoy plenty of outdoor life here, in a climate that is dry and sunny and somewhat of a compromise between the hot summers of the Southwest and the colder winters of the Northeast. Many physicians recommend this climate for asthma, sinus, bronchitis and other ailments. For fishing there are the Roosevelt Dam, the Coolidge Dam and the mountain streams. Hunters find deer, elk, antelope, turkey, dove and quail in the mountains. Globe is the center of early Indian culture and life. Many ancient ruins are still preserved. A number of retired families are reported to be living comfortably on $150 a month, but to do so they must have this income assured as there are limited opportunities for employment.

Prescott. Pop. 6,764. Alt. 5,014 ft. County Seat of Yavapai County, Arizona. This "Mile High City of Health" is one of the few Western cities that retains much of the flavor of the frontier days. It is located in an area of the nation's largest pine forest and is noted for the relief of many forms of allergic sensitivity, sinus and respiratory conditions. Many of its prominent citizens went to Prescott seeking relief from asthma and remained to make it their permanent residence. The results of a survey to determine the effects of the local climate on asthmatics indicate that, out of six thousand people questioned, one in every thirty-five had come to Prescott suffering from this ailment and 93 per cent had found relief.

Winter temperatures average fifty degrees maximum to twenty-five degrees minimum. Due to the low humidity and light winds, these temperatures are not uncomfortable. Summer temperatures range from eighty-nine degrees maximum for short periods to fifty degrees about daybreak. Relative humidity ranges from a high of 66 per cent in December to a low of 26 per cent in June. Snowfall in winter usually amounts to twenty inches but disappears rapidly due to the dry air.

For recreation there are many scenic and picnic areas, such as Granite Basin, Granite Dells, Mingus Mountain, Castle Hot Springs and Thumb Butte. Miles of valleys, mountains and wilderness offer excellent fishing and hunting as well as all kinds of outdoor sports. Those who like an active, social life may find the Prescott area rather quiet. The outstanding annual events are the Frontier Days Rodeo in July, and the Smoki Indian Ceremonials.

New Mexico

Las Cruces. Pop. 12,325. Alt. 3,860 ft. County Seat of Dona Ana County, New Mexico. Las Cruces is situated in the fertile Mesilla Valley of the Rio Grande, forty-four miles north of El Paso, Texas and Juarez, Mexico. The city has attractive residential houses of Pueblo, Spanish and hacienda style on its quiet, well-shaded streets. Winter temperatures average seventy degrees. For the summer months high temperatures are in the low nineties with nighttime averages at sixty-two degrees. Average annual rainfall is less than eight inches. The almost constant sunshine (85 per cent of daylight hours) and the clean, dry air are beneficial to health seekers.

Recreation and social activities include 257 social and civic clubs and organizations, golf, swimming, horseback riding, Billy-the-Kid Museum and fishing and boating on Caballo Dam and Elephant Butte Lake. Close by is Radium Springs, famous for its hot-water mineral baths. College background is supplied by New Mexico College of Agriculture and Mechanical Arts. Thirty-two churches represent nearly every denomination. The White Sands National Park and the White Sands Proving Ground, where experimental rockets are fired, are nearby.

Dona Ana County, of which Las Cruces is the county seat, produces 25 per cent of all crops grown in the thirty-two counties of the state. A ten-acre farm will sustain a family if properly farmed. The cost of land is high with prices ranging from about $800 per acre up to $1,500 per acre, depending upon productivity. The Memorial Library and the College Library have 18,300 and 75,000 bound volumes respectively.

Deming. Pop. 5,672. Alt. 4,321 ft. County Seat of Luna County, New Mexico. Deming is located on a semiarid mesa, in the heart of the 80 per cent sunshine area. The mean temperature for the year is sixty degrees, ranging from an average high of seventy-nine degrees in July to an average low of forty-two degrees in December. Average relative humidity is 35 to 40 per cent. Annual average rainfall is ten inches. The climate is beneficial for arthritis, sinus disorders, tuberculosis, asthma and allergies, and for people susceptible to harsh, damp weather. Healthful sunshine is available 355 days of the year.

Cultural facilities consist of an excellent school system, seventeen churches, a small but excellent library, community concerts, cantatas, annual talent shows, band concerts. For recreation there is the Country Club with golf course and swimming pool, a municipal swimming pool and tennis courts, several parks with picnicking facilities, various fraternal and civic organizations and an active community house. The Gila National Forest, largest in the United States, a vast sportsman's paradise, is one-hour's drive away. Thirty-five miles south of Deming is the fascinating land of Old Mexico. Living expenses are about the same as those in the Middle West, and slightly lower than those in the East. Taxes are lower and, on the whole, real estate costs less.

Truth or Consequence. Pop. 7,500. Alt. 4,200 ft. Sierra County, New Mexico. Formerly named Hot Springs, this town was made famous by Ralph Edwards and his radio program Truth or Consequence. It is one of the health capitals of the nation. The healing waters of its hot mineral springs are famous for their value in the treatment of arthritis, rheumatic complaints and similar diseases. There are twenty regularly operated mineral spring bathhouses. The healing waters of Truth or Consequence are supplemented by a healthful climate with sunshine during 80 per cent of daylight hours. The winter temperatures average forty-six degrees with a high of sixty and a low of twenty-eight degrees. In summer the average temperature is seventy-seven degrees with a high of ninety-two and a low of sixty-two degrees. Relative humidity averages between 10 and 15 per cent. Annual rainfall is seven inches. Truth or

Consequence is the home of the famous Carrie Tingley Hospital for Crippled Children. The Community Center is the gathering place for residents, tourists and visitors interested in card games, shuffleboard and dances. Elephant Butte Lake, three miles away, and nearby Caballo Reservoir offer boating, fishing and swimming and an annual outboard motor regatta. A golf course is open for residents and visitors. Other forms of recreation include horseback riding, rock hunting and picnicking. There are churches of eighteen denominations, a well-stocked library, a good school system and many service and social clubs. Truth or Consequence is a good location for those seeking a retirement mecca, for those seeking relief from illness, for those seeking recreation.

Santa Fe. Pop. 27,998. Alt. 7,000 ft. County Seat of Santa Fe County, New Mexico. This is a favorite retirement location, but not recommended for those suffering from heart diseases or nervous disorders. The high altitude accelerates respiration, increases the metabolic rate and tends to produce conditions of excitability. However, you will find many retired people living here. Winter temperatures average forty degrees maximum to twenty degrees minimum. An average of thirty inches of snow falls during the winter months. Relative humidity in winter averages 60 per cent. Less than one inch of rain falls each month during the winter. There is no excessive heat in summer, the average highest temperature in July is eighty degrees and average lowest is fifty-seven degrees. Summer nights are cool enough to require wraps and covers. On an average, the sun shines during 74 per cent of daylight hours. Living expenses in Santa Fe are not low, since nearly all food and merchandise are shipped in from outside the state.

There are approximately one hundred active artists in Santa Fe's thriving art colony. Several schools and private art classes provide unusual facilities for art and craft study.

There are more than a dozen square-dance clubs in the city. Santa Fe has three fine museums and a state art gallery. The Community Concert Association, Sinfonietta Chorale Society, Philharmonic Orchestra, Cinema Club and Little Theatre provide opportunities to enjoy music and dramatic presentations. The Santa Fe Fiesta held over the Labor Day week end is a colorful spectacle. There is excellent fishing in nearby trout streams and lakes. Hunters find a variety of game within a few miles of the city. For golfers there is a nine-hole Municipal Golf Course. Santa Fe offers many interesting and educational sidelights on Indian culture and relics.

Real estate costs are relatively high. The sources of income are the state capital and Federal Government pay rolls, the craft industries and the tourist trade. It is estimated that two-thirds of Santa Fe's residents draw their livelihood directly or indirectly from the tourist trade.

Texas

El Paso. Pop. 130,485. Alt. 3,920 ft. County Seat of El Paso County, Texas. The City of El Paso, "Sunshine Playground of the Border," located in the far western corner of Texas on the upper Rio Grande, is one of the leading cities of the Southwest. For many years El Paso has boasted of its four C's—climate, copper, cattle and cotton. The climate is basically warm and dry; humidity is extremely low. The average daily temperature during winter is fifty-seven degrees maximum to thirty-two degrees minimum. During the summer, the daily average is ninety-three degrees maximum to sixty-nine degrees minimum. The city has sunshine during 79 per cent of daylight hours. There are, on the average, only thirty-four cloudy days per year. Rainfall averages nine inches a year. Relative humidity around noon averages 30 per cent. The area is free from blizzards and cyclones. The climate is recommended by medical authorities for its health-giving attributes. Many people who suffer from various pulmonary diseases, such as asthma and tuberculosis, move to El Paso to regain their health.

The city and vicinity offer many scenic and historic attractions. These include old Spanish missions, Carlsbad Caverns, Indian ruins, Big Bend National Park and Old Mexico. Tourist expenditures are estimated to run as high as twenty-five million dollars annually. Throughout the year there are many events which attract more than local interest. These include the Sun Bowl Football Game, the Sun Land Rodeo, the Sun Carnival and bullfights across the border in Juarez. There are in El Paso some eighty-five active clubs and organizations, exclusive of fraternal orders. Among the important ones are the El Paso Country Club with swimming pool, tennis courts and an eighteen-hole golf course, a municipal golf course, the Skeet Shooters Association, symphony orchestra and the Little Theatre. Texas Western College with the El Paso Centennial Museum on its campus, Loretto Academy for Girls and the Cotton Memorial School of Art add college atmosphere to city life.

The city has a cosmopolitan population and attractive residential sections. Homes of brick, stucco or adobe, suitable for retirement living, are priced from $10,000 up, depending on location and size. Most homes have no basements because big heating plants and coal bins aren't necessary. Small natural-gas heating units are sufficient to take the chill off winter nights. Heating fuel for the average home costs about $50 for the entire season. El Paso is a favorite retirement location for Army personnel. The trend toward more domestic travel and more travel to Mexico will continue to offer increasing opportunities for business enterprises serving the tourist trade.

CHAPTER XVI

Retirement Planning Schedule

Your retirement can mark the beginning of a rich new life free from the financial cares, the rigid time demands, the confining influences of the workday world—a life in which you can devote your talents and abilities to the pursuits that interest and excite you. Like so many others have done, you can make your retirement years the happiest, most productive years of your life.

To make them so, however, you must plan ahead. The following suggestions are meant to guide you in organizing your planning schedule for a carefree, happy retirement.

Thirty-five to forty-five. This is an ideal age to make plans to meet your financial requirements in retirement, to adopt a program of living that will equip you spiritually, mentally and physically for a purposeful life during your harvest years.

The attitudes, hobbies, talents and skills you develop during your middle years, your savings program, the diet you follow, the care you give your health, your philosophy of life —all will greatly determine your well-being after retirement. Retirement should not be a complete break with the past. It should be merely an extension of your plan for better living, conceived and developed during your pre-retirement years. If you make life worth living before retirement, you won't have difficult adjustments to make to enjoy retirement.

Keep a checking account balance equal to two months' income, reinforced by an emergency cushion fund sufficient to cover three-months' living expenses. Be sure you have adequate life, health and hospital insurance. When you have attained these goals, the next step is to buy your own home.

Now, if you still have a cash surplus, consider investing it in fixed assets like Government E Bonds or in the purchase of additional insurance or an annuity. Other possibilities are stocks and real estate.

Before deciding where to invest your surplus, determine first what your long-term debt situation is. If you have a large mortgage on your home invest more heavily in fixed assets. Should you, on the other hand, be in a liquid cash position, with only modest long-term debt obligations, you can afford to invest a larger share of your surplus savings in more speculative investments. Next, decide the objective of your investing. Do you want to get the largest possible income from your capital? Do you want to increase the size of your capital? Do you want to protect your capital at a higher income than you would get from fixed assets? After you have decided your objective, talk to your banker or a reputable broker, and ask for advice.

One suggested method for investing your surplus is to put one-third of your surplus into buying E bonds, one-third into buying high-grade common stocks or mutual funds and the other one-third into "growth" company stock. Be sure to diversify your holdings.

Now also is the time to devote some of your spare time to developing hobbies. Perhaps you would enjoy being a weekend painter like Winston Churchill. You might choose to devote your spare time to public service as Bernard M. Baruch did as a young man. Or you might prefer to take up gardening, photography or amateur radio, etc. Time invested in these creative activities will be rich assets when you retire.

Observe the rules for healthful living. Overeating and poor diet can result in shortening your life. Rest and relax; avoid emotional tensions. Begin to formulate a positive philosophy of life. Regular attendance at church or synagogue, spiritual reading and a genuine interest in life will enrich your outlook and fortify you for retirement.

If you plan to change jobs to increase your income, this is probably your best chance. After forty-five, it is often difficult to make new employment connections, especially with the larger organizations.

As to vacations, try going to a different place each year. Use your vacation time as an opportunity for a personal investigation of retirement locations that might appeal to you and your spouse.

At Age of fifty-five. You are probably at or near the peak of your business or professional responsibilities and earning power, with possible retirement ten years away. With your children grown and educated and on their own, you face decreased family responsibilities.

Begin to clean up your fixed, long-term debts and get your financial structure into a more liquid position. While still maintaining a respectable checking account and cushion fund, you can afford to take a little more risk in investing. Continue to save, but don't begrudge yourself and family the right to some of the fruits of life that can be enjoyed now.

Confine yourself to easy-to-digest foods. Give up eating heavy meals and watch for overweight. Cut down on sweets, drink more milk and fewer alcoholic beverages. Build up health reserves against chronic illness.

Develop the kind of hobbies that appeal to you now and which potentially could be your bread and butter in retirement. Collect all the information and assistance you can to develop the hobbies of your choice.

Use vacation time to make a more serious survey of the states you would like to retire to. Look over possible locations with an eye to low-cost living, climate and health advantages, facilities for leisure-time activities, opportunities to establish a part-time business or farm. You might use a vacation or two to get practical experience in your retirement avocation.

At Age of sixty. You have five more years in which to build up your financial treasures. Make an analysis of your financial net worth. Review your entire estate program in the light of retirement income needs and income sources as you see them.

You can still do something about increasing your retirement income, if you have not done so already. But you will have to take greater risks. First, clean up mortgage and other long-term debts and don't contract for any additional ones. Work toward financial solvency. Use about half of your surplus cash in growth stocks, always remembering you have little time to recoup any losses. A good mutual fund is an alternate way of spreading the risk. Don't put all your money in this type of investment and all in just one stock.

Be sure you carry enough accident, health and hospital insurance. The need for these increase as you get older. Also investigate your coverage of fire, automobile and personal-liability insurance. Your retirement estate could easily shrink if you are not protected against possible property loss and court damage awards.

You should know by now the kind of part-time employment, small business or farming activity you plan to follow after retirement. Become more active in your hobby and other interests. Now is the time to bring them into full bloom.

Consider adult educational courses being offered in your community. One or two evenings a week devoted to a course in arts, crafts, trade or business training, agriculture, retirement preparation, etc., will reward you well for the time spent. You will discover that you can learn how to do new things and enjoy doing them.

Look upon your vacations as a period of semiretirement. Spend the time getting personally acquainted with a few families who have settled permanently in the area where you plan to retire. You will then not be a total stranger in the community when you take up retirement residence. Investigate real estate possibilities with an eye to buying a lot, and building, buying or renting a home. Begin to wean yourself away from too close associations with your family and friends and familiar locations. This will help make future adjustments easier.

At Age of sixty-five and Over. Welcome retirement as the beginning of a new career. Accept retirement and make the most of it.

Get a complete geriatric checkup and follow your doctor's advice on living in the later years.

You'll need financial security and solvency from this point on. The period has passed for risking your savings to increase capital growth. This is the time to start liquidating some of your growth stocks and putting your money into more assured dividend-paying stocks, high-interest bonds and other stable income producing investments. Consider selling some of your stocks or properties and converting some of your insurance into an annuity.

Increase your emergency cushion fund to the amount needed to cover your cost of living for at least two years.

Make application for Social Security. As payments are not automatic, you must apply for your retirement benefits.

Put your hobby and leisure-time program into effect within a reasonable time. Too long a period of idleness invites despondency and robs you of the contentment and satisfaction you should enjoy in retirement.

Work out a budget of expenditures that will keep you

within your retirement income. Stay out of debt. Avoid time-payment or installment buying. Buy only needed items in economical quantities during sales as often as possible. Don't cut down on quality foods to save money. Provide a substantial part of your food requirements from home-grown production.

Now it's up to you. The years you will spend in retirement are valuable to you and to the community you live in. They can be fruitful, active, productive years. You alone can make them so.

City	Eleva-tion (Ft.)	Temperature °F				Precipitation		Relative Humidity %	Sunshine Hours
		Winter	Summer	Highest	Lowest	Rain (in.)	Snow (in.)		
Albuquerque, N. Mex.	5,310	36.4	74.4	104	-16	8.06	7.0	30	3,408
Amarillo, Tex.	3,590	36.9	74.0	107	-16	20.99	20.1	-	3,695
Atlanta, Ga.	1,050	46.0	77.9	103	-8	49.79	2.3	72	2,715
Asheville, N.C.	2,192	39.2	71.6	99	-6	38.09	10.5	75	2,916
Bismarck, N. Dak.	1,670	12.0	67.7	114	-45	16.09	34.3	70	2,658
Boise, Idaho	2,842	33.2	69.8	109	-15	12.66	0.7	63	2,748
Boston, Mass.	15	29.7	69.4	104	-18	40.34	43.1	72	2,561
Brownsville, Tex.	16	61.2	83.3	104	12	31.05	-	81	2,763
Buffalo, N.Y.	693	25.5	69.8	97	-20	36.00	76.9	77	2,346
Burlington, Vt.	331	20.2	67.4	101	-29	32.30	63.9	75	2,147
Charleston, S.C.	9	51.3	80.4	104	7	45.22	4.5	79	2,064
Cheyenne, Wyo.	6,144	27.1	64.2	100	-38	14.99	56.7	58	2,966
Chicago, Ill.	594	27.0	70.9	105	-23	32.81	33.4	73	2,645
Cincinnati, Ohio	761	33.5	75.1	109	-17	38.40	18.2	76	2,678
Cleveland, Ohio	787	26.7	69.9	103	-17	33.56	41.9	72	2,444
Denver, Colo.	5,221	31.7	70.2	105	-29	13.98	55.1	52	2,968
Des Moines, Iowa	800	24.0	73.6	110	-30	31.74	32.3	72	2,765
Detroit, Mich.	619	26.4	70.4	105	-24	31.47	39.7	74	2,367
El Paso, Tex.	3,920	45.0	80.3	106	-8	8.88	2.3	41	2,947
Fort Worth, Tex.	658	47.5	85.0	113	-8	31.16	2.5	67	3,610
Galveston, Tex.	6	54.5	82.6	101	8	46.35	0.2	80	2,890
Helena, Mont.	3,893	23.1	64.5	107	-42	12.69	54.4	60	2,666
Huron, S. Dak.	1,285	16.0	70.3	111	-43	19.91	28.5	-	2,658
Jacksonville, Fla.	18	56.6	81.8	104	10	54.49	-	81	2,802
Jackson, Miss.	316	49.5	80.8	107	-5	51.44	1.5	-	2,530
Kansas City, Mo.	741	31.9	77.1	113	-22	36.32	21.4	68	2,630
Knoxville, Tenn.	949	40.2	76.1	104	-16	48.10	9.4	75	2,607
Little Rock, Ark.	265	43.6	79.8	110	-13	47.61	6.4	71	2,831
Los Angeles, Calif.	312	56.4	69.9	109	28	15.40	T.	68	3,217
Memphis, Tenn.	271	42.0	81.7	107	-8	41.42	3.2	71	2,608
Miami, Fla.	11	68.4	81.4	96	27	58.81	0.0	76	2,931
Minneapolis, Minn.	830	16.7	70.4	108	-34	27.19	41.1	72	2,618
Montgomery, Ala.	201	50.0	80.8	107	-5	51.90	0.7	72	2,865
New Orleans, La.	8	56.0	81.6	102	7	60.97	0.2	78	2,627
New York, N.Y.	10	32.9	71.9	103	-14	42.69	30.0	70	2,685
Norfolk, Va.	11	42.5	76.9	105	2	42.85	9.1	76	2,754
Oklahoma City, Okla.	1,254	39.5	79.8	113	-17	31.65	7.6	68	2,009
Omaha, Nebr.	978	23.2	74.6	114	-24	27.83	27.7	-	2,817
Pensacola, Fla.	11	54.2	80.6	103	7	58.07	0.1	78	2,914
Philadelphia, Pa.	26	34.3	74.1	106	-11	40.44	22.4	70	2,637
Phoenix, Ariz.	1,107	53.7	88.1	118	16	7.81	-	49	3,792
Pittsburgh, Pa.	1,242	32.0	72.4	103	-20	35.95	34.2	71	2,505
Portland, Maine	63	23.7	67.4	103	-21	41.14	70.5	75	2,585
Portland, Oreg.	30	40.9	65.3	107	-3	41.63	12.9	73	2,155
Raleigh, N. C.	400	42.9	77.5	104	-2	46.35	7.6	75	2,726
Reno, Nev.	4,397	34.1	67.5	106	-16	7.16	20.6	71	3,370
Roseburg, Oreg.	505	42.6	65.8	100	-3	32.58	6.6	47	2,592
St. Louis, Mo.	465	31.7	75.3	110	-22	35.89	17.5	68	2,693
Salt Lake City, Utah	4,200	29.8	75.7	106	-30	15.72	56.2	58	3,065
San Antonio, Tex.	792	51.4	82.9	107	4	27.00	0.5	68	2,721
San Diego, Calif.	19	55.7	67.0	110	25	10.03	0.0	71	3,015
San Francisco, Calif.	52	51.4	59.0	101	27	20.08	0.2	76	2,935
Sault Ste. Marie, Mich.	724	14.1	60.3	98	-37	29.94	79.5	80	2,125
Seattle, Wash.	14	41.8	62.9	100	3	33.55	11.2	72	2,040
Spokane, Wash.	1,958	30.0	67.5	108	-30	15.78	55.8	64	2,584
Tampa, Fla.	6	61.9	81.4	98	19	48.92	T.	79	3,019
Washington, D. C.	72	35.2	75.0	106	-15	41.89	20.5	70	2,583
Wichita, Kans.	1,372	34.2	78.1	114	-22	30.13	13.7	67	2,887

Index

325